"I really think I love my parents, but I hate visiting them. You see, it's not them that I hate. **I hate the way I am when I'm with them.**"

How can you stop your parents from hurting you? From aggravating you? From passing judgment on your life?

How can you avoid getting involved in their problems?

How can you be compassionate and responsive to their needs—without being overwhelmed by their demands?

You can begin by
CUTTING LOOSE.

"Lucid thinking and fine writing . . . I unreservedly recommend this book."
—Robert A. Harper, Ph.D.
Former President of the American Association of Marriage and Family Counselors and of the American Academy of Psychotherapists

"Clear, concise . . . helpful . . . free of jargon."
—Harold Greenwald, Ph.D.
Professor, School of Human Behavior
Ur

CUTTING LOOSE

An Adult Guide to Coming to Terms With Your Parents

Howard M. Halpern, Ph.D.

BANTAM BOOKS
TORONTO • NEW YORK • LONDON • SYDNEY • AUCKLAND

CUTTING LOOSE

*A Bantam Book / published by arrangement with
Simon & Schuster, Inc.*

PRINTING HISTORY

Simon & Schuster edition / January 1977
2nd printing . . . January 1977   3rd printing . . . . March 1977
Literary Guild Book Club edition / July 1976
Serialized in the Washington Star / January 1977

Bantam edition / April 1978
2nd printing . . . . . April 1978   5th printing . . . . August 1981
3rd printing . . November 1978   6th printing . . . February 1983
4th printing . . . February 1981   7th printing . . . . August 1983

ISBN 0-553-23553-2

Published simultaneously in the United States and Canada

*Bantam Books are published by Bantam Books, Inc. Its trade-
mark, consisting of the words "Bantam Books" and the por-
trayal of a rooster, is Registered in U.S. Patent and Trademark
Office and in other countries. Marca Registrada. Bantam
Books, Inc., 666 Fifth Avenue, New York, New York 10103.*

PRINTED IN THE UNITED STATES OF AMERICA

H   16 15 14 13 12 11

Acknowledgments

Many years ago, when I published a book for parents about children,* a ten-year-old patient of mine said, "How about writing a book for us kids about dealing with our parents. We need it!" That lodged in my mind, evolved, and emerged as a book not for kids but for adults because often they too have formidable difficulties in their relationship with their parents. So I want to thank that little boy who sowed the seed, and the many patients who nourished the idea by sharing with me their struggle to become individuals separate from their parents and to discover their own wholeness. Thanks to Fred Hahn and Marlon Brenner, who in their critique of my first efforts spurred me to add more substance and theory rather than keep it an anecdotal "how-to" book, and to James Ranck for suggesting a title that almost was and that also captured what this book is about, Love Them But Leave Them.

I particularly want to acknowledge the help of Ruth Kaplan Landa. Speaking of parents, if I am the father of this book, Ruth is the mother, having been my muse, my typist, my unofficial editor, and astute critic and commentator, a wellspring of ideas, and a continuing source of inspiration through her own enthusiasm and excitement about what I was doing. Her caring was beautiful, and the book and I are grateful.

Thanks, also, to my editor, Diane Harris, for having faith in the book and going beyond the call of duty with her chapter-by-chapter counsel.

*Howard M. Halpern, *A Parent's Guide to Child Psychotherapy* (New York: A. S. Barnes, 1963).

For my daughters, Shari and Dina,
who will probably find me on many pages of this book,
with the hope that it will help them to deal with my
Inner Child
with firmness but compassion,
so that they and I
can grow our own ways.

Contents

1 | SHALL WE DANCE?   1
What Are These Dances?   *How did we get into them? How do they damage us? Can we stop them and still maintain a relationship with our parents?*

2 | BLEST BE THE TIE THAT BINDS   13
Parental Double Messages   *How do they keep us tied to our parents? How can we undo the bind?*

3 | YOU ALWAYS HURT THE ONE YOU LOVE   29
The Martyred Mother   *Her use of guilt provocation to control us, and our vulnerability to her maneuvers.*

4 | THE LITTLE MAN WHO ISN'T THERE   45
The Unavailable Father   *The father so weak or withdrawn he offers us no real alternate parent, but we may be intensely involved with his weakness.*

5 | THE HIGH AND THE MIGHTY   63
The Despotic Father   *He rules through fear and belittlement, but we*

can get free if we see the insecure little boy who needs to wield such power.

6 | THE SAINTS GO MARCHING IN   82
Moralistic Parents   They have the word on how you and everyone else should behave and will withdraw their liking and respect if you don't go along with their injunctions.

7 | I DON'T KNOW HOW TO LOVE HIM   107
Unloving Parents   Parents who, for a variety of reasons, mostly their narcissism, were not able to love us very much, and the deficits and weak spots this has caused make us vulnerable to all kinds of songs and dances.

8 | DON'T SIT UNDER THE APPLE TREE WITH ANYONE ELSE BUT ME   130
Seductive Parents   Mothers and fathers who stimulate rather than defuse our Oedipal feelings, sow conflict in our relationship with them and impair our relationship with others.

9 | DON'T FENCE ME IN   148
The Family Song and Dance   The old, scripted interactions among family members have a compelling power to draw us into outworn but familiar roles whenever we come within the family orbit.

10 | TWO DIFFERENT WORLDS   172
Divorced (Separated) Parents   A

marital split brings the child within our parents forcefully to the surface so that we are called upon to engage in all the old songs and dances plus some new ones based on the new situation.

11 | DARLING, I AM GROWING OLD   189
Aging Parents   The increasing incapacity of advanced years is another factor that brings forth the child in our parents, and here we must come to distinguish the old song and dance from the realistic and appropriate need to be dependent on us.

12 | THE SONG IS ENDED (BUT THE
MELODY LINGERS ON)   202
Dead Parents   It can be more difficult to stop a song and dance with a dead parent than with a living one, because our memories of him or her are frozen in the past, and so are our emotional reactions.

13 | LET IT BE   220
Giving Up   Though we have stopped our end of the old songs and dances, our parents have taken a rigid adversary stance that forces us to the sad but liberating decision to terminate the relationship.

1 | Shall We Dance?

We're adults. We've got all the credentials and scars to show for it. There's a birth certificate in our drawer that says we're old enough to vote or drink at a bar. Maybe in the same drawer is a diploma and possibly the kind of degree that marks us as professionals. There is probably a marriage license and the birth certificate of our kids. There might even be a divorce decree or two. There have been lots of experiences chalked up to experience. There are lines around our eyes that weren't there last year. It's all there. The stuff of life that makes a child refer to us as grown-ups.

But a grown-up is supposed to possess himself, to be his own person, to make decisions according to his wishes and his best judgment. Too often we find that this is not the case with us. Frequently we are so limited by habitual ways of acting and thinking, so needful of the approval of others, and so afraid of their disapproval that we don't own ourselves at all. We are like a corporation that has gone public, and other people own controlling shares. And for many of us in that position, the biggest shareholders are our parents. We may have all the trappings of adulthood and live much of our lives as responsible, competent people, free to make our own decisions and create our own lives. But with our parents, we may feel at the mercy of old patterns of response that, though deeply unsatisfying, frustrating, and draining of our energies, seem beyond our ability to change. We are not free and can't be free when we're still more concerned with taking care of our parents' feelings than our own and when we are still caught up in trying to win their love or avoid their displeasure. And we may feel dismayed that here we are, adults in an adult world, still unable to escape these patterns from the past.

We feel it's appropriate when we hear a group of adolescents talk endlessly about their parents with bitterness, complaints, exasperation and ridicule. That is a part of what adolescence is all about. They are engaged in the developmental task of becoming separate, self-directed individuals. But have you noticed how frequently groups of adults—young, middle-aged, sometimes even elderly—when chatting over coffee or a drink or sitting around the living room after a dinner party, will begin to talk about their parents in a similar deeply involved, complaining or condescending way? I am not surprised by this when I recognize that becoming an individual psychologically is not completed in a single developmental period such as adolescence. We are always in the process of becoming, and part of that ongoing process is the job of getting disentangled from those interactions with our parents that place them at the center of our thoughts, our tensions and our talk. This process takes time, but the more we understand it, the more we can hasten it, and then we can call back those outstanding shares of stock so we can claim full ownership of ourselves.

How did we come to turn over so much of who we are to our parents? The fact is, we had no choice. Our helplessness as infants places our survival in the hands of our caretakers. We are dependent on their ministrations to our physical needs, and we are dependent on their loving concern if we are to maintain a sense of contentment, well-being, and feeling welcome in the world. It does not take us long to learn that our experience of well-being depends on the availability of our parents' loving attentions, and it takes us only a little longer to discover what we must do to keep that affection available and to avoid chasing it away.

We know that if mother (or the mothering person) is happy and unhassled, not only do we enjoy, even in infancy, the more tender attentions she is able to direct toward us, but her happy state is transmitted to us directly, through a process that the psychiatrist Harry Stack Sullivan (*Conceptions of Modern Psychiatry,* New York: Norton, 1953) calls a "mysterious emotional linkage." Through this "infantile empathy," mother's unhappiness, anger and anxiety are also directly transmitted to the infant-us in the form of tension, discomfort and fear. So our stake in keeping mother happy starts early, and our repertoire of behavior to achieve this grows as our understanding and knowledge of what makes her happy expands with time.

As we grow up, our physical survival depends less and less on our parents. Increasingly, we can take care of ourselves—but our dependence on our parents for having good feelings, particularly about ourselves, decreases much more slowly. The emotional umbilical cord not only remains uncut but often twists into a Gordian knot that ties us fast to our parents' reactions to us. At times we may come to take a rebellious stance against our parents' demands or to rail bitterly against their shortcomings. But this is only another indication that powerful, energy-draining emotions are still revolving around our parents. It also matters little whether we live thousands of miles from our parents or under the same roof, whether we rarely see them or see them every day. In fact, it sometimes doesn't matter whether they are dead or alive. What does matter is that we may be caught up in a dialogue or interaction with them that stunts our growth and restricts our autonomy.

All of us have been dependent for survival on our parents. All of us have experienced feeling good when our parents approve of us and awful when they disapprove. Why are some of us so much more caught up in freedom-limiting interactions than others? This depends, to a considerable extent, on our parents and their need and expectations of us. If our parents have a clear understanding that the parental job is to help their offspring to develop into autonomous, self-sufficient people and if they have enough maturity to act on this understanding, they will largely function in a way that will support our individuation. But even if our parents believe that their role is to encourage their offspring's growth, there may be a part of them that has failed to grow up enough to really act on this. Inside our parents, as well as within us, there is an *inner child,* and this inner child frequently directs our parents' behavior just as it directs our own. Recorded in the brain cells of every person are the "videotapes" of every childhood experience and feeling, including fear, love, anger, joy, dependency, demandingness, insecurity, self-centeredness, inadequacy feelings, etc. Dr. Wilder Penfield,* a neurosurgeon, found that when he stimulated certain areas of the cerebral cortex, memories of past events came back in full detail, as if they were being played back on a videotape, complete with sound and the emotions that were in the scene at the time of the original event. It would seem that everything that ever happened to us, including those countless moments we thought were forgotten, has been recorded and stored. There are indications that these memories can be triggered to come back and influence our feelings and behavior in the present. Also registered in our neurons from childhood are the commands, prejudices, injunctions and rules for living of our parents (and our parents' neurons contain the voices of their own parents). The combination of those tapes of all our early childhood feelings and reactions and the tapes of all the ways our parents behaved and all the injunctions and prescriptions for living they gave us compose what I have referred to as our inner child. These stored transcriptions from our childhood can at times be "switched on" and replayed in the present as current feelings and behavior without being modified by our more grown-up experience, knowledge and wisdom.† For example, we may react to another person's being cool or distant with

---

*Wilder Penfield, "Memory Mechanisms," *AMA Archives of Neurology and Psychiatry* 67 (1952): 178–98.

†Transactional analysis, an approach to psychotherapy that has much to say about the child within us, proposes that we are all made up of three states of mind, or "ego states"—Parent, Child, and Adult. The Parent ego state consists of the "tape recordings" stored in our brain of all the rules, injunctions, and ways our parents told us we should act. When we are "in our Parent," we are behaving like one of our parents. The Child ego state consists of thoughts, feelings, ways of seeing, and modes of behaving that existed in us in early

a powerful childhood fear of abandonment that is totally inappropriate as a reaction to the current situation. The emotional state of the frightened inner child has taken over and overruled our judgment.

Often our parents' inner child is not pleased by our being strong and independent. The child within them may be apprehensive and angry at the separateness and the loss of control over us implied by our autonomy. It is in the nature of the young child that dwells in our parents (or us, or anyone) to want the sustained and dependable intimacy of those they are close to, because their inner child depends on that involvement for their feelings of well-being, worth and adequacy. When we behave in ways that mark us as individuals separate from our parents, individuals with our own ideas, feelings and lives, the child within our parents feels an overwhelming threat of losing us and may react with disapproval, upset, hurt or anger. The child within us, seeking to avoid the disapproval or anger of the demanding child within our parents, may then enter into an unconscious collusion with the maneuvers of that child and develop specific ways of relating to our parents that keep us perpetually and placatingly reactive to their spoken or implied injunctions.

What all this adds up to is that when we are hung up with our parents long after we know that we are functioning as self-sufficient adults who have the capacity to be independent, we can be sure that our interaction with them is based on our early discovery: "If mother (father) feels good, I feel good. If mother (father) feels bad, I feel bad. Therefore I'd better find out what makes mother feel good and do it. And I'd better find

---

childhood. When we are "in our Child," we are actually being ourselves as a child, reliving the childhood feelings and actions. There is an Adult ego state, which is likened to a computer, dealing with the data in the situation logically, rationally and without emotion (Eric Berne, *Transactional Analysis in Psychotherapy*, New York: Grove Press, 1961). The division that transactional analysis makes between Child and Parent ego states is valid and useful, but for our purposes it will often be helpful to think of all childhood material that lives in us and can be called into action in the present as manifestations of our *inner child*.

our what makes mother feel bad and not do it." *The child in us* is trying to make *the child in our parent* feel good (or not feel bad).

I call the specific interactions that develop between the inner child in us and the inner child in our parents *songs and dances* because they have a repetitious, almost rhythmic, pattern. The same words, the same music and the same dance steps are performed over and over.*

Perhaps there's a song and dance that you and your parent(s) have done together for so long you think it's the only way you two (or three) can relate. As long as that dance doesn't change, you're all unable to grow because you are locked into a precisely choreographed pattern of response between the childlike part of them and the childlike part of you. For example, if your parent is being the demanding narcissistic child who insists that you center your life around him or her, and you are responding as the compliant child (or the rebellious child or the guilty child), you are engaged in a *pas de deux* that can go on till the end of time. If your parent should change the song and dance and grow up, then maybe you would. You'd both be free to grow because you wouldn't be lock-stepped together

---

*These songs and dances bear similarity to what are called games in transactional analysis. Eric Berne (*Games People Play*, New York: Grove Press, 1964) described games as a series of transactions between people that have a well-defined, ulterior, but quite predictable outcome. The reason the outcome is predictable, even though the game players may not be consciously aware that it is predictable, is that the people are unconsciously motivated to reach that particular outcome. The game is always dishonest, usually self-defeating, and frequently painful, but it persists because it makes the players feel they are combating feelings of worthlessness by repeating an early, time-tested way of getting others involved with them. For example, a man who constantly complains about his wife to his friends, receives their varied advice, and then tells his friend why each suggestion is no good is playing the game of Why Don't You, Yes But. After a while his frustrated friends may give up, leaving him feeling misunderstood and unlovable. But his game has brought him lots of caring attention and then confirmed his familiar feelings of worthlessness, thus granting him some security.

Whereas "games" are the transactions the young child learned to do with his parents and then continued to do with *other* people, "songs and dances" are the repeated interactions that persist *directly between parent and offspring* as the offspring grows to adulthood.

repeating those unproductive mechanical and draining interactions. But the truth is nobody has to make the first move. It can go on like this all their lives, and yours. Often that's exactly what happens, because changing the song and dance seems about as easy as changing the course of a deeply channeled river using a demitasse spoon. Your old responses are also deeply channeled. They have worn pathways in your behavior that go back to your earliest history and have cut further and further into your ability to flow in other directions. This habituation is reinforced by your inner child's powerful fears that changing in ways that your parents disapprove of would cause them to be angry at you or abandon you, with catastrophic effect. Your more objective judgment may tell you that their reaction would not be so drastic and that if ever it was, you could survive it very well. But it can be difficult to make the vulnerable inner child believe that.

So there is no underestimating the difficulty in modifying the song and dance routines you have developed with your parents, but as you become aware of just what the song and dance is that you and your parents perform so ritualistically, then you can begin to change the tune. Recognizing the nuances of interactions so habitual as to be almost beyond self-observation is no easy matter, but once you see the dance you can begin to change the words, the music and the steps.

Part of what I hope you get from this book is an awareness of the most common parent-child songs and dances, so that you will be able to recognize the pertinent patterns in your own life. It is important not only that you recognize the patterns with your intellect but that you permit yourself to be in touch with the child you once were and *to feel it when that little child in you is taking over and reacting* to your parent. It will also be important to look behind your parents' paternal and maternal adult roles and see in their facial expressions, their gestures, and their words the child in them that has not changed since they were very young. (You may find it difficult and even painful to see the child within your parents, because the child in you needs to see your parents as the big people that you can come to and lean on, and fears that seeing their inner child will make this impossible. So it is important to keep in mind that your parents are more than the newly discovered child inside them and that you are really more than the needy child in you.) As I review the various patterns that seem most common between parent and child, I will offer suggestions to help you achieve this kind of awareness. But even this insight is just a starting place, for, as psychotherapists have discovered, insight is not enough. Many people have become discouraged when they found that knowing the "whys" of their hang-ups did little or nothing to change them. You can know exactly why you are doing some self-defeating thing and then keep on doing it. The fact is that change is always an *exchange,* and there is often great fear in exchanging the security of the familiar, no matter how constricting, for the risks of the unknown.

Where is the motivation to make this exchange to come from? It derives mostly from your pain and dissatisfaction in repeating the old songs and dances. And your determination will become stronger as you realize how much is at stake if you fail to make changes. Because what's at stake is whether or not you will really own yourself, whether you will be self-animated or a puppet jerking to an endless song and dance, whether you will grow up or just grow older, whether you will spend uncounted time and energy hassling with and about your parents or whether you will free those energies for the realization of your own pleasures and potentials. A life is to be gained. New possibilities will emerge as the fear becomes less, for fear beclouds options. Alternative ways of interacting with your parents can open to you when you stop the old, limiting ways. But the hard work of change, the actual doing it differently—that will be up to your resolve.

At times, dealing with your parents may seem so difficult that you may wish they had never been born. But, to paraphrase the humorist Theodore, "Who among us is so lucky?—hardly one person in a thousand." Often we may want to chuck the whole relationship with our parents so we can be free to go our way without them on our back. After all, if our primary job in life is to become an autonomous person in touch with our own needs and preferences and effective in fulfilling them, what do we need our parents for if they are going to be such drags? Why not simply break with them?

With some parents, even if you discontinue the old song and dance and invite them to relate to you more appropriately and honestly, and even if you give them some time to absorb and deal with the shift, they will not change. In some instances, parents become so threatened by the loss of the old status quo that their behavior becomes even more destructive and hurtful —not just as a temporary reaction but more lastingly. But many parents can and do change when the old routine is stopped, so if you can grow and encourage your parents to grow along with you, then you can communicate with them on a more honest and authentic level. After all, the parent-child relationship is a primary source of who we are, and the mutual emotional attachments are derived from countless interactions, conscious and hidden memories, and profound feelings that go back to our days of oneness with them.

While each of us must be the main carrier of the twisting thread of his or her own history, the numerous relationships, activities and places that come and go in our lives produce so much fragmentation that there is a special value in maintaining our first relationships as a manifestation and marker of the continuity of our own existence. Our parents bespeak our roots, and with viable roots we feel less alone and vulnerable.

Besides, it is condescending to write off your parents as stuck and unable to grow unless you've tried to make the relationship more real. They may have more flexibility than you ever realized. And from the point of view of your own fullness, such dismissal of them can make you smaller rather than bigger. As Baba Ram Dass writes in *Be Here Now:*

If you never got on well with one of your parents and you have left that parent behind on your journey in such a way that the thought of that parent arouses anger or self pity or any emotion . . . you are still attached. You are still stuck. And you must get that relationship straight before you can finish your work. And what, specifically, does "getting it straight" mean? Well, it means re-perceiving that parent, or whoever it may be, with total compassion . . . seeing him as a being of the spirit, just like you, who happens to be your parent. . . . It's hard work when you have spent years building a fixed model of who someone else is to abandon it, but until the model is superseded by a compassionate model, you are still stuck.*

Baba Ram Dass points to the "stuckness" involved in maintaining anger at a parent as a way of relating to him or her. In fact, when it is anger that has been the leitmotif of our particular song and dance, antagonism signals no change in the old bond. In some instances, newly erupted anger may be a defiant refusal to go along with an old, compliant, suffocating song and dance and may be a helpful step in breaking with that type of interaction. But there is always the danger that angry rebelliousness or even a disruption of all communication may be a powerful tie in itself. I recall a patient who broke all contact with his mother and, on Mother's Day, expressed his sentiments by sending her a lemon. Is he less or more tied to her than someone who sent his mother a bouquet of flowers?

This book is a grown-up's guide to parent rearing. It assumes that your primary job in life is becoming your own person and realizing your own potentials. But we have noted that success at this job is often elusive because the child part of you is doing a song and dance routine with the child part of your parents that keeps you both from growing up because it keeps you emotionally dependent on each other. The task becomes one of helping your parents and yourself to stop responding to each other with voices from your respective childhoods. You can do this by recognizing when you

---

*Lama Foundation, *Be Here Now* (New York: Crown, 1971), p. 55.

are replaying words and music recorded in your head when you were very young, clicking off that old recording, and responding with your adult voice.

At times your adult voice will address itself directly to the child within your parent, perhaps guiding, nurturing, structuring, or setting limits. For example, if you find that one parent or both want to visit you with much more frequency than you wish, you can say, as you might to a clinging child, "I love you and enjoy your company, but I need to have more time for myself. Let's make the visits less frequent. Now, how about a week from Thursday, can you make it then?" Such behavior would be more mutually liberating than continuing an old compliant-child interaction in which you feel programmed to say, "Drop in whenever you want to," or a rebellious-child response like "You are always on my back. I don't want to see you again."

At other times, you will be more effective if you bypass the child's voice in your parents and respond to them as the adults they really are. For example, a possessive child within your parent may be trying to persuade you not to move into an apartment of your own and may, like a child screaming when the baby-sitter arrives, reject all attempts at reasonable discussion or reassurance. You may then have to address yourself directly to the reality-oriented part of your parent: "I'm moving Friday. That decision is definite and the arrangements are made. I'd like help from you with some aspects of the move if you care to give it to me." This would be telling the adult in your parent where it's at. If the adult part of your parent listens, he may outweigh the demands of his possessive inner child, accept your decision as a fact of life, and see in your request for assistance that you are not rejecting the entire relationship. Communication can then move to another level.

Ending the old song and dance routine can release an enormous amount of energy. You are finally free to change your movements and direction. Your new movements may be with your parents or without them; either way, a blocked potential for self-realization in you and them is liberated. But once you've reached this point, you've discovered that whether you are both growing and changing so that you can have honest and open communication, or whether they have chosen not to change, you are now more free to move to your own inner rhythms.

2 | Blest Be the Tie That Binds

In every parent there is a wish that his or her children grow up to be strong, independent, effective people. And in every parent there is a wish that his or her children remain weak, dependent, ineffectual people. The relative power of these two wishes can vary greatly, but if your parents' wishes that you be dependent and inadequate have been dominant, or anywhere near dominant, then you are probably in trouble, because the pressures on you to obey their "Don't grow up" wish may be irresistible.

The parental wish to have his child become strong and independent doesn't need much explaining. That is what parents are for, and throughout the animal kingdom parents train their offspring for autonomous survival and then unceremoniously push them from the nest. Kahlil Gibran talks of the parents' being the bow and the child's being the arrow.

The parents' wish to have his or her child remain weak and dependent needs a lot more explaining, because it contradicts the basic biological reason for parenting. We can understand it more clearly when we realize that the parent's desire to see his offspring grow and be independent comes from the mature parenting part of himself, while *the parent's desire to have his offspring remain attached and dependent comes from the little child within the parent.*

IF YOU GO AWAY

A parent is not a "bad" parent for having an inner child that wants her or his offspring to remain safely close. All of us have such an inner child and it would be asking too much of anyone to act always on the basis of the more mature goal of launching the child. To want to hold on is deeply human, and we can only hope that a given parent can more often than not make the hard adult choice of supporting the offspring's growth. But in our own interest, it behooves us to look very closely at the child inside the parents and see what makes them act the way they do. We may see a little girl or boy who clings in fear of abandonment; or a child who feels so inadequate that he (or she) grasps at a synthetic feeling of power by keeping his (or her) children close as if they were security blankets or teddy bears; or a child still echoing to the "Don't grow up" injunctions of his (or her) own parents. This child part of the parent speaks through the same mouth as the mature part of the parent and with the same parental authority. The two parts may at times fuse, mask each other, each rationalize for the other, and otherwise present themselves as a single, integrated person. The result is a *double message,* hidden from the parents, hidden from and confusing to their children.

At times the mature part and the child part of the parent want *contradictory* things, so that the parents' double message puts the children into a *double bind* —i.e., if the children obey one message, they will be disobeying the other message. It is a "Damned if you do, damned if you don't" situation. And the overall double message of importance here roughly translates as "Grow up strong" versus "Don't grow up," with the first message usually obscuring the latter.

One of the most common forms of the double bind is "I want you to be self-reliant, so do as I say." This is not to be confused with the parent who insists that his or her sick child take medicine or who sees to it that his or her child doesn't run out into traffic; in these examples the parent is probably speaking solely from his nurturant concern and mature judgment of consequences. But when a parent of a young adult says, "I want you to do what's best for you—I can bear the loneliness," there are clearly two messages emanating from that one mouth. The first represents the mature parent, aware of his offspring's need to develop his own independence and strength; the other is the message of the little child, afraid of abandonment and separation, using a guilt-provoking maneuver to stifle the offspring's bid for separateness. This offspring, receiving the double message—"Do what's best for you" and "If you do you'll make me unbearably lonely"—is in a double bind. If he does what he knows is best for him, he is causing pain to his parent and this is distressing. If he doesn't do what he knows is best for him, he is avoiding his parent's hurt, anger and guilt provocation; but he is likely not only to experience the frustration and dejection of not doing what he feels is best but also to find that the part of his parent that really meant the "Do what's best for you" message is disappointed in him.

This disappointment of the parent when his or her offspring gives in to the "Don't grow" messages is usually unexpressed. In fact, the child within the parent will probably be expressing pleasure at having won, but parent and offspring are often secretly aware of the parent's disdain. One patient, a man in his early thirties, had just had a run-in with his mother, who was a domineering and belittling woman. He had backed down and let her have her way and she seemed delighted. That night he had a horrifying dream that his mother, contemptuously denouncing him for giving in to her, literally castrated him while screaming, "You don't need these. You're not a man anyway!" Again, damned if you do, damned if you don't.

The double-message theme of "I want you to be strong and self-reliant, so do as I say" takes many forms:

"If you really want to get ahead in this world, listen to me."

"Of course you have good taste, but I still think I should go with you when you pick out a coat."

"I want you to do what you want, but if you come into my business you'll be set for life."

"I brought you up to make your own decisions, but if you marry a black man you're no longer welcome here."

"For someone with your intelligence, you're always screwing things up."

"Do it your way, but don't come to me when everything collapses."

"So now you're a doctor. I'm so proud. Daddy always told me not to worry, that between him and me it was impossible that we could make something bad."

And how's this for a double bind? I was once helping a young woman settle into a new apartment after the movers had deposited the furniture. Her mother was also there to help. Everyone was working very hard, particularly the young woman whose apartment it was. At one point the mother began insisting to her daughter, "You look terribly tired. Lie down and rest for a while." Finally the daughter agreed and did lie down. About every three minutes her mother came into the bedroom to ask, "Where does this go?" or "Do you really need this?" Finally the daughter said, "Look, you told me to rest, yet you keep disturbing me." Her mother walked away angrily and called back over her shoulder, "I don't see how you can rest with the apartment in such a mess." The mother was completely unaware of the double message.

Why did this mother convey such conflicting messages? There was a concerned, nurturing mother there, genuinely wanting her daughter not to exhaust herself. And there was a mother there whose own tyrannical father once had her sweep her room twelve times, making her do it over again if there was a speck of dust even though he knew she was in a hurry to go out (see

Chapter 5). It was this father, embedded in her head in early years, who was now saying, "I don't see how you can rest with the apartment in such a mess."

Many double messages use guilt provocation as a way of saying "Don't grow up and away." And many double messages use the theme of *belittlement* as a way of trying to so damage the adequacy feelings of the offspring as to keep him forever hobbled. The hackneyed parental statement "Your grades are good but you could do better" can be a realistic appraisal, but it is more likely the double message of approval and undermining. Take this bit of dialogue: before Martin went for an important job interview, his mother told him, "You have nothing to worry about. With the qualifications you have they'll be lucky to have you." Several hours later Martin called excitedly, saying, "I got the job."

"Really?" his mother said with amazement in her voice. "You really got the job? You're sure? When did they tell you to come back? You're sure it's no mistake?"

A young man was running for political office. He was not supposed to have a chance, but he campaigned vigorously, and when the election returns began to come in, he was doing surprisingly well. His mother took him aside and said worriedly, "If you get elected, how will you know what to do?"

Perhaps my favorite tragicomic anecdote of this kind of double message occurred when a friend opened his medical practice in a luxury building in Manhattan. His mother called to congratulate him and ask him how he liked his office.

"It's just fine. I like it here."

"Tell me, son, do they know you're there?"

"What do you mean? Does who know I'm here?"

"The people who own the building. The authorities there."

"Of course they know I'm here. I pay rent. I'm a tenant. This is my office."

After a long pause his mother asked, "And they don't mind?"

There is one particularly confusing type of double

message reflected in these two segments of a conversation between a mother and the grown daughter who lives with her.

MOTHER: Do me a favor and write out a check for me.

DAUGHTER: Why can't you do it?

MOTHER: You know you do it better than I do.

Within the same week the following conversation took place.

MOTHER: I'm tired. I did all your laundry today.

DAUGHTER: Why didn't you leave it for me?

MOTHER: That's silly. I'm home.

Besides the obvious double bind in this last segment ("I'm tired"—"That's silly") there are contradictory messages *between* the two conversations. In the first ("You know you do it better") the mother is saying, "I am dependent on you." In the second ("I did all your laundry") the mother is saying, "Be dependent on me." But as we think about these seemingly contradictory messages, it is clear that they are mirror images of the same statement: "Don't leave me (because I need you and/or you need me)." Getting caught up in the variations on this theme means a debilitating participation in a song and dance that goes round and round in endless circles.

Deeper than the injunctions "Don't grow," "Don't be strong," and "Don't be successful" is the most secret and deadly injunction of them all. This is a message from the parent indicating a wish that the child had never been born or would now die or disappear. The child may have heard about how his mother almost had an abortion but then decided to go through with it or about how his birth almost killed his mother. Or it may take other forms:

"How can I take a chance on a new career now that I have a kid?"

"If I didn't have children I would have left your mother long ago."

"If I didn't have you I might have been a star by now."

"You're nothing but aggravation."

"Life was pleasant around here until you came."

"I'll call the rag man and have you taken away."

"You tore me apart when you were born and you've been tearing me apart ever since."

The "Don't exist" wish is almost always buried beneath messages from the mature, nurturing part of the parent that wants his child to live and be strong. The two messages combine, often in a form that has as its underlying statement, "I really wish you didn't exist, but it will be acceptable to me that you exist if you: don't bother me; don't leave me; don't grow up; do become successful and thus bring me glory; do become successful enough not to lean on me or disgrace me but not so successful that you may leave me behind," etc. In other words, to try to make a parent who is sending you a "Don't exist" message love you or tolerate you, there is a price you must pay. And that price is to go along with your parent's terms for acceptance of your existence. Often, these terms directly enjoin you to be immature, unsuccessful and dependent; the terms themselves demand a close tie to the parent. In other instances, the terms may enjoin you to grow away from the parent ("Be successful," "Don't bother me") but your involvement in fulfilling these terms so as to be granted your right to live is itself an ongoing, powerful involvement with that parent. So you might be striving ambitiously, piling up many gains in fame and fortune to show as trophies to your parent, as if saying, "Now do you love me? Now is my being alive all right with you?" Or you may try not to bother them by becoming withdrawn, quiet and passive, as if telling them, "See how good I am? I don't make any trouble for you so please let it be okay that I live."

In either case, the "Don't exist" injunction that is masked by the acceptable terms for your existence hooks you in an addictive way into a lifetime task of trying to win your parent's dispensation. It is a futile task, like Sisyphus' being doomed to roll a rock up a mountain only to have it roll all the way back down just before reaching the top. Being hooked into this task is being hooked into an exhausting pursuit of an unrealizable hope.

You may be much more bound to your parents than you'd like to believe, and since the first step in ending a song and dance is always to see if you are indeed doing one, it may be helpful to look over certain aspects of your relationship with them from the past to the present. Usually, a too dependent tie with parents begins very early, as the small child starts to move about and into the world. While all parents must give certain injunctions at this point that have to do with the safety and health of the child, some parents anxiously portray the world as a dangerous place:

In some instances, there may be a payoff in money and material goodies. Overall, since your parents' end of the song and dance has been to make you feel weak, inadequate, and needful of them, and your end of the song and dance is based on believing that message, then their continued involvement in your life seems essential to your well-being even though you may know it's not. Your response to their message of "Don't leave me" (often disguised as "You can't function without me") has been some form of "I need you, I'll stay."

Perhaps your "I need you" is expressed directly by turning to them for help in little things, like bringing your laundry home for them to do or having them baby-sit with your child (despite the complications it often means) or having them advise you in shopping for clothing and furniture as if their taste and judgment were better than yours. Or perhaps it takes the form of needing their approval in big things—your choice of a mate, a career, a house. (If you are hooked into them through a continual rebellion, your emotional dependence may take the form of choosing a mate, career or house that they would disapprove of.) Sometimes the "I need you" may come out in screwing up, always going from one crisis to another so that your parents come back into your life to rescue you, scold you, advise you, cluck worriedly over you, etc. Adolescents often do this by getting involved with drugs or getting into school difficulties and having a crisis with authorities so that suddenly the parents they are supposedly gaining independence from are brought heavily back into their lives. Others may sabotage a relationship with someone they have fallen in love with so that they can avoid either physically or emotionally leaving their parents. Others may make a bad marriage, involve their parents in their marital difficulties, and even "run home to mother." The ways of living that say "I need you" to your parents seem infinite, and the price you pay is to live as a cripple.

If you recognize that you have been bound to one (or perhaps both) of your parents in a song and dance that resembles a three-legged race, keeping you and them from moving freely, you've taken one important step out of the bind. The next step occurs when you can recognize that your parents have been giving you a "Don't grow" message that has been enforced by specific techniques: belittlement and undermining of your self-confidence; making themselves seem indispensable to them; provoking guilt if you move away from their control; threatening you with withdrawal of their love, and so on. Then, it's important to see that the "Don't grow" message is coming from the frightened or possessive little girl or boy in your parent and is being responded to by the frightened or insecure or guilt-ridden little child in yourself and has nothing to do with the mature needs and requirements of either of you.

But the most important recognition is that in almost all parents, with the exception of those severely disturbed, the "Don't grow" message does not stand alone but is paired with a "Grow up strong" message that comes from the mature, parenting part of them. *It is this mature, nurturant aspect of your parent that you must respond to.* Child therapists, working with parents who have been undermining their child's growth and autonomy, have often prefaced their suggestions to parents that they change their parenting behavior with a statement such as "I know you are very interested in your child's growth and development . . ." At times, when I used to do this in my own practice I would feel gimmicky, because I was putting the parent in a double bind—either they go along with me or they are admitting they are not interested in their child's growth. But it was not a gimmick. I was bypassing the parents' inner child, who was opposed to his or her offspring's growth, and talking directly to the concerned, nurturant parent. This is precisely what you must do if you are to end the old song and dance.

I have seen countless examples where someone does respond in an adult way to the adult part of his parent, and the parent's response is also surprisingly adult. More than once I have seen a patient agonize about the Christmas visit: "A whole group of my friends are going to Vermont for skiing. They've rented this big house and it would be so much fun. But I've *always* been with my family for Christmas. They'd be crushed and furious." Then, finally, they would decide to tell their parents their intention to be away at Christmas. At times, there would be a hurt and angry reaction, although this would usually dissipate if their offspring continued to express the intention in a mature and understanding way. But very often the response was something like, "I'm so glad you said that. Dad and I have a chance of going on this special holiday charter flight to Barbados with a group of our friends, but we were going to turn it down because we felt it would hurt your feelings if we didn't spend Christmas with you!" What had been going on here? The child part of the offspring was feeling guilty and afraid of causing anger and abandonment feelings if he (or she) told the parent he would prefer to do something else. The child part of the parents was feeling guilty and afraid of causing anger and abandonment feelings if they told their offspring they would prefer to do something else. If one of them hadn't spoken up they would have spent Christmas together, the offspring daydreaming about Vermont, the parents daydreaming about Barbados, each wondering why they couldn't recapture the spirit of bygone Christmases with stockings over the fireplace.

"Don't play with that, you'll get germs."

"Stop running all the time, you'll tire yourself."

"I don't care if your friends are allowed to cross the street, I don't want you to."

"You may not have a fever, but you don't look right to me so I want you to stay in bed today."

"I know all the kids on the block have a bicycle, but you can wait a year."

"Let me see your bowel movement."

"I don't want you to go ice skating with your friends if there is no adult along even if it is a supervised rink."

"You haven't been eating right the last few days so I made an appointment with the doctor."

"I know it says you're supposed to take a knife on the camping trip but you can do without it."

"I don't like you eating at other people's houses."

"No, you cannot go to the slumber party. Nobody gets any sleep at those things."

"You don't need to go to the zoo with Julia's family. We can take you."

"Never tell anyone what goes on in this house."

Probably everybody has heard his parents say some of these things sometime, but was it a pervasive theme in your family? Did you have the feeling that the other kids always seemed to be allowed to do more than you? Did other kids sometimes say to you, "Gee, your mother (or father) won't let you do so many things"? When you first heard the term "overprotective parent," did you feel it described your parents?

If you did have an overprotective parent (overcontrolling is a more accurate term), you were always faced with the decision of giving in or rebelling. This decision becomes particularly acute during adolescence when the pressures from inside and outside are toward greater independence from the parents. How did adolescence go for you? Were you a "good" adolescent, going along with your parents' overcontrolling injunctions? Were you deceptive, seeming to go along but secretly doing your own thing? Were you overtly rebellious, having a "stormy" adolescence? Did your rebellion get you out from under or did it become a career that maintained an intense and angry bond with your parents?

If you are still emotionally dependent on your parents as an adult it may take many forms. Here are some questions you might ponder to help you check out whether there's a song and dance going on.

Why do I still live with them (if you do)?

Why do I live near them (if you do)?

Have I more contact with them than I would really like? In person? On the phone?

What would I feel if I had less contact—guilt? anxiety? loneliness? relief?

Do I include them in more of my life than I feel is best for me?

Am I still very involved in their lives? In their marital conflicts? Do I play marriage counselor or side with one against the other?

Do I take care of things for them that they can do for themselves, like balancing their checkbook or being their chauffeur?

Have I been avoiding steps that would mean moving toward greater independence? greater risk? success? growth?

When I choose ways of acting that are counter to my parents' wishes, is there a lot of anxiety? Do I start eating a lot or smoking more? Do I get physical symptoms? Do I have difficulty telling my parents about these choices?

If something came up on Christmas (or Thanksgiving or Mother's Day or Father's Day) that I would much rather do than spend the day with my parents, could I?

Do I still seem to *need* the approval of one or both of my parents? Do I get upset when I do something that gets their disapproval?

There's a lot of security in being emotionally bound to your parents. You remain in touch with the early primal source of all your security. It is deeply familiar. It is knowing that there is somebody out there who has always been there for you, so you are not alone. Continuing the dependence may bring an ongoing flow of affection and concern, or at least the ever-present hope that some day, if you hang in there and show how much you care, you will get that affection and concern.

I recall treating a woman in her mid-twenties, Carol, who was living with her parents in a house in Brooklyn. As therapy progressed and she began to feel more independent, she had thoughts of moving into an apartment of her own in Manhattan. For months Carol was tortured by this decision, talking of how devastated her mother would be when left "alone." I would question why she would say "alone" when her father was there, but she would insist on seeing her mother as totally abandoned. I would also question her about her own feelings of fear at being alone and independent, and she would acknowledge some such feelings but always return to "How can I do this to my mother?" Finally she took courage and wrote a long letter to her mother, the gist of which was, "I love you so much but there comes a time in the life of a young woman when she must find her own way. . . . Please don't take it as my being against you . . . I wouldn't want to hurt you for anything. . . . I'll call every day and come often for dinner. . . . Please understand this is something I must do." Carol left the note for her mother and went off to work sick with anxiety. She came home that night literally trembling, and when she walked into the house there was her mother, sitting in the living room looking at the classified ads and saying, "I'll miss you a lot but I think it's about time you struck out for yourself. I've circled some ads for apartments that you might be interested in." Carol's first reaction was a wave of relief. Then she began to feel her mother was abandoning her and in the next weeks we were able to deal with all her own terrors of moving out, loneliness, and being more independent, once her concern about her mother could not be used to mask these feelings.

A young man had married and lived with his wife. He had fallen into the pattern of calling his mother in another part of the city every Tuesday night. Each time he called his mother would say, "How come I never hear from you? Your sisters call every day." They would then do variations on that theme. One Wednesday, something came up that he had to tell his mother about and he called her Wednesday, though he had just spoken to her the night before. Immediately she began, "How come I never hear from you?" He exclaimed in surprise, "But Mom, I just spoke to you last night!" "You did?" she replied, taken aback. He thought about this and realized they were caught in a ritualized song and dance that had no meaning. The next time he called, about ten days later, she went into her routine, "How come I never hear from you?" This time he did not say he had been busy, that he was not one of the sisters, that she was trying to make him feel guilty or any of the other things he had been in the habit of saying. Instead he said with slow seriousness, "Mom, I never want you to say that again." There was silence, and then she said quietly, "Okay," and she never did. He had spoken to the adult in her, telling her to override the inner child that was behind the song and dance, and the adult responded.

Not all parents react so maturely to their offspring's moves to break the tie that binds. I recall another young woman, Sarah, who also presented her parents with her plans to move out. Her father was deriding her and called her a whore. Her mother collapsed into a minor depression. But Sarah courageously stuck by her decision, found an apartment, and arranged for the move. On the day she was leaving, neither parent was around to help. Her mother left her a note that read:

> Dear Sarah (*picture of a smiling face*),
>   Sorry I couldn't be here to help you move. Good luck.
>
>   Mom
>   (*picture of a sad face with
>   tear rolling down cheek*)

What guilty feelings of being an abandoner and fearful feelings of being abandoned were stimulated! And what anger was evoked! But at this point, Sarah knew enough to regain perspective and see the reaction as coming from the frightened and angry child inside each of her parents and was not thrown by their behavior. She went about doing what was best for herself, knowing that if there were mature parts of her parents that were truly concerned about her development and happiness, those parts would emerge after the child inside her parents had finished its tantrum, just as good parents often have to wait it out patiently till their two- or three-year-old finishes a tantrum.

These final steps in ending the song and dance, then, mean not only bypassing the child within your parents and responding to their maturity but also being ready to cope with the hurt, angry, anxious child that may begin to scream because you are no longer gratifying them in the old familiar way. This requires you to take a nurturant attitude toward the child in your parents, not out of guilt but out of understanding and caring.

I think of Johannes, a young man who had received verbal messages from his parents to live an active and useful life but also was given countless nonverbal messages to live passively, cautiously, and dependently close to them and their constricted life-style. He finally chose to follow their admonition to step to his own drummer more adventurously. Despite the fact that this was what they had preached, they were confused and frightened as he moved into a life that they feared would exclude them. Soon they became hostile, but he empathized with their reaction and weathered a long period of animosity and distance. He stood his ground but made it clear he was available for a better relationship. Finally they began to accept him as he really was and he expressed his feelings in a long letter which read in part:

> Dear Mom and Pop,
>   The real reason I wanted to write this letter to you both is to say "thank you" for being so understanding. I know that my life-style is often hard to understand ... but it does feel right to me. It is nice to know that your main concern is whether I am happy. . . . The point of my letter is to thank you both for giving me the moral background and philosophy for my thinking and behavior. . . . On the basics of leading a good life I know we agree fully. . . . Between the two of you I have learned a great deal. . . . I wanted you both to know.
>
>   Love,
>   Johannes

Calling forth the nurturing parent within yourself can be a vital step in your own development, because in strengthening your own good-parenting ability, not only will you be able to respond in a caring way toward the child in your parent, but you can use this nurturing capacity to be a caring, concerned parent to yourself. This is crucial because, particularly at a time when you are breaking the tie that binds, the hurt and frightened child within *you* will need all the nurturing you can give it. And if you are able to give yourself this nurturing and to sustain it during what may be the long night of your parent's hurt and disapproval and your own pain and despair at the death of the old tie, you can come to a new day with yourself and, most likely, with your parents.

3 | You Always Hurt the One You Love

One of the most enduring song and dance routines is the gavotte between a martyred mother and her guilt-racked offspring. With a little distance from Mama Martyr she's quite comical—a living satire, an obvious cliché. She is the fabled Jewish mother of all religions, races and nationalities. But, if she's your mother, getting that distance is not easy, and you won't find the manipulations engineered by her suffering very funny because the chances are that she's got you by the guilt.

NOBODY KNOWS THE TROUBLE I'VE SEEN

There are two broad categories of maternal martyrs —Noisy and Silent. The Noisy Martyr's suffering can be measured in decibels—sighs, groans, stage asides, shouted recriminations, shrieks. It's not the decibels, however, that reflect her effectiveness, but a rather ingenious way with words composed to make you feel that you are responsible for causing, or at least not alleviating, the suffering.

If your mother was a Noisy Martyr, some of these experiences may also be part of your résumé:

You may have heard how she was in labor for —— tortured days when you were born. ("The doctor said that in twenty-five years of delivering babies he never saw anything like it.") Or, maybe, it was the six months she had to stay in bed during her pregnancy. Or the caesarean. Or some other agony that you inflicted on her before or at your birth. You started your mother-hurting career early, and don't you forget it.

You were told that you got sick just to make her suffer. ("Don't you get sick on me again. I've had enough this winter." "I told you to take a jacket but you knew better.") Any variation of the sick-on-me theme gives you many points toward proving that you did indeed have a genuine martyred mama.

Beyond being born and sometimes getting sick, you often felt yourself to be the cruel cause of all her other suffering. ("A mother tries so hard to do right by her child, and this is the reward she gets.") One particularly gut-gripping variation is that you may have been told, in either words or music, how unhappy she is with your father, and you have the uneasy feeling that it is all your fault. ("You know how your father is. If it weren't for you children . . .") Sometimes you may not be the sole cause of her tragic unhappiness; perhaps you're part of a general conspiracy to misuse her. ("What does everyone want from me? People are tearing pieces from my flesh.")

Maybe you've teetered from the brink of one of her fatal illnesses to another, always with that vague sense of not having done enough to prevent it or support her. ("I may need another operation. What do I care if I come out of the hospital this time? You'll all be better off without me.")

You've hated it when your mother did you a favor. ("I had nothing to do while you were gone so I washed and ironed your things and straightened your room out a little. I hope you had a good time.")

You've become wary about inviting your mother to a happy occasion. ("I don't know if I can make it. I've been having those dizzy spells. I wouldn't have said a word to you about it if you didn't invite me. Just forget about me and enjoy yourself.")

You dread occasions that call for buying her a present. ("What do I need it for? You know I'd never go anyplace where I'd wear something like this. Why did you spend so much?" Or, if it's an inexpensive present, "What do I need it for? I'm going to bring it back and get you a refund." If you have decided to go along with her and not get a present, "You should see how many beautiful presents I got. It's nice to know that some people care.")

You feel panicky when you hear her voice on the phone, heavy with pain and accusation, and suddenly you realize you forgot to call her all week. ("I was so sick, I never thought I'd pull through. Everyone else in the family called every day but you're too busy to pick up the phone.")

You've often felt that wanting to do something completely on your own was a malicious assault on your mother. ("Go ahead, see if I care. My opinion never meant anything to you.")

YOU'LL NEVER KNOW

Now, if your mother is a Silent Martyr, you've been receiving the same messages but they have been wordless, harder to pin down, harder to fight. She plays it cool. If you had not called her while she was ill she would mention nothing to you—she'd let somebody else tell you how sick she was. If you went somewhere she disapproved of, you might return to find her lying on the sofa with a cold compress on her head, and if you asked her how she felt she might ignore you or simply mutter, "Better." If you planned to do something that would make you more independent of her she might be thunderously silent. If pressed to respond she might say, "Look, you decided already so that's it," or "If it makes you happy." If you buy her an elegant item of apparel and months later ask her why she never wears it, she might then tell you that she exchanged it for a vacuum cleaner.*

---

*I am making our martyred mother a caricature with little to commend her at this point, but the purpose of this is to sharpen the focus on just those aspects of her that are causing you trouble if you have such a mother. We'll see her in a bit more depth further on.

The songs and dances may vary, then, from the pounding flamenco rhythms of the Noisy Martyred Mother to the soft-shoe subtlety of the Silent Martyr, but the goal is always the same. It is to make you feel sufficiently guilty so that you'll let her be in control. And if she's really good at it, then you're carrying a little old lady around on your back much of the time.

If you have decided that you have to get her off your back you have probably joined battle with her on more than one occasion. But the chances are the battles have not gone well for you, because no matter what you seem to do to win, you lose. But that's the whole devilishly clever beauty of the martyred mother's technique. The winner loses, the loser wins.

Let me zoom in on that more sharply. If the grand strategy is to keep you under her sway through provoking guilt, then what happens if you have finally had it, become enraged, and lash out at her? If you've tried it, you know very well what happens. If her aim is to make you feel responsible for her pain, then each blow you strike is one up for her. Attempting to get free through open warfare is fighting on her terms, and those terms are that the winner is the one with the goriest wounds. Only the greater sufferer has the victor's right to control the other. So since she gets valuable guilt-provocation points each time you attack her, and since you probably are not cured of your vulnerability to feeling guilty in relation to her, you might find that you slip into martyred maneuvers yourself. For every "Look what you've done to me" that she hurls, you might find yourself saying, "But look what you've done to me!" For every illness she flings at you, you might throw back your own headaches, depression, cancer phobia, or whatever. After all, if she is making you feel guilty about not calling her when she was sick, what could be more "natural" than saying you were unable to call because you were laid low yourself. But it's not just saying it that has a pernicious effect on your selfhood; it's the possibility of actually becoming a sick, masochistic loser in order to outbleed her. Even in that position, though, you can't win, because now the rules are changed: if you're such a mess then you obviously can't handle your life so you'd better let her handle it for you.

If that sounds bad, I'm afraid it isn't even the whole dismal picture. Because the chances are that not only have you been tempted at times to do battle based on her weird masochistic ground rules, but you have doubtless often tried to allay her suffering by striving to make her happy. What a futile exercise! She'll cling to her hurt the way a queen grips her scepter, for it is the source and symbol of her power. She fears, quite unconsciously, that if she gives it up she has no other way of having a hold on you or anyone else whom she controls through guilt.

Remember, too, that you won't make her happy by giving up little bits of your selfhood. She wants all of you. So if you start surrendering your autonomy in order to get her to stop her noisy or silent accusations, it will only work until the next time, which may be five minutes later. You can twist yourself out of shape trying to fulfill her wishes. It's like the story of the man who goes into the bargain clothing store. The salesman is trying hard to sell him an ill-fitting suit.

"This suit doesn't fit right," the man says. "The left shoulder is too high."

"So, raise your shoulder a little."

"Okay, but now the suit sticks out too much over the right hip."

"So stick out your right hip."

"All right. But the left pants leg is too short."

"Bend your leg a little at the knee."

The man decides to buy the suit and leaves the shop wearing it. Two women watch him leave. One says to the other, "Look at that poor man. He's so deformed."

"That's true," the other woman replied, "but look how nice his suit fits."

How much are you willing to deform yourself in the effort to allay your guilt?

I WANT A GIRL JUST LIKE THE GIRL . . .

The most self-destructive part of being in the masochistic song and dance may not be in your relationship with your mother but in your transferring these patterns to others. In fact, mother may be long dead, her music may have stopped, but you keep on dancing.

How often I have seen women with martyred mothers develop relationships with friends, lovers and husbands in which they repeat the old steps. They will not dare, for example, to choose a man who will help them toward growth and contentment; or if they by chance do choose such a man, they will frustrate whatever fulfillment he might help bring to them. After all, how can they dare to be happy if mother is suffering so? How can they dare enjoy sex when mother seems so bitterly unsexual or so sexually frustrated? If someone were groaning in agony on the rack, could you walk by whistling?

Besides denying herself happiness as a "guilt tax" to her mother, it's not too uncommon for a woman to duplicate the same dance with her man. I have seen a woman flee from mother's grasp into a relationship with a man in which she experiences the same old feeling of guilt whenever she tried to be herself in ways he doesn't like. Even if he were not too much of a guilt provoker before, he is likely to become one when he sees how well it works to control her. He, too, can become a martyr, silent or noisy. She can try to outmartyr him. They are soon spiraling downward, feeling misunderstood, misused and trapped. And the woman who feels so trapped has got to feel enraged, and one way or another she will thrash about in her rage. She may feel that the only way she can get out of the trap is to get rid of her man, while what really needs to be eliminated is her own proclivity to respond to her man as if he were her mother, with the same vulnerability to being strangled by his pain and disfavor, real or imagined.

Men who have spent a lifetime trying to bring a smile to the gothic face of a martyred mother will not only be afraid to reach out for happiness while mother is suffering but may, with uncanny accuracy, find women who are also terribly unhappy and need rescuing. A man with this mission will often don the apparel of a gleaming white knight, striving to rescue his sweetheart or wife from her own inner dragons, often losing sight of his own wants and needs, often driving himself into greater and greater despair. I have frequently told a joke to patients of mine who are involved in such quixotic rescue efforts. It is about a man whose wife has been slowly, excruciatingly dying. The end is obviously near, and as he sits by her bedside she whispers, "Darling, as a last request, make love to me one more time."

He feels squeamish about this, as she looks so weak and skeletal, but how can he refuse? So he climbs into bed with her, and as they make love she begins to move with increasing vigor, the passion mounts to a frenzy, and it is by far the best sex they have ever had. After it comes to a screaming climax the wife, who has been bedridden for months, jumps up and pirouettes around the room, her face full of color, her eyes sparkling. "Darling," she shouts, "you've saved me. I'm going to live."

Her husband is still lying in bed, disconsolately sobbing.

"Aren't you glad, darling," his wife asks, "that I'm not going to die?"

"It's not that," he answers. "But if I only knew, I could have saved my mother."

Rescuing martyred mothers and their substitutes later in life is one of the most perilous and profitless pursuits a man could engage in, but if you have had a martyred mother, you may well be unwittingly addicted to it.

I'M MY OWN GRANDPA

From our earliest days our parents have been the big people, their ways and rules have stood for the injunctions of that powerful world of the big people, so it is easy for us to lose sight of the fact that *often it is the most immature part of our parents that has played such a commanding role.*

Let's look at the martyred mother in this light. What is she expressing in her maneuvers to control her offspring through guilt? What kind of little girl dwells within? First we can see a little girl who has, in some important ways, been failed or disappointed in her own needs for parental loving. This has left her with such doubts about her own lovableness that she can't believe that anyone, even her own children, would care about her, listen to her and wish to be with her because they *wanted* to, but would do so only if they were somehow *forced* to do so. And the hungry space in her, the vacuum left by whatever early deprivation of love she experienced, produces such desperation that this little girl will bleed herself and blackmail others in order to extort a pitiful pseudo-love.

The unhappy little girl within your mother cannot see that it is just these efforts that now drive away the people whose love she wants, and that it is her maneuvers that make her children want to put more distance between them and her; she sees only that unless she binds them with guilt, they will disappear. The pits of bottomless yearning that riddle your mother because she did not receive what Winnicott* has called "good enough mothering" from an "ordinary devoted mother" lead her to attempt to get the mothering she wants from her own offspring, a reversal of the usual parent-child relationship that we will see often. It is as if the little girl in her is saying, "I'm scared, Mommy (or Daddy). Nobody loves me or cares about me and I feel so alone. If you stay with me I feel much better so please don't go away, don't get interested in other people and other things because I become afraid you'll forget all about me. Take care of me. Pay attention to me. If you don't, I'll get sick and maybe that will make you care. And I'm also angry that you don't pay enough attention to me, that you don't give me the loving I want. I'm so angry that I will show you how hurt I am to make you feel bad. I may even die to make you feel guilty. You *must* love me. And if you love me you'll do what I want."

Why did this love-starved little girl in your mother choose guilt provocation as a way of trying to get love? Probably because she learned it from her mother

*Donald W. Winnicott, *The Maturational Processes and the Facilitating Environment* (New York: International Universities Press, 1965).

(Grandma) who may in turn have been love-starved and learned it from her own mother. It can become an accepted mode of relating as martyred mothers, themselves deprived children, try to wring from their offspring what they couldn't get from mother. They pass their crippling craft down like an heirloom with a curse. Looking back along the time track, daughter complains about having to load and unload the dishwasher. Mother says, "You think that's bad? I had to wash the dishes by hand."

Grandma says, "That's nothing. I had to heat the water."

Great-grandma says, "Hah! I had to go to the pump."

And so on till the beginning and end of time. There are some subcultures where this mode of childrearing, this "I'm suffering so you owe me" attitude is so widespread and indigenous that your mother, if she came from this background, learned it as naturally as any other social skill. It is difficult for people brought up in such a milieu to conceive that there is anything damaging about controlling their children through guilt, and if you have such a mother you will receive and might pass along that tragic heirloom to your offspring unless you can step back, see what's going on, realize its destructiveness, and work on moving out of that kind of interaction.

DON'T BLAME ME

The first step toward ending a song and dance with a martyred mother is to recognize that you are participating in it. Do some of the descriptions here sound familiar? Are you controlled by your mother's guilt provocations? Sometimes it is difficult to know if you are responding to her suffering with inappropriate guilt or appropriate compassion. Because she is another human being who has a long and close shared history with you, it certainly would be a genuine loving response if you reacted to give her support or sympathy, or to do whatever you could to alleviate her pain. It *is* compassion when you can see that the pain is real and not self-inflicted and/or a chronic way of provoking a de-sired response. It *is* compassion where there is no sense of her accusing you of either causing or failing to rescue her from her pain. It *is* compassion that you feel when her acknowledgment of her pain and her asking you for succor is straightforward and not laced with blame or demand.

But it is guilt that you feel and *not* compassion when this is her usual and time-honored way of getting you to respond automatically the way she would like. It is guilt and *not* compassion when your reason tells you that she will not fall apart if you don't honor her wishes but your guts react as if she will. It is guilt, *not* compassion when her actions lead you to feel enormous unease, as if you've committed a malicious injury, when all you've done is behaved other than how she would have wanted you to behave. It is guilt and *not* compassion when you feel the discomfort of a transgressor for acts that really harm no one. It is guilt and *not* compassion when you end up feeling callously selfish for simply doing something that pleases you though it takes nothing of importance from her or anyone. The guilt that you feel is provoked by your mother's manipulations, and the response you then make to keep yourself from being accused is your end of the song and dance. If something is to change, you first have to become aware of the predictable movements of each of you.

This awareness of how you have been manipulated by guilt may initially make you furious and may trigger you to attack your mother, but this would be just another variation on the song and dance, because the attack would make mother even more martyred, might make you feel even more guilty, and could leave you as involved as ever in the "who's hurting more" entanglement. It would be more helpful if at that point you could bring the little girl in your mother into focus, if you could look at her and listen to her when she is in her martyred role and then push aside her mask of adult, self-righteous parenthood and see beneath to that frightened, angry, demanding brat. How much less formidable she then seems! What a paper dragon-lady! It opens up whole new possibilities of how to react to her. When you see that it is the child within your mother who is trying to control you through guilt, the question is raised, what should you do with this child? How would you deal with an actual child that was making these demands?

The situations of raising a child and raising the "child" in mother are not exactly comparable. A real child's dependency is more appropriate to his age and it expresses needs that must be met before he can move sturdily to the next stage. Mother's dependency is not appropriate to her age, expresses needs that can no longer be fulfilled by others, and blocks her from finding other ways to fulfill herself. But even with a young child, you would not go along with any method he used to make you meet his needs. It would be destructive to you and your child to reward his whining, injustice collecting, accusing and manipulating because these rewards would reinforce the continuance of such unpleasantness. And it is destructive to you and your mother to reward her whining, injustice collecting, accusing and manipulating by entering into a song and dance with her that does reward this behavior.

Recognizing that it is the demanding child within mother that is provoking guilt, and at the same time realizing that mother is, chronologically, not a child, can lead to a crucial insight: *You can never make up for what your mother didn't have, and trying to satisfy the "child" in her is futile to the point of exhaustion, despair and the slow erosion of your self's integrity.* You must give up the myth that you can rescue or fulfill her. In fact, only if you (and others) stop trying does she have a chance to try out new ways of being.

If you are with me up to this point, then you have recognized the song and dance and your part in it. You clearly see the "child" within your martyred mother; you accept that you cannot make up for what she didn't have; you're tired of being manipulated by guilt and you want, finally, to refuse the invitation to the waltz. It should be simple now that you see it all, so why, when you try it, is it so hard?

First of all, knowing that you're in a song and dance in the abstract is different from knowing at a given moment that you are caught up in it. When you're actually in it it feels familiar and natural, like the pollution you breathe, so you may not refuse the invitation simply because you haven't yet learned to recognize immediately when you *are* accepting it. This takes practice and vigilance.

Even seeing it immediately is no guarantee that you won't fall into the old song and dance. The pattern is etched in your neurons. It has been repeated so often that it is automatic. But above all, it is not the adult part of you that is hooked into such a profitless interaction, but the little child, and that little child in you is vulnerable to mama's control. Your inner child's prominence in your interaction with the child in your mother leaves you with two weak spots in your emotional foundations—your dependency feelings and your own personal packet of guilt.

The child in all of us has dependent yearnings. How predominant a part of us it is, is largely a function of how successfully our early dependency needs were fulfilled. If we are postulating that a martyred mother has enormous unresolved needs for maternal nurturing herself, then it follows that it was probably difficult for her, when you were very small, to help you feel secure in the constancy of her loving and caring. A longing to win mother's loving and hold on to it can then become a compelling force in your inner child, and can be felt at times as a hunger so desperate that you would be willing to pay a high price for the hope of having it gratified. And gratification cannot come from a suffering mother, particularly if you have made her unhappy.

The other weak spot abiding in your inner child is your private parcel of guilt. It is filled with all the things you ever did or thought that you felt were wrong. It contains some of your shameful secrets. But above all, it contains all your early training that to want, do or be something that mother would not approve of will upset her, and that you, as the cause of this upset, are therefore bad. Not only have you received the message "Do what I want and I'll love you; don't do what I want and I won't love you"—an injunction of enormous power to the dependent child—but martyred mother has added another message: "If you don't do what I want it makes me suffer and you are selfish and hurtful." These messages, striking at the dependency and guilt of your inner child, put termites in the underpinnings of your selfhood.

So, beyond the recognition of the song and dance and all that goes into it for her and for you, you are confronted with a monumental inner conflict in your attempt to avoid the old pattern of guilt-appeasing responses. You must be prepared to weather the possibility of mother's anger, of her accusations and of her withdrawal of love. You must be prepared to test whether you can survive feeling guilt-racked and abandoned. Where does the strength come from to bear the threat of her anger, her blame, your anxiety and your fear of losing her caring? It must be remembered that while it is the child within you that is locked into the old reactions, there is more to you than that shaky, desperate child. You are a grown person, with complex skills, countless experiences, and a capacity for much more actual and emotional self-sufficiency than the child in you knows about. But it's there. It's been in the best interests of the child in your mother that you not know it's there. It's been in the best interests of the child in you to not know it's there, so you could keep open your claim on mother's caring. But it is there, you can take care of you, and you can reassure the child in you of this.

Having a great capacity for self-sufficiency and for taking good care of yourself does not mean a retreat into ascetic or lonely solitude. Part of taking good care of yourself is finding people you can depend on for certain gratifications and emotional sustenance—people who have it to give, wish to give it to you, and do not demand that you surrender control of your life to them in return. You can go from twisting yourself out of shape in order to avoid being accused to standing up straight and getting fulfilled. This knowledge, which you will have to gain bit by painful bit, can sustain the child in you when he cries out in terror. It takes courage to endure the lonely agony of refusing to participate in the old dance, and you will find that not only will everybody survive, but you will also begin the process of strengthening your foundations and of finding ways to fill the termite holes by giving nurturance and guidance to that child in you.

And mother? She may be driven to more and more obvious, even bizarre ways of trying to maintain control through martyrdom. This can make for a very difficult period, but it has the advantage of driving out into the open the hidden motivations and maneuvers, making them so blatant that they are undeniable to you and maybe even to her. If you maintain your refusal to dance despite these crises, and mother finds it too threatening to relate to you as adult to adult, she may angrily withdraw. And she possibly may stay that way. But it is more likely that she will in time respond to your stopping the old pattern in a way that will indicate that you have taken a major step toward helping the "child" in her grow up.

I recall a young single woman who taught high school math. She usually brought her lunch to school as she didn't like the food available there. One day her mother, a near invalid, noticed that she had left the lunch at home. Being a bona fide, certified martyr she traveled almost an hour by bus to leave her daughter's lunch at the school office and then return home. In the past this performance would have led to many familiar lines like "Mother, you didn't have to do that," or "What a surprise when I found the lunch in the office. But you know the doctor said you shouldn't travel." These lines are manna to mother, and she would eat them up along with her daughter.

On this particular day, maybe because the daughter had in her therapy become increasingly aware of the guilt provocation in her mother's kindness, maybe because she had begun to realize the high dues she was paying in her life for this kindness, something different happened. The daughter said nothing about the lunch when she came home. The mother tried to wait out this strange omission on her daughter's part but could stand it no longer and asked, "You got the lunch?"

"Yes, thank you." Followed by another unorthodox silence.

"Was the lunch okay?"

"Yes. Could have used more salt, but okay."

The mother was too stunned and confused to say, "After I travel by bus for an hour with my veins all you can say is that the sandwich needed more salt." She heard, in the words and tone, that her daughter was sitting this dance out.

This was not, of course, the end of that kind of song and dance between this pair. Such deeply entrenched, well-rehearsed patterns are not unlearned easily. But it was a trumpet sound, clearly heralding the possibility that something new was coming.

A third step is to persistently make it clear to martyred mother that if she chooses to suffer when you don't do as she would have you do, it is her choice and that you will not accept the blame. Of course, you really have to believe this in order to do it. You have to see clearly that dividing line between her responsibility for herself and your responsibility for your self.

When you act without malevolence in your own behalf, and that action is counter to mother's wishes, her guilt provocations must be met by a firm position that you refuse to be held responsible for her suffering. And this must be coupled with an insistence that her claims for attention and interaction be in the context of her recognition of you as a separate person and her respect for your right to say no.

I am reminded of a woman in her late thirties who was once my patient. She was very much a puppet of an expert martyred mother. We had been talking in therapy about her servile role in the family and her wish to break with it. The particular issue that had brought this to a head was that she was expected, as usual, to make a huge birthday dinner for her mother. She was so locked into this role that none of her siblings or other relatives ever thought of offering to do it, or ever questioned whether it should be done. Nor, until now, had she. She wanted to say no. She wanted to say, "Let's all go to a restaurant where I could sit and be waited on, too." But how could she stop the old dance? How could she withstand the angry disapproval of her aging, sick, demanding mother?

One afternoon, the day after we had had a session in which she was struggling painfully with this conflict, she phoned and said, "I must see you tomorrow." I checked my schedule and told her I had no time available.

"But you must," she insisted. "I've got to make a decision. I didn't sleep at all last night."

I repeated that I was sorry but just had no free time to see her. She hung up crying and angry.

When she came for her next appointment she was cheerful, even beaming. "I told them that I wouldn't make the dinner, that I wanted to be waited on like a lady for a change, and that if nobody else wanted to make it we should all go to a restaurant. They were surprised but said 'fine.' "

I congratulated her, and asked how this decision had come about. She answered, "After I talked to you on the phone I was very upset. Then it hit me that if you could say no with all the pressure I put on you, then I could say no."

So in the nonmalevolent assertion of your reality needs, you do not damage but help the other become aware that she/he, too, has a right to say, "No, this is not acceptable." The myth that because one person has a need the other *must* meet it is challenged. And it is in feeling the right to say no to the coercive pressures of this myth that you free yourself to grow, and probably help mother grow, too.

4 | The Little Man Who Isn't There

What's a father for, anyhow? After he's done his brief biological stint, what's the use of him? He has no warm womb to incubate and nourish the fetus while it unfolds according to its prearranged blueprint. His aid is not necessary to thrust the child into the world. He has no breasts to feed and assuage the infant, and the child's other needs for physical care can be met adequately by a competent mother or other caretaker. Does the father have no important developmental role with his offspring?

Mother is the primal parent, the source, the nurturer, the parent who, in most cases, holds the child's day-to-day survival and well-being in her hands. As the child grows, the inner urge toward separation and autonomy stirs and gets stronger, but it is always in a struggle with the deep attachment to the safety and familiarity of mother. Mother's willingness to help the child detach, first by letting him be sufficiently attached and filled with the assurance of her caring presence, then by permitting him to take steps away from her, to come back, and to step out again, is crucial in the development of his autonomy. But both mother and child often need help, the mother because she may have deep needs of her own to hold on to the child, the child because separation is always beset with anxiety. And here it is the father who must take the child by the hand and stroll with him into the larger world, showing him its joys and bedazzlement, teaching him to deal with its dangers, imparting to him the courage and confidence to be out there. At his best, the father is also available to the little child within the mother who may be upset and threatened during this time of separation. *The essential job of the father, then, is to help the mother and child separate from each other*. This is a role of quiet strength, of ordinary heroism.*

Fathers vary greatly in their fulfillment of this role. There are fathers who are not able to take their child's hand, are not available as a helper and guide in separating from mother or imparting the confidence to step into a wider life. There are many reasons that fathers may be unable to do this fathering job adequately. They may be too narcissistically self-involved, they may be ignorant of what is required of them as fathers, or they just may not give a damn about their child. But the father I will discuss in this chapter is the one who fails his offspring because he is, in some essential ways, a weak man.

A father can be weak in many spheres and in many ways. He can be weak in his dealings outside the family and within the family, and unless the child deceives himself in order to uphold an image of father as being strong, he will have untold opportunities to see that weakness. The weakness I speak of here is not in those occasional times when father fails at something or doesn't handle a situation capably, or when he backs away from a confrontation or makes a fool of himself. This happens to all fathers and it may make their children cringe when it does, but the child still has a reservoir of evidence that there is a basic paternal potency.

---

*Whether it is biological or a function of this time and this place, whether it is a good arrangement or a poor one, in the nuclear family an intense bond often develops between a child and its mother based on the nurturing role the mother *usually* has with the infant or young child. When she breast-feeds, she may be the sole feeder. Usually she spends more time being with and taking care of the child than the father. The father, then, is the "other" parent and is equally important not only because he too can be a nurturer and take care of the child, but because he offers an *alternative* relationship that can also be close and powerful but is different because he is different. Because of this alternative relationship, not all the child's emotional eggs are in one basket, and that is desirable no matter how loving and effective the basketkeeper may be.

What I refer to here is the father whose core of confidence, courage, competence and self-respect is shriveled so that his actions are often ineffectual, his thrust is blunted and his presence is underwhelming.

The child may observe that his father is weak in many situations *outside* the family. For example, father's being a poor provider, when it reflects a dedication to an unremunerative calling, may actually be a strength; but where the child perceives his father's inability to provide well for the family as being a product of father's irresponsibility, laziness, poor judgment, passivity, or a tendency to clash repeatedly with authorities, to undervalue himself, to avoid risks, or any other defects that arise out of a fault (almost geologically speaking) in the structure of the father's personality, he will have feelings that his father's earning difficulties reflect weakness.

When the child, watching his father in action with neighbors, landlords, repairmen, clerks, friends, authorities and other people encountered in day to day living, sees his father as wishy-washy, unassertive, ineffectual, or unable to stand up for his rights, he learns that his father cannot be either a pillar of or a model for strength in his life. If he sees his father, in discussions of current issues, large or small, seem to have no opinions and no consistent point of view, or sees him shy away from putting forth or defending his beliefs, except perhaps angrily put down those he disagrees with, he will feel that his father is lacking solidity. If he sees his father as having few if any interests, and as being withdrawn into a narrowly circumscribed area, such as the TV set, or gambling, or sleep, or aches and pains, he cannot see him as a guide to the larger world. And if he sees his father as morally defective, knows that he cheats others, gets away with whatever he can, has little sense of ethical responsibility to his fellow men, will do almost anything for a buck, and sees nothing wrong with this approach to life, he knows he cannot count on his father to help him develop a useful moral rudder to steer him through life's ambiguities.

Within the family, the growing child has even more

opportunity to see his father's weakness. He can see his father be ineffectual with his mother, his siblings, and/or with him. If you have had a father who places himself in a subordinate position to your mother you may have seen him—

—go along with her on a wide range of decisions, including where to live, who their friends will be, how they will spend their time together, what foods are good for him, what he should wear for a given occasion, what movie or restaurant they will go to, and even how he should spend his time alone. ("While I'm away I've arranged for you to eat at my sister Lucy's Saturday night and to spend the day at your mother's on Sunday.")

—lose argument after argument to her either by passively and quietly going along, by raging loudly and impotently and then giving in, or by surrendering to a particular maneuver of hers—*e.g.,* he may be unable to tolerate tears, or her sustained fury, or her sullen withdrawal, or her collapse into depression, etc. ("All right, all right, have it your way—it's not that important.")

—pretend that anything she wants is okay because he has no strong desires or preferences of his own. ("It makes no difference to me.")

—give the illusion of strength, perhaps deriving his strength from her, as the Prime Minister from his Queen, but you felt he always knew the Queen could have him beheaded. ("My wife doesn't like this table. Could you find us one further from the door?")

In his interactions with you, you may have known the sinking futility of feeling his weakness very directly.

You may have been yelled at or punished by your father not because he felt you did wrong, but either because mother egged him on to it, or because the rage that he was too frightened to express at her was diverted toward you. ("Next time you'll listen to your mother.")

You may have given up turning to him for help in dealing with your mother when she seemed unreasonable because he would not offer any support, even when you knew he agreed with you. ("If your mother says so, then that's the way it will be. What can I do?")

You may have stopped turning to him for advice about dealing with the bully down the block, a difficult teacher, a problem with friends, guidance about relating to the opposite sex, or career choice, because his advice was ineffectual. ("Don't worry. Time will take care of it.")

You may have stopped arguing with him about politics, social issues, your generation, etc., because he would either be frustratingly passive ("Maybe") or would have a tantrum ("What do you know?").

You knew you could never discuss ethical issues, like cheating on tests, petty stealing, or taking advantage of others, because you felt his moral sense was feeble ("It's dog eat dog") or that he lived according to inflexible codes handed down to him and never questioned ("There is *never* a good reason to lie").

You had the feeling, when there was a confrontation with him, that he was a fortress of farina, that if you punched him your fist would sink into the softness of his belly and disappear or that if you came on too forcefully he himself might go "pop" and disappear like a helium-filled parade balloon (or choose a metaphor closer to your own experience).

I recall a group therapy session in which Carl, who had been struggling for months to keep from being controlled by his girlfriend, Pia, recounted another experience in which Pia had suddenly withdrawn and become cool and distant just at a point when Carl was feeling confident and assertive with her. And as always, Carl's proud but precarious strength toppled like a tower of children's blocks when the bottom is kicked out. He felt that old desperation—you must love me, you can't leave me, you can't do this to me, Pia, please, please. The group tried to help Carl. Some showed him what Pia was up to, some indicated what he was repeating, others told him why he was doing it, others got angry at him for letting it happen over and over again with no attempt to use his knowledge of what was going on to stop it. Carl listened to everyone, looked miserable, and said nothing. Then he turned to the therapist, who had been silent, and said, "We've been all over this so many times and I still keep doing it. When are you going to help me to stop?" The therapist still was silent. "Are you going to just sit there?" Carl wanted to know. Still no reply. "Oh, I'm sorry," Carl said. "I know you want me to work it out for myself."

THERAPIST: Then you're not really angry at me for not helping you with that?

CARL: No, I'm angry at myself.

THERAPIST: So why do I get this unmistakable feeling that you are furious with me?

CARL: I'm not. It's not your fault I'm a slow learner.

THERAPIST: *If* you were angry at me, what might you say?

CARL (*laughed, then*): That you're an ineffective SOB who's taking my money and not helping me with my problems; you don't know how to help, yet you pretend it's my failure.

THERAPIST: That's what you would say *if* you were angry at me.

CARL: I'm not, really.

THERAPIST: You shouldn't be but you are.

CARL: Why shouldn't I be? Oh, hell. It's as hard to tell you I'm angry as it is to stand up to Pia. But damn it, I am! I hate having this problem and I hate your giving me cliché answers and sitting there like a smug Buddha while I suffer. Get off your ass and do something!

The floodgates had opened and Carl loosed a torrent of stored complaints against the therapist. Then after another silence he said, "You don't look at all destroyed."

THERAPIST: Disappointed?

CARL: No, relieved. And exhilarated.

JEANNE: I never saw you let loose like that, particularly with a man.

CARL: I stopped showing my anger to my father years ago. I remember once I was in a screaming rage at him for being my mother's puppet—I was about sixteen—and as I yelled I caught this look on his face—sad, helpless and pathetic. His whole being was an impotent shrug. I just stopped as if someone had grabbed my throat, and I turned away. I haven't yelled at him since. And I could never tell off the doc, here, either, until today.

JEANNE: I know the look you mean. I've seen it in my father many times when I get mad. Except he not only looks helpless but terrified, as if I were going to kill him. Christ, he's a foot taller than me and built like Sonny Liston.

THERAPIST: When he looks like you're going to kill him, and acts as if you can kill him, how do you feel?

JEANNE: Like I'd really like to kill him! And *that* scares me. So between *his* fear of my anger and *my* fear of my anger I back off. But then I feel the rage and the guilt continuing to war inside me till my guts feel like the battlefield at Little Big Horn the day after.

CARL: With me it's not even a feeling of wanting to do anything violent to him. It's more the feeling that he's so unsubstantial that just expressing my anger, just telling him off, will make him vanish! Poof! Not even dead, just gone, blown away.

JEANNE: Sometimes my father would vanish behind his eyes and look blank. But mostly it was a beagle look.

CARL: I stopped expressing anger to my father that time because I already had found that I'd feel worse and worse after. When I was a kid and felt I hurt him I would begin to feel so guilty that I'd run and beg his forgiveness and he'd say "all right" but he looked like he didn't know what I was talking about!

JEANNE: Exactly the same with me! I'd feel this compulsion to go to him and make it right. I couldn't concentrate on anything else till I did it. He knew what I was talking about but he'd just look more hangdog, like even the emotion in my contrition was too much for him.

THERAPIST: So it's not just your angry feelings he couldn't take?

JEANNE: No, all feelings. I was always afraid to tell him how much I loved him, because that could also make him crumble.

THERAPIST: What power!

JEANNE: Oh, yes! For years I couldn't see it as his being weak. I didn't want to see him as weak. So I thought that he reacted that way to me because I was too strong, too intense. I started to feel that I was a storm, a cyclone of love and hate and all kinds of swirling feelings that could destroy everybody.

CARL: I've had that feeling. It scared me so that I began to walk around gingerly, as if I were carrying a bomb through a busy playground. But worse than that was trying to hold on to some image that my father was really strong. I could see myself not only holding myself back but keeping down just to pretend my father was up.

JEANNE: If I could have felt sure that my father didn't care about me it would hurt but I would have stopped trying to make him something he's not. But for all I know he cared a lot, or maybe he didn't. He was a blob, a Rorschach inkblot, and I could fantasy anything about him. And did I! As a child I saw him as the grandest and the greatest. I elevated his passivity to a saintliness, I saw his submissiveness as chivalry, and I twisted his weakness into a gentle strength. Then there were two incidents that smashed the illusion. I was about ten and I was riding in the car with my father when a policeman stopped him for passing a red light. My father at first denied it although we both knew he was guilty. Then, when the cop started to write out the ticket my father began to cry, and he told the cop he passed the light because he was upset because he had just found out my mother had cancer!

CARL: Did she?

JEANNE: No. Although at the time I wasn't sure—even though my father told me right after that it wasn't true I worried about it for a long time.

CARL: Did he get the ticket?

JEANNE: No.

CARL: That was a pretty neat maneuver!

JEANNE: You would say that! And I tried to tell myself, "Isn't Daddy clever," so I could maintain my pride in him even though I felt like puking whenever I thought of it. There were probably hundreds of other little things that were making it harder and harder to keep him up there.

There something happened when I was fourteen that shattered my image of him as surely as if I had thrown a brick into the bathroom mirror while he was shaving. In school we were outside during a fire drill and I got slightly bitten by a dog. The school nurse kept trying to call my mother at home but the line was always busy. She had the operator check and found the receiver was off the hook. So she called my father at his dry cleaning store and he came right over and took me home. When we got there he opened the door but the chain lock was on from the inside so he rang the bell. My mother called, "Who's there?" We told her and we told her what happened. She took over five minutes to answer and there was this man there who she said was an interior decorator with whom she had been discussing redoing the living room, but she was all flustered and the man was awkward and left quickly. It was all so obvious, but my father acted like he bought the whole thing. I swear, I thought he was going to ask the guy to stay for coffee. I knew that he knew but that he was keeping himself from really knowing because then he might have to do something or say something or whatever and he was scared to confront my mother. I'm sure it wasn't because he was "liberated" or unjealous. He just let it go because he was always so afraid to make waves.

THERAPIST: Can you feel how you felt then?

JEANNE: I hated my mother, but I felt more betrayed by my father. I had been idealizing him, creating an illusion and then suddenly I couldn't anymore. Suddenly I saw him as a pathetic shmuck. [She started to cry.] It's still painful! All those wasted years of propping him up. What a sad, stupid waste! [She cried for a while.]

CARL: I felt the same thing when I had my moments of truth. They weren't as dramatic as your incidents, Jeanne, just little things, like the time I mentioned before when I yelled at him and saw that helpless look. But I was bitter when later on, in therapy, I began to see all the ways I had stunted myself so I could look up to someone who didn't deserve it. I had my mind jumping through hoops to preserve the image of his power. At this moment I'm more angry than sad and more determined than angry. No more jumping through hoops to keep anyone up there.

JEANNE: And no more being dependent on anyone whose strength is a mirage growing from my thirst for a father I can count on.

So we see in this dialogue how a weak father can make you feel afraid of overwhelming him with any kind of strong feelings or emotional needs and can make you feel that if you are too much for him, then there must be something wrong with you.

For a young girl, not only the hope for an alternative to mother but the wish for an intense Oedipal* intimacy with her father is painfully disappointed when his weakness makes him unavailable for support, trailblazing or closeness. For a young boy, his father's weakness not only deprives him of a model and teacher, but carries the threat that he can defeat his father in the Oedipal rivalry if he lets himself. The ramifications of these feelings may have led you to distort your own perceptions of him, as did Carl and Jeanne, because you did not want to see his weakness. Perhaps you are still mentally trying to prop him up and have not yet gauged him realistically. If so, what price are you paying for that song and dance? Are you making him big by keeping yourself small, him strong by keeping yourself weak, him reliable by keeping yourself irresponsible, him competent by keeping yourself ineffectual, him a success by keeping yourself a failure?

Or perhaps you have already been disillusioned, recently or so long ago that you cannot remember ever seeing him as strong; maybe you've already seen him life-size but, perhaps rushing in angry disillusionment to the opposite pole, now see him as smaller than he is! That, too, has a price—the burden of ongoing contempt, which precludes the development of any relationship of value with him.

There are many ripples emanating from the turbulent interactions that pass for relationships between a weak father and his offspring. Perhaps you are locked into a pattern of finding enfeebled "father figures" and then dedicating yourself to overlooking their weakness

---

*While Oedipus was the boy who killed his father and married his mother, and Electra represents the girl's rivalry with her mother for her father, I follow the common psychoanalytic tradition here in using "Oedipal" (or "Oedipus complex") to stand for the attachment of children of either sex to the parent of the opposite sex.

or to forever propping them up to look strong. Men sometimes do this with friends, supervisors and bosses. The danger is even greater for women who do it with lovers and husbands, thereby entering into a possible lifetime replay of the old song and dance with the only change being the name of the male partner. I have seen women with weak fathers unerringly and repeatedly select, out of a large number of men who cross through their life space, men who are little boys in basic ways—perhaps alcoholics, drug addicts, love addicts, failures in careers, inept at earning a living and unable to assert themselves except perhaps in a little-boy demandingness, tantrums and sulkiness. Sexually they are often passive and constricted, although some may be sexually vital when body hedonism is more an expression of their little-boy feelings than of confident worldly strength. And oh, how good they are at their end of the song and dance if you play your part. And if you've had a weak man for a father, you know your part very well.

Initially, at least, it's to deny your man's basic weakness, either by blinding yourself to it completely or by seeing it as some cute or perhaps mildly troublesome quirk. Then, when your face or rear end is sufficiently bruised from falling on one or the other every time you thought your man was strong enough to lean on for occasional emotional, moral or practical support, it may gradually dawn on you that there's some pretty basic defect there. This would be a good time to re-evaluate the whole relationship, but if you were hooked into a rescue and rehabilitation fantasy with your father, you'll swiftly and unthinkingly don the uniform of whatever rescue mission is called for—nurse, social worker, vocational counselor, benevolent mother, policeman—and begin the soul-grinding process of lifting up, pumping up, propping up, shoring up and giving up; and then, after briefly resting up, return to lifting up, etc.

The question is, what's in it for you, both with your father and with other men with whom you continue that pattern? You have this empty place in you that your father's weakness left unfulfilled. His not having a strong hand to clasp yours and introduce you to the world has left a crevasse in your confidence you may not yet have found a way to fill or bridge. So there is an unfinished task. Some perceive this task as finding a strong person they can identify with, learn from, be guided by and thus fill the crevasse. They are lucky, because this is an achievable task that may lead to an enriching goal. Many others see the task differently (and I use "see" here not as a deliberately thought-out view of the job that needs to be finished but as an unconscious, automatic perception). They see the unfinished task as having to "cure" and strengthen their weak father, and if they transfer this task to other men, then by definition these men must be weak in order to be strengthened! The pull to complete this job is powerful and basically unachievable because, as you may see now if you are caught up in this, you are not out to *succeed* in this task but simply to keep *working* on it. The game is played to bring you back to Square One, feeling let down, disappointed, victimized and still seeking a strong father. (A similar version is played by men who are dependent on an inept boss who may get fired and leave them floating anchorless, if they don't get fired with him, or who place their trust in a man they believe to be dependable but who, for example, gives the important contract that he should have given to them to someone he didn't know how to refuse.) Once you have returned to Square One as the victim, you can start all over again as the rehabilitator; but this time you can feel self-righteous about nagging and controlling the man to be raised up. Control! That's one thing the weak man allows you to have. It seems like you can walk all over him. What power! Only after you've finished walking all over him you may notice that your shoes are missing. Maybe even your feet!

So it is the addiction to completing the unfinished task of raising up your father, the hope that if you do you will have someone strong to lean on and learn from, the repeated disappointments and hurts that lead you to claim the victim's right to persecute and push around, that set the rhythm for your end of the song and dance. And breaking it, as in all other songs and dances, begins with the recognition that you are in it.

There is a story about a frail, aging little man who answers a "Man Wanted" ad he had seen in the newspaper. The ad called for a "strong, experienced outdoorsman, expert marksman, horseman and mountain climber." When he arrived for the interview the interviewer was stunned.

"You don't look strong."

"To tell you the truth, I'm sickly."

"You're an experienced outdoorsman?"

"Sundays I go for picnics."

"You shoot, ride horses, climb mountains?"

"I never touched a gun, I'm afraid of horses and I get dizzy when I'm high up."

"So why did you answer this ad?"

"I just came to tell you, on me you shouldn't count."

Rarely if ever does a weak father come out into the open with his weakness and tell you, "On me you shouldn't count." (I have been amazed at how many people with weak fathers tell this as their favorite joke.) Most weak fathers don't see themselves as weak —they see themselves as "too easy," "giving in because it's a short life and who needs trouble," "what does it cost you to be nice," "I've had a lot of disappointments"—so you may have to define for yourself the areas of weakness where he failed you.

If you suspect you are in an insidious song and dance with a weak father, then a good, hard look at the reality of your father is called for. What are his strengths and weaknesses as a man? Have you blown him up too big, or shrunk him too small? Is your perception of his strengths and weaknesses yours or your mother's? (There are mothers who are perpetually raising their husbands up, and others who unfailingly tear their husbands down, in the eyes of their children. It will be necessary to wash mama out of your eyes and see father as accurately as one person can view another he is close to.) Trying to see your father accurately means going over your storehouse of memories of him—not just the few that are favorites because they seem to characterize what you feel about him, but all that you can recall—and put yourself in his place, feel yourself into him in these memories. Then look at the overall picture of his life—what you know of his childhood, his struggles, his reasons for marrying your mother, his ambitions, his disappointments. Some people who have deluded themselves by ignoring his weaknesses may have to face their own hidden disappointment; others who have seen only his weakness may find a core of strength and resolve there, a vein of hard iron or flexible steel buried beneath the soft muck, that they may never have noticed.

If your end of the song and dance has been to prop him up in your own eyes and in the eyes of the world, this is what you will have to stop doing, but this is incomparably harder than to stop scratching a poison ivy rash. You will have to face the fact that in certain ways he never could be counted on and doubtless never will, and that this indeed has left you with a crack in the foundations of your own self-confidence. You will have to give up the old pattern and thus surrender the hope that you can turn weak father into strong father and thus have him repair the crack in your foundation.

The recognition that father has failed you in basic ways may lead you into the reverse type of song and dance with father; instead of raising him up you will be forever tearing him down, angrily berating him, treating him with contempt. How vindictive we can get when our god's clay feet are exposed! This is the usual reaction, but one that we can challenge by asking, who made him a god in the first place?

After the upsetting recognition of your father's weakness, how it has affected you, and the songs and dances you are still futilely involved in with him, it will be useful to ask what kind of little boy in him you are dealing with, for here, even more clearly than in other songs and dances, it is the parent's inner child that your own disappointed inner child is hooked into. I think of a young woman who was expecting a visit from her parents. When the doorbell rang she called out, "Who's there?" She heard her father's voice answer, "Mama!" She was enraged at her father's castrated reply and at all the memories it brought of being let down by her father's submissiveness. But in thinking about it later she realized that her father's reply of "Mama" represented not only his identity-less relationship with his wife but also was a product of a fused identity with his own mother, and she saw her father sympathetically, as a man still responding as a little boy because his sense of self was shattered very early in his life, perhaps in infancy, by parents who did much to make him feel worthless, to drain his self-assurance, discourage his separateness and to clip his wings. If you try to look at your father and peel away the years so you can see him as a child, you might intuit that perhaps he cried a lot the first day of school, and maybe the second and third, unless his submissiveness took the form of being the "good little soldier." Probably he was at the edge of the group, most likely he was taken advantage of by the other children, possibly even made fun of. He probably did what he was told by the teachers unless he resisted by passively messing up. Picturing your weak father as a little boy might have two beneficial results for you. You might realize the impossibility, the sad ludicrousness, of trying to lean on or pretend you could lean on such a small child as if he were a big man. The preponderant little child in him can't ever fully grasp that he is a parent, and what emotional responsibility that carries with it. He still feels *he* is the one that needs taking care of. And you might feel some compassion for this hurt child that will help you get out of the recriminative, angry song and dance based on accusing him of failing you. That refrain only pushes him down, reinforcing his profound feelings of ineffectuality, and probably leaves you feeling guilty. So if you give up both the push-him-up and tear-him-down songs and dances that are so tempting to do with weak fathers, and you have the courage to face that his weakness did indeed deprive you of something basic and has left soft spots in your functioning, the question becomes, how can you best make up for what he didn't give you? Or do you just resign yourself to those soft spots?

First, in the actual relationship with your father it is particularly important to relate to the mature, strong part of him, no matter how small a part this is, not by the old, disastrous maneuver of inflating his strength, but by recognizing what is strong there and communicating with it. This not only serves to stymie his end of the song and dance ("I can't, it's too heavy, I don't know how, it's too hard, help me, leave me alone (sigh), how can you leave me alone") but enables you to tap into whatever adult strength has brought your father through life to this point. To the extent that you can tap into this strength, you can begin to fill in the soft spots, or add new tape messages where the old tape was blank.

You can also become aware of the fatherly strengths in yourself, the thoughts and wishes that encourage you to dare, to risk, to leave mother's psychological force field, to stick to the pursuit of your goals and ideals, to pick yourself up and keep going. Certainly there is some of this kind of fatherliness there. And some of this fatherliness can come from other men, not weak men you have to prop up but men of real strength who may be in your life as friends, teachers, colleagues, lovers. Levinson has found that for a man (perhaps because he is less likely than a woman to have the experience of having a male lover), having a mentor can be crucial.* A mentor is usually an older man, often successful in your kind of work, who has qualities and an approach to life you admire and who seems willing to share these strengths with you. For women, lovers and husbands as well as friends, colleagues and others can help fill the blank areas in the father tapes with new messages that impart courage to grow from the real or internalized constricting mother. But this very possibility carries with it a crucial ques-

*See D. J. Levinson *et al.*, "The psychosocial development of men in early adulthood and the mid-life transition," in David F. Ricks *et al.*, *Life History Research in Psychopathology* (Minneapolis, Minn.: University of Minnesota Press, 1974), Vol. 3, pp. 244–57.

tion: What of missed fathering can I legitimately ask for of a husband or lover without setting up another out-of-balance parent-child relationship? You can ask for and get quite a lot provided that the parent-to-child mode of relating is not all one way but reversible (we all need to have our inner child responded to), that you choose a man who is willing and able sometimes to assume a fathering role, and that the parent-to-child mode of relating can give way to a more frequent mature mutuality.

5 | The High
and the Mighty

Despite our talk of weak fathers, shadowy fathers and absentee fathers, the despotic father is still alive and unwell, wreaking his own particular kind of havoc. He seems formidable and frightening because he doesn't rely on guilt provocation like mama martyr. Naked power and arousal of fear are his methods of controlling and he usually starts using these techniques at tender ages in the lives of his children, when size and strength and power are decidedly unequal. So this fear, often under the guise of "respect," is implanted early and can sit forever in his offspring like a little pool of gelatin waiting to quiver.

I have seen grown men, men of considerable accomplishment, literally tremble when questioned by their fathers about why they are getting a divorce, and I have seen adult women, women with grown children of their own, run to put out their cigarettes when daddy, who abhors smoking, rings the doorbell.

YOU BELONG TO ME

It's important to clarify just what a tyrannical father is, so we don't get him confused with just plain strong fathers who require their children to aim for certain standards and who offer active guidance and appropriate discipline. The differentiating factor is simple: *Daddy the despot believes he owns you. For the tyrannical father, if you are his child, you are his possession.*

To help you to identify despotic daddyness I have

constructed a specialized test, the DDI or Despotic Daddy Inventory. Now perhaps this test would not pass the strictures of widespread sampling, reliability and validity that the psychological profession requires testing instruments to meet. It comes instead from what psychotherapists like myself enjoy calling "clinical intuition," which usually means we want to make a point and back it with scientific mystification. So I would like to suppose that:

1. if we gave this test to a random group of fathers and asked them what was the correct response to the given statements by their young adult offspring, most fathers would give responses scattered evenly over multiple choice items "a," "b," and "c," and

2. if you find yourself frequently resonating to answer "c" with a feeling "that sounds like my dad," then we can assume that, as far as you are concerned, you had a true despotic daddy.

DDI (Despotic Daddy Inventory)

1. "Dad, I'm going out to meet my friends."
   (a) "Have a good time."
   (b) "I want you back by midnight."
   (c) "Friends, hah! They'll lead you into trouble."

2. "I've changed my mind about my major."
   (a) "How come?"
   (b) "Are you sure this is what you want?"
   (c) "You'll never amount to anything the way you sway with each breeze."

3. "I'm going to the movies."
   (a) "What are you going to see?"
   (b) "Don't get back too late."
   (c) "Where are you really going?"

4. "I've been invited to my friend's house for dinner and I'd like to go."
   (a) "That sounds like fun."

(b) "Which friend is this?"

(c) "Are you asking me or telling me?"

5. "I thought about the trip and I really want to go ahead with it."
   (a) "Okay, if that's what you want."
   (b) "I think it's a mistake, but I wish you luck."
   (c) "Do it your own ridiculous way."

6. "Do I have to spend all day Sunday helping around the house?"
   (a) "Yes, I need your help."
   (b) "Sure. You're part of the family."
   (c) "Just remember who pays for the food you eat."

7. "I got the test results back and I went down in math."
   (a) "Did you really study?"
   (b) "You'll have to get down to work now. Would a tutor help?"
   (c) "You can't go out or have a friend over until you bring that grade up."

8. "I know I had the tickets but now I can't find them."
   (a) "Keep looking."
   (b) "You'll have to pay for them."
   (c) "I can't believe a son of mine could be so stupid."

9. "He's my closest friend."
   (a) "It's good to have close friends."
   (b) "That's surprising. You haven't known him long."
   (c) "Just be sure he's not taking advantage of you."

10. "I have to hurry or I'll be late for the concert."
    (a) "Next time try to time things so there isn't such a rush."
    (b) "Drive carefully."
    (c) "First you'll stop at the store and buy me some cigarettes."

If your father scores high on the DDI then you'll recognize the man in this chapter. You'll see that his view of the world is perhaps a bit less paranoid than Captain Queeg's. For example, look at the responses, "Where are you really going?" and "Friends, hah! They'll lead you into trouble," and "Just be sure he's not taking advantage of you." He has become convinced that nobody can really be trusted. He makes it clear he doesn't trust what you're up to and that you'd better not trust people either because trusting is naive and the naive get shafted.

To feel safe in a world where people can't be trusted, DD has probably mastered the put-down to be used with people below him in status, like you. ("You'll never amount to anything the way you sway with each breeze," "Do it your own ridiculous way.") Belittle is the technique. Be little is the message.

I WAITED ON MASTER AND BROUGHT HIM HIS PLATE

And then, of course, there's the message making it very clear just who the boss is and where your position is in relation to him. ("Are you asking me or telling me?" "You can't go out or have a friend over until you bring that grade up.")

The quote "First you'll stop at the store and buy me some cigarettes" was spoken by a father who had several cartons of cigarettes in the drawer. And like Hitler (Chaplin) seating Mussolini (Jack Oakie) in a little sawed-off chair in *The Great Dictator,* daddy, too, will often drop any subtlety: "Just remember who pays for the food you eat."

If your father scores high on the DDI then you know that his kind of statements, statements you've grown up with, have added up to a set of simple commandments that have been scorched into your cerebral hemispheres as if by Jehovah. They read something like this:

I. I'm your father and no one comes before me.

II. What I say goes.

III. My needs and conveniences come first.
IV. I get respect and gratitude.
V. Go along with these rules or else.

The "or else" may change as the child matures: "Or else I'll spank you, beat the hell out of you, stop talking to you, confine you to your room, stop your allowance, throw you out, cut you off, etc." But the commandments usually remain, perhaps paler as the child becomes an adult, but rarely erased completely.

If you have or had a despot daddy, it is important to see not only the song and dance you have entered into with him but how he has shaped your way of relating to the rest of the world. *Basically, your style depends on whether you chose to fight him, surrender to him or join him.*

HIGH NOON

If you decided to fight your DD you may have become a real scrapper. Perhaps your childhood and adolescence was a sequence of showdowns, shootouts and duels in the sun parlor. You were defiant, you were punished; you were remorseful or simmered; you were chastened or glowered, and then you were defiant again. Maybe at times the fight even got violent. Maybe it was one-sided (he "taught you a lesson"); maybe it was two-way (you "taught him"). Possibly a grudging respect has grown out of these battles. Or maybe your adolescent anger and hatred has hardened into a coldness and distance as you've gotten older.

And what about your attitude toward the rest of the world—particularly that part that has been identified with him because it also tells you what to do, like teachers, supervisors, bosses, rules, laws? Are they subject to the same defiance? Are you still fighting the old battle in new arenas? As you get old enough to have rebellious children of your own, are you getting tired of being a rebel without a cause?

And if you're a woman, does your defiance of DD carry over to other men in your life? Do you battle your sweetheart or husband as if his wishes for your affection, sexuality and givingness are demands for the unconditional surrender of your separateness and your selfhood? Do you long for a tender, loving, warm and understanding man and then dismiss such a man as a schnook while you pursue the excitement of battle with a contemptuous bastard? And did I hear you say you've resolved this problem with your tyrannical father?

Some women go another route. To be sure they will never again know the tyranny of a DD they seek a man with little need to dominate. But then they may feel him to be ineffectual, either because he really is, or because compared to their domineering father he seems that way. So when it looks like she is stating, "I can't stand a tyrant like my dad and I'm going to find a man who treats me nicely and respectfully," it may soon become "My husband is passive and weak, not strong and manly like my father." In other words, when a woman with a DD feels her man is beneath her, she is often setting it up so that nobody will dethrone her father. And that is setting up trouble.

I SURRENDER, DEAR

If you took the route of surrendering to him you're in another kind of trouble. But surrendering to him may have been hard to avoid, because if DD has really wanted your surrender, he knew how to get it. I mentioned earlier the woman who told me how her father had made her sweep her room twelve times, inspecting carefully after each time, making her do it all over again if there was a mote of dust. All this while she was in a hurry to go out—and with the threat that if she didn't, she couldn't go out at all.

A man tells me how when he was a child, his father would provoke him into a tantrum. He would swing his small fists wildly at air while his father laughingly held him at arm's length with the palm of his hand against his face. After a while the son would collapse in tears of humiliation and exhaustion. Then his father would hold him and comfort him.

I can feel the frustration and fury they must have

experienced, but I can also feel the despairing sense of futility and inadequacy in a childhood replete with such incidents. And so there is often a surrender. Let daddy be the boss. After all, father has power, father really knows best. The fear-bedeviled woman who told me of sweeping the floor twelve times and of other incidents, some even brutal, showed no warmth toward her father but was quick to assure me that she "looked up to him and respected him." And for her submissive role she was able to count on his help whenever life got tough. When defiance is punished and surrender is rewarded, the shoulders begin to stoop, the head begins to look down, the legs are less firmly grounded than they should be.

This stance is not assumed before father alone. If you have surrendered too much of yourself there, it is unlikely that you hold to a firm and assertive posture anywhere but with your dog or in your daydreams. And I'm not so sure about with your dog. Surrender has bought freedom from Father's kind of terror, but the yoke's on you.

I know many people who think they fought their despotic fathers but who actually gave in to them. Take those hordes of bright youngsters, mostly males, who were labeled underachievers—kids who, everyone was forever saying, "could do better." Daddy and the daddy figures represented by school, requirements, and so on told them "do well"; their own experiences told them that "do well" meant "do what we tell you," and they were determined to save their selfhood by defying that enslaving stricture. They fought by not doing. They failed courses, flunked out, dropped out. For some it worked to preserve their separateness. Too many others deprived themselves of the intellectual muscle, of the informational strength, of the knowledge and skills that could make them truly independent of their parents. They weakened themselves to be defiant and only ended up weak. So it is important to question: Was defiance their only motivation, or was there some hidden drive toward defeat and surrender? The most striking examples of this are the many young men I know who have gone the whole defiance route, dropping out, running away, bumming around. Then, finding they haven't prepared themselves for anything else, they go back to work in father's business. It is often beautifully choreographed—the fights, the departure, the return, the surrender, the burying of the past. Who is to say that this denouement wasn't planned in advance by the father and the part of his offspring that longs to surrender to father?

PRAISE THE LORD

Maybe you've worked things out with your father not by high-spirited defiance or broken-spirited surrender but by getting into the spirit of his thing. "If you can't fight him, join him" is often a workable basis for a relationship with a DD. Every general needs his colonels, every boss his executive assistants, every DD his adulators and imitators.

Joining this kind of father has many advantages. First, you don't get chastised, beat up or otherwise punished as you would for fighting him. Secondly, you don't become ineffectual and vacuous as you would from surrendering to him. And after all, isn't it part of the mental hygiene rules for healthy development that a child, particularly a son, identifies with his father's strengths? Well, not exactly. It makes a difference what it is that causes a child to identify with his father— and love and respect are better motives than fear and trembling. But where a child has assumed a "satellite" relationship with a despotic father, not a groveling or placating one but where he revolves around him in an admiring and emulating way, it is not fear alone that has made him choose this way of relating. In most instances, the child has learned that his or her father approves those qualities that are most like himself and therefore the child is rewarded for being aggressive, egotistical and domineering (so long as he does not fight his father's authority). I have seen authoritarian fathers wink at their child's hooky playing and even covertly twinkle when a child broke all the windows in the schoolhouse or beat up the kid down the block. It is when a despotic father encourages self-aggrandizing behavior in his child that he pushes the child toward being merged in identity with him rather than being subservient or defiant. If you have gone this route, you've avoided the dangers of a fight, you haven't abjectly surrendered and you've bought yourself some safety. But you are still paying a price.

For one thing, you may still have not achieved the closeness with your father that you've always wanted. There may be something unreal, not quite right, vaguely phoney, not really warm or harmonious beneath the surface alliance. And though you may not feel you surrendered to him, you may occasionally detect a note of contempt in him that makes you wonder if he sees it the same way.

But even more distressing are the times when you are not quite sure if that voice you are speaking with is your own voice or his, if the words are your own, if the melody is your own. Sometimes you listen to yourself with your friends or, even more unsettlingly, with your own kids, and you can hear his phrases, his tone. And how does it feel when you want to try out new songs, songs different from his? Are you still afraid of his reaction? Are you so afraid that you quickly rejoin him, convincing yourself that what he wants of you is what you want for yourself?

Men who join their fathers in this way often have trouble establishing really loving relationships with women. Their strongest bond is with a man, their father, and it is a bond forged more of power and fear than of tenderness. If you've joined your DD there's a good chance you want a woman who will stay in her place, and you can get pretty upset when your woman wants equal time and treatment. And, particularly these days of women's consciousness raising, she's going to give you a hard time if you try those DD songs and dances on her.

WHO'S AFRAID OF THE BIG BAD WOLF?

If the first step in ending a song and dance is usually recognizing the child within your parent, how do you go about recognizing a child inside an adult man of formidable mien and a long-standing position of power? Hal, a young man who had spent his life alternating between trying to please his patriarchal father and pretending he didn't give a damn about pleasing him, returned home for his first vacation from college. At dinner, Hal's father asked how college was going. After talking awhile about his classes and friends Hal reported, as if casually, but with barely concealed pleasure, how he had dropped into the college chess club one evening and asked someone sitting there for a game.

"It was a good game but I beat him without too much difficulty . . . Then I found out that he was the captain of the college chess team!"

There was a long pause, and then his father intoned, "Some captain."

At the time it happened, it was another of a series of putdowns and belittlements by his father that had been crushing Hal since infancy, when his father had totally ignored him. He would tell Hal's mother, "When he's old enough to talk and think, then I'll do business with him." The business he had in mind seems to have been the wrecking business, so this latest undercutting was nothing new but was as devastating as ever because Hal still clung to the unyielding hope that maybe this time it would be different. Maybe this time he'd say "Great" or "Wonderful" or wordlessly smile with pride. This was Hal's end of the song and dance—to keep expecting and trying for his father's approval as if his self-worth depended on it. So there was that old sinking feeling when his father shot him down again but now, when Hal told this story in therapy, he was overwhelmed by rage at his father's consistent efforts to castrate him. Hal ranted, poured forth similar incidents and relished being in touch with all that anger.

When Hal's fury subsided, the therapist said, "Tell the story again." He did, but this time he was empty of emotion. It came out flat. The therapist said, "Tell it again." He told it once more and now, by the time he got to "Some captain" he was convulsed with laughter, and so was the therapist. The two of them sat together, roaring with mirth, tears streaming down their cheeks. The father's overbearingness—till then such a source of fear and pain and rage—suddenly flipped into perspective as the absurdly funny pomposity it was.

In that change of perspective is the key to understanding DD and to begin to deal with him more effectively than fighting, surrendering or joining. Because with that change in perspective we see clearly that we are dealing with the child in the father, with the little boy behind all that thunder, and suddenly he's not frightening.

After all, what makes an adult man, often an intelligent, educated one, need to see his own child as a possession? What makes him need to promulgate such childish, self-centered rules and commandments? Certainly it's not the mature part of him. Nor is it the concerned-parent part of him. Look closely and you will see, leaning in the corner of the throne, a little boy in a playsuit, his crown so big it's slipped down over his eyes, his hand clutching a pinwheel, his high voice piping, "Remember who's the big man around here." It is often difficult to permit yourself to see the child inside your authoritarian father, or any weakness in him, because you also have a stake in seeing him as powerful, even when his power has been destructive to you. There is a security in seeing him as strong, a need to protect both him and yourself from seeing his foibles and vulnerabilities. A young woman told me of the tears that welled in her eyes when her father, whose domineering she despised, became unnerved in an upsetting situation and was for a while transformed into a fumbling, frightened, inept little boy. She felt herself yearning to have him back in his old tyrannical role.

But if you dare to see the child in your despotic father you can, perhaps with compassion, look further and see what you can learn about how he got stuck being a spoiled child for so long. Was he pampered? Or was he not taken seriously so that he had to yell and demand attention? Did the other kids like him, or did he try to get his way by pushing them around? Is he really powerful or is he like the Wizard of Oz, an ordinary, life-size man hiding behind the curtain and controlling the big voice?

As you see the insecure, frustrated, angry boy in your father your feelings may begin to respond more realistically. This view does not have to be a contemptuous or disrespectful one. It may make you like him more by seeing his humanness in fuller dimension. Nor does this view mean that his power should not be taken seriously because, even if he is part little boy, he can have the kind of clout that often derives and accumulates from living longer—experience, wisdom, money, position and know-how. But the power he has with you is probably not a product of his real power, but of his old and early ability to frighten you. If you begin to see that the little child in you is frightened of another little child, the little child in him, why then there's no reason that your "child" can't handle his "child." And once your "child" has unfrightenedly dealt with his fist-shaking "child" then the adult you are can go about your business.

I DID IT MY WAY

Several years after Hal, our student chessplayer, was devastated by his father's imperious "Some captain!" and after considerable growth in self-esteem through psychotherapy and rewarding life experiences, the following dinner-table dialogue took place on another visit from college.

"I'm not going to law school."

"You're not what?" Hal's father glared at him. The young man felt a twinge of the old fear lightly spasm his gut. He noticed that his father seemed older, thinner, smaller. The spasm flickered away.

"I've decided not to apply to law school. It's just not for me."

"Not for you! Why not? Why the hell did you take all those pre-law courses for?"

"I thought that's what I wanted, but now I know it isn't."

"You know. You don't know anything."

Hal was silent.

"So, what are you going to be, a bum?"

"I'd like to be an English professor."

"Like I said, you're going to be a bum."

"Dad, could you please pass the butter?"

"What?"

"Could you please pass the butter?"

The butter was passed and Hal spread it in silence. His father stopped eating, letting his fork clatter onto the plate.

"English teachers are a dime a dozen. I have a Ph.D. in English working for me writing letters to customers who complain. We call him 'Professor.' "

"Some professor," Hal muttered.

"What?"

"Nothing."

"If you become a lawyer I would throw more business your way than most lawyers get when they're in practice ten years."

"I know. I've thought a lot about it. And I know it's hard getting academic jobs. But it's what I really want and I think I'll be damn good at it. If I don't make it, well, then we'll see."

"And who's going to pay for this foolishness?"

"I knew you might not want to support me in this line of study. You had been counting on my going to law school. So if you'd rather not, I'll take a year off after graduation to work and put some money together. Then I can get a part-time job while I'm going to grad school."

"Work! What can you do?"

"Something."

And his father didn't pay, and Hal got a job. As Hal's father saw that his son would make it he was uneasy about his loss of control and offered to give Hal an allowance, offered him a better-paying job working for him, offered to buy him a car to get to work more easily, etc. But by now Hal was enjoying his sense of responsibility for his own life and politely refused. He entered graduate school the next fall, paying his own tuition and fees. Then he spoke to his father again about finances.

"Dad, I can maintain myself working part time

about twenty hours a week. But if I didn't have to work I could take more courses, begin my dissertation early and finish up sooner. Either way is okay, but if you'd like to lend me the money I'd appreciate it."

"Okay, you can have the money."

"As a loan."

"I don't lend money to my son."

"That's the only way I'll take it."

"What are you afraid of? That if you take the money I'll think I own you?"

Hal grinned. His father sighed. "Okay, okay, a loan."

The essence of this story is that Hal felt and communicated a competent ownership of himself. He didn't get involved in an intensely defiant struggle, which would have been another kind of song and dance that would have reflected more of a need for his father's capitulation than for freedom. He hadn't begged or bargained with his father as if his autonomy was something his father could grant or withhold. He hadn't been inept and self-defeating in his bid for separateness, which would have again invited his father to call the tune. He simply became, in matters pertaining to his own goals and needs, his own authority.

Sometimes it's easier to stop a submissive or placating song and dance, as Hal was able to do, than to stop a defiant one. If you have an overbearing father you may feel that all is lost if you permit him to get one up on you or to win a single argument. It feels imperative that you never acknowledge his strengths or accept the merits of his suggestions. Granting him any victory brings back all your childhood feelings of being helpless, belittled and controlled by him and you must defend vigilantly against this possibility. I saw this clearly as I got to know Craig, a young orthopedic surgeon who had been in a power struggle with his father since his earliest memories. His father was a farmer, and many battles centered around his demands that Craig work long hours in the fields and Craig's resentment at what seemed to him the tyran-

nical way his father treated his mother. As Craig got
older, there was distance between his father and himself except for times they matched physical strength, as
measured in arm wrestling, chopping wood, lifting
weights, hitting a baseball, etc. His father would invariably win, and would gloat disdainfully. When
Craig decided to go to college his father sullenly sup-
ported it at the urging of Craig's mother. Once, on a
visit home from college, Craig's car got into a ditch.
His father came with his own car, pulled Craig's car
out and charged Craig five dollars! A few months later
his father's car got stuck in the same ditch. Craig
pulled his father's car out and charged him ten dollars "because it was Sunday." This story typified their
relationship.

When I met Craig he was a father himself, a successful professional who had come into psychotherapy
with me largely because he found himself in repeated
power struggles with the directors of the hospital
where he was on staff. He had been warned by several
colleagues that his abrasiveness and his rebellious responses to those in authority were jeopardizing his
career but he couldn't seem to modify this behavior.
Despite rare contact with his father, Craig talked of
him often in therapy, usually with bitterness and rancor. His father had made several efforts to be closer to
Craig, but Craig had rebuffed them all. In one session
Craig was expressing much anger at his father, who
had just invited him to visit for dinner. For Craig, the
invitation had many of the earmarks of a command.
I asked Craig to stand up, make believe his father was
facing him, and tell his father all the things he hated
about him. Craig began eagerly.

"I've hated you almost all my life. When I was a
kid I'd be home talking to mom in the kitchen or playing with a friend in my room and then you'd come in
from the fields and everyone would become tense.
Everyone could sense the anger you brought in with
you and all fun would stop. You wouldn't be in the
house two minutes when you'd find something to criticize or yell about. You'd put down mom if dinner
was a few minutes late. You'd throw out my friends

if you wanted it quiet even if we were playing quietly. You'd find something for me to do just to make me do something. You hated me for getting good grades and wanting to become a doctor and get off the damn farm. And you never took the trouble to talk to me about anything that I was interested in. It hurt a lot, and then I decided, the hell with you, and I became your enemy. I dreamed of beating you in everything, and the day when I was fifteen and we were throwing stones across the stream and I could throw them further was the happiest day of my life, and you got so quiet and couldn't look at me. I really wanted you to be proud of me but I settled for your looking defeated and I thrived on that instead. And now you want to be close to me, particularly since mom died, and you invite me over and ask about my work. Why? Because you're lonely? Because now I'm successful and you want a piece of it? Suddenly I'm your son so you can brag about me. Well, the hell with it. It's too late, dad. Way too late."

I interrupted Craig to point out that all the time he talked to his father he was looking up, as if his father were towering over him. Craig was tall, six feet three, and so I asked him how tall his father was. He answered, "about five feet eight or so." It was obvious that he still felt like a little boy with his father and that it was the child in Craig who was talking. To try to break this perspective, I asked Craig to stand on the chair, to see his father as standing down below, smaller than him, and to continue the conversation. Craig began to tell me he wouldn't stand on the chair just because I said he should, then he stopped himself and got up on it.

"Like I was saying, it's too late, dad. You were always against me and trying to control me and . . ." Craig's voice trailed off. He looked "down" at his father and for a long time wouldn't say anything. "Christ, you're little! I never realized how little you are. And you're really getting old, aren't you? If I stop looking up from down below you I can see you've been a hard-working, bossy, insecure, threatened little guy. And you're smart. You were right when you warned me off buying that house three years ago and I'm glad I didn't but I almost bought it because you said I shouldn't. I've hated you so much, but you really are small and shaky. I see the little kid in you feeling frightened and inadequate and acting like a big shot to cover it up. I see the kid in you having a tantrum when you don't get your way."

Craig sighed and looked at his "father" for a long time. "Okay, pop, take it easy. Now you're getting old and weak and you're afraid that the scared kid in you will be all that's left. So you want to lean on me a bit now, and feel good about yourself through my success. Okay. From up here that's all right with me. From down there, from the child in me, it's not been all right because I'm still scared of you and I hate you. But from up here you look different. I might even be able to hug you. No, that still feels like too much right now. But I could call you on the phone tonight to find out how you're making it. And to tell you what's happening with me. Maybe I'll say okay about coming over."

Craig stepped down from the chair. "Let's see what it's like down here now, not looking down at you as your parent and trying not to look up at you as your kid. I'm looking you even, right in the eyes." Craig paused a long time, looking intently straight ahead. "Man to man, you're okay. If I don't have to be afraid of you, or to convince you what a bastard you some-times were, it feels all right. Yeah, I'll still call you to-night."

When Craig was really able to experience that it was the child in him reacting to his father, and to recognize that it was the child in his father that he hated, his continued hostility felt like it made no sense because his father now, in reality, was doing him no harm. And if his father tried to be controlling, Craig was now a competent adult who could easily handle his father's bossiness. Besides, on a man-to-man basis, there was much that was admirable in his father that Craig could enjoy. Craig could then let himself feel something he had till then recognized only with his intellect, that he was taking the same defensively antagonistic stance with the authorities at his hospital, for much the same inappropriate reasons. It did not lead to instant modifications of his reactions to either his father or the hospital directors, but he began to move in that direction.

There are difficulties in ending a satellite song and dance with an authoritarian father to whom you relate as admirer and emulator. Denise, a nineteen-year-old woman, had striven to model herself after her father to the point of almost merging her identity with him. Her primary definition of herself was as his daughter, and she was quite happy with this until several friends, particularly young men, began pointing this out and told her they were finding it extremely irritating. It ruptured some close relationships. She was upset by this and began to question her relationship with her father, being glad of the feeling of specialness she felt with him, but wondering about what she was giving up for this. Denise was a good tennis player and learned much about how her personality worked by observing herself on the tennis court. She now became aware that although she was clearly a better tennis player than her father, she invariably lost to him. She would defeat herself, as if the only way she could share in his power and glory was by helping him keep it, even if it meant losing to him. When we talked about this in therapy she became fiercely imbued with the desire to win to prove that her power did not depend on standing in the light of his. She was so tense and over-anxious that she pressed too hard, made many errors, and lost badly. The next time she played with him she found her jaws actually aching with the clenched determination to win and her playing was tight and forced. She told me, "I was so frustrated. Then I suddenly realized that instead of being afraid to beat him or desperate to beat him, we could just have fun together. I became aware that it was beautiful day on the tennis court, the sun was shining but not too hot, the birds were chirping like crazy and it was good just to be there. I began to play just to feel the joy of it, and to be sharing it with my father. I began to move easily and loosely, I hit the ball well, I played smart tennis and I won easily."

Denise's tennis court discovery became a prototype for changing her relationship with her father. She saw that she could not enjoy her own separate effectiveness and freedom if she continued in the original song and dance based on the need of her inner child to be her father's reflecting satellite, nor could she be free if she tried to overcome the old song and dance by getting into a struggle to defeat his authoritarian inner child. Both endeavors were equally father-centered. So she shifted her focus to her own feelings, her own strength, her own experiencing and then shared this experiencing with her father as one person to another. Just as he was disconcerted by her first victory in tennis (no longer could he say, "You'll have to go a long way to beat your old man"), he was at first uncomfortable with her new way of being with him, but he came to appreciate her relaxed directness in time.

Whether it be Hal's making a clean-cut declaration of independence, or Craig's assuming a friendly, almost parental role toward his father's bossy inner child, or Denise's sharing her experiences with her father as a peer, they have in common ending a lifelong song and dance with the despotic, controlling inner child inside the father of each of them. It is an opening move toward a new way of relating.

If you end the submissive or defiant or satellite song and dance with your father and if he is inflexibly fixed in his dictatorial role, he may not be able to relate to you anymore. Or maybe he'll grant a grudging respect. He may even enjoy your autonomy because it's a damn attractive trait.

It's a risk.

But consider the alternative.

6 | The Saints Go Marching In

Some of us have been blessed by parents who are saints and we still may be trying to recuperate from this blessing.

Parents need not even be religious in order to function as priests, ministers, rabbis or gurus. To be ordained they simply must be in touch with the absolute truth about how people ought to behave. Once so ordained, elevation to sainthood involves just a few more fairly easy steps. They must preach their truths to you and all who will listen. They must show they have suffered very trying life experiences, such as raising you. They should have achieved some position of respect such as housewife, parent, provider, salesman, foreman, teacher, rich man, P.T.A. president, so that they have the necessary stature. And to complete their canonization, they must be able to show how professing these truths has aided the moral development of others, particularly their offspring. Having achieved all this, they need only tilt their head at the right angle for their flashing halo to blind you to perceptions of reality other than theirs.

An important aspect of parenting is imparting values and morality to your offspring. Does this make every parent who does this a saint? Not at all. "Good enough" parents teach you the importance of judgment and making different choices; saints teach you ready-made codes and rules.

Good enough parents teach you to make your decisions flexibly, basing them on your assessment of the whole picture; saints present you with a rigid system of shoulds and should nots.

Good enough parents teach you that it is often difficult to know what is the better, more effective, more moral, more self-actualizing thing to do; saints teach you that there is right and wrong with no in-between. (In fact saints couldn't easily accept the term "good enough parent." You are a good parent or a bad one.)

Good enough parents teach you to differentiate among life's big questions and little questions, to establish a hierarchy of what's important; saints tell you that there are no little questions. Saints can often be as morally outraged about an unmade bed or a fashion color clash as they'd be if you wrote a bad check.

A good enough parent is aware that you are different from him, that you have your own needs and ways of looking at the world that help determine what's best for you; a saint can't see a clear boundary between him and you so he expects you to live by his perceptions and values.

Good enough parents can accept the possibility that their values were largely swallowed whole when they were children, and they attempt to subject their values to rational scrutiny; saints have no awareness that the rules, fears and prejudices they live by are not built into the order of things but, rather, are early childhood indoctrinations.

Good enough parents try to indicate the reasoning and life experiences that go into their positions on morality and social protocol; saints often try to connect their injunctions with a greater power such as God, church, gospel, absolutes, historical imperatives, public opinion, etc.

Finally, when good enough parents use ordinary words they do it to communicate information; saints can shape these same words into barbs that provoke guilt and fear. Commonplace terms become commands, belittlements, narrowers of perception, limiters of alternatives, prescriptions for salvation. For this reason, before proceeding further in our discussions it will be useful to take a look at the semantics of saint-hood.

GLOSSARY OF SAINTLY WORDS AND TERMS

ALWAYS—as in "We always," "One always"

"We always" denotes a rule your parent lives by and you will always live by, with no exceptions, no maybes, no sometimes. This rule is forever.

Variation: "You always" says that stretching from your past and into your distant future, you everlastingly mess things up and do things wrong.

Examples: "One should *always* be courteous." "We must *always* be careful not to let others take advantage of us."

"I *always* keep the house spotless."

"I *always* put on a cheerful face."

"You *always* try to get out of anything difficult."

ASHAMED—as in "You should be ashamed," "I am ashamed."

"You have done something that makes me feel small, wormlike and embarrassed (or would make me feel that way if I had done it) and I hope you feel like you want to disappear into a hole because people are looking at you. In fact, I wish you would disappear into a hole and then maybe people will stop looking at me."

Examples: "You ought to be *ashamed* to go around dressed like that."

"I was so *ashamed* when you didn't say a word to anyone at the party."

"I was so *ashamed* when you made yourself the center of attention at the party."

BAD—as in "That's bad," "You're bad."

Your parent wants you to believe that you are breaking an important social taboo ("that's bad") and you should feel that you are an awful person ("you're bad") for doing it. Freely translated it means, "I don't like what you're doing."

Variation: "He's bad": Don't be like him or I will

turn this same angry, disapproving countenance in your direction.

Examples: "It's a *bad thing* to be closer to your friend than your family."

"I never thought a child of mine could be so *bad*."

"He's a *bad egg* and he's having a bad influence on you."

BEST—as in "I know best," "Do your best."

"I know best" means that "compared to you or anyone else you invoke, I have a particular insight and knowledge about what should be done that is clearly superior."

"Do your best" means that although the saint really believes only perfection will do, he is willing to concede to your obvious limitations as long as you always do things as well as you are capable of doing them.

Examples: "Buy the heavier coat. Believe me, I know *best*."

"I don't expect you to be the top in the class as long as you do your *best*."

DIRTY—as in "That's dirty," "You're dirty."

"What you are doing or saying makes me feel revolted and nauseated and I can assure you my parents would have felt the same way if I did it, which only goes to prove that there is something in the very nature of such behavior that is filthy and disgusting."

Examples: "Hearing you talk about sex so blatantly makes me feel *dirty*."

"Anyone who picks his nose is a *dirty pig*."

"He's a *dirty old man*."

FOOLISH—as in "Don't be foolish," "That's foolish."

Any behavior that's just for fun, that "wastes" time or that is frivolous—*i.e.*, behavior other than what your parent wants you to do, but not a serious enough transgression to be labeled sinful, bad or shameful. Similar to "silly," "childish."

Examples: "Going to a hockey game is a *foolish waste* of time."

"Spending that much on a dress is *foolish*."

GOD—as in "God wants," "God will. . ."

Often used simply to express a belief in a higher power or holy spirit. But sainted parents may also invoke it as the ultimate in elevating and transforming their preferences into the wishes of a divine and omnipotent authority.

Examples: "God wants you to have children."

"God will punish you if you are mean to your parents."

"God doesn't like liars."

"God knows when you are doing something wrong."

"Don't be bitter—it is *God's will.*"

GOOD—as in "Be good," "That's a good boy."

This simply means your parent is made happy by that behavior. Do more of it and you will be smiled upon all the time.

Variation: "He's good" stands for someone your parents approve of. Be like him and they'll be happy.

Examples: "Be good and stay out of my way."

"Look how *good* and quiet Mary is."

GRATEFUL—as in "You should be grateful," "We should be grateful."

"You should be grateful" means "don't want too much from life or from me because there are people in the world, like me, that are or were much worse off. So instead of being angry, disappointed or demanding, be thankful for what you do have and what I have done for you."

"We should be grateful" means "See how resigned I am? How about you?"

Examples: "So you have a limp. You should *be grateful* you can walk."

"Why do you want to go back to work? You should *be grateful* your husband makes a good living."

"We must *be grateful* she didn't suffer."

GUILTY—as in "You should feel guilty."

You have violated a major parental injunction that has been set out for you as social protocol, the word of God, tradition, etc. You should feel self-loathing and remorse. Admit your transgression and repent.

Examples: "You should feel *guilty* for not calling your father when he was sick."

"You should feel *guilty* for letting your children go out without sweaters on a day like this."

"You should feel *guilty* going out with a married man."

MUST—as in "You must," "One must. . ."

A strong, no-nonsense command. Similar to "should" but more immediate. The clear implication: "You'd better or else."

Examples: "You *must* always make the bed before leaving the house."

"One *must not* cancel a social engagement."

NEVER—as in "We never," "I never," or "Never!"

"We never" applies to behavior that is so beyond the pale that it must never occur to you as a possibility.

"I never" is spoken with smug pride by the parent who is telling you that he has wiped from his repertoire all possibility of this errant behavior.

"Never!" is an ultimate imperative, a no-no reaching to eternity, and violating it chances losing parental love and respect—at least for a while.

Examples: "We never talk with food in our mouths."

"I never buy in expensive (or cheap) stores."

"Never discuss family matters with friends!"

"Never marry a black (white, yellow, brown, Jewish, gentile, poor) man!"

ONE—as in "One doesn't," "One must. . ."

The implication here is that there are rules everyone must live by that are quite impersonal and certainly do not arise from your parents' own beliefs, thoughts and hang-ups. And it doesn't leave much room for recognition of your individuality, does it?

Examples: "*One* isn't seen in places like that."

"*One* doesn't wear those shoes with that dress."

"*One* doesn't get angry at his parents."

"*One must* have children."

PEOPLE—as in "What will people say?" "People will talk."

"There's a whole world of others out there, and I am afraid that those others, known or anonymous, will disapprove of me. I want you to be afraid of others disapproving of you because, since we are connected, if they disapprove of you, they disapprove of me."

Variation: "The best people." These are not only the judges of our merit, but you should emulate them as they rate high on your parents' value scale.

Variation: As in "People can't be trusted." Note the paradox—often parents who are most concerned to have the respect and high regard of others feel that these same others are not to be trusted.

Examples: "If you go away with him for a weekend, you know what *people* will say."

"Only the *best people* go to that hotel."

"Never tell *people* your problems."

RIGHT—as in "Do it right," "That's right."

There is always a prescribed way that you should act and your parents know exactly what it is. Always do right and you will become the kind of person they will be proud of.

Variation: "I am right" usually means "end of argument."

Examples: "Now that's the *right way* to set a table."

"Can't you ever do anything *right?*"

"I know I am *right* so there's no use discussing it."

SHOULD—as in "You should do, think, believe, etc."

It really means "I want you to do it that way." But look how much more mileage a parent can get by presenting it as a "should." It becomes an injunction, a given rule, instead of a personal preference or prejudice.

Examples: "You *should* always love your parents." "You *should* visit Aunt Helen."

SHOULDN'T—as in "You shouldn't do that."

Translation: "If you do that I'll be anxious and upset because I wouldn't like it, other people may not like it, and if they don't like what you do they won't like me."

Examples: "You *shouldn't* wear your dress so short."

"You *shouldn't* travel alone."

"You *shouldn't* turn down a good paying job."

SIN—as in "It's a sin."

This is worse than doing something "bad" or "wrong" because here you are not only breaking cultural taboos or social protocol but God's own word, as perceived and interpreted by your parents. The appropriate reaction is *guilt*.

Examples: "Throwing out food is a *sin*."

"Going away with a man for a weekend is a *sin*."

"It's a *sin* to play with yourself."

THEY—as in "They say. . ."

This is similar to "people" except that it has a more mysterious and global quality, as if "they" carry the omniscience of correct social protocol. It really means "This is what I'd like you to believe and do but you may not accept it if it just comes from me. However, if I can make you believe that everybody else agrees with me, or that I'm just agreeing with everybody else, then maybe what I say will have more weight."

Examples: "*They* are wearing dresses longer this year."

"*They say* if a woman is too easy, men will never respect her."

TODAY—as in "People don't know how to live today."

This means that morality is going to the dogs. "People (you) are now doing things that I was brought up to know were *wrong* and therefore they (you) are *bad*."

Examples: "Young people have no respect for anything *today*."

"There's no patriotism *today*."

TOMORROW—as in "You must think of tomorrow."

Sometimes means "plan ahead." But it often translates: "Don't enjoy yourself today because that's sinful and scares me. So live for the ever-receding future and you can guarantee not living too fully in the here and now. That will make me feel less anxious."

Examples: "If you don't worry about *tomorrow* you'll have plenty to worry about *tomorrow*."

"Forget about having a good time. *What about tomorrow?*"

UNGRATEFUL—as in "You are ungrateful."

Usually means "After all I've done for you, you ought to feel terribly guilty if you (1) don't appreciate it; (2) want anything more from me; (3) question my motives."

Example: "It took me all day to clean and rearrange your room. How can you be so *ungrateful?*"

WE—as in "We never" or "We don't. . ."

There's no separation between mommy (or daddy) and you. You are part of them, like an ankle, thumb or jawbone. And "we" must always do what "we" are programmed to do.

Examples: "We never leave dishes in the sink."

"*We* mustn't be silly."

"*We* don't talk to strangers."

WRONG—as in "That's wrong," "You're wrong."

This applies to behavior that your parents know to be incorrect, inappropriate, harmful or sinful. They expect you to accept this knowledge as gospel. If you do "wrong" things, or question whether doing the "wrong" thing would lead to dire consequences, you are "bad."

Examples: "*It's wrong* to go out to a party when your child isn't feeling well."

"You're so obviously *wrong* I won't dignify your behavior with a comment."

SHAME AND SCANDAL IN THE FAMILY

Few behavior modification psychologists are as adept in the use of rewards and punishments for shaping behavior as are saints. Starting with the earliest childhood comprehending, saintly semantics structure the range of permissible behavior through the ubiquitous, built-in praise and condemnation. In fact, their rewards and punishments not only set limits on permissible behavior but on conceivable behavior. It is not enough to say that the saint enforces his values by his approval or disapproval, because all parents do that, willingly or unwillingly. When parents are being saintly the threat to their offspring is not that they might make them feel guilty, as when parents are being martyrs, nor is it making them afraid of parental rage, as when parents are being tyrannical. The threat is in their attempt to make their children feel *shame.* The child thinks he has done something unthinkable, beyond the pale. His punishment for deeply disappointing the parents is not the withdrawal of love, but the withdrawl of their *respect.* The granting and withdrawal of respect are enormously powerful enforcers. We need to feel that our parents value us as worthwhile human beings, and do not simply love us because we are theirs. We need to feel our parents *like* us. Saintly parents communicate that if we don't follow their rules, they may still love us, because, after all, as parents they *should,* but they won't *like* us. And that's heavy.

In addition, the very personality of the saint, the righteousness that is conveyed in his bearing, becomes a very early model for the child to identify with. And the young child may have no way to discover that alternate values and ways of behaving even exist because the people his parents would tend to associate with, the family members and friends that are around most, often share the parents' way of seeing the world.

IT AIN'T NECESSARILY SO

The structure of the parent's values will meet some baffling challenges as the child runs into people who see things differently from the saintly parent. Sometimes this occurs concurrently with the saint's teachings, as when the other parent may not agree with the saint. Sometimes it is another family member, a friend, a friend's parent, a teacher who presents the child with alternative possibilities. What often happens is that the child rejects these possibilities because they carry the threat of the saint's disapproval and disrespect. These new ideas are labeled "bad," "wrong," "sinful," etc., by the child, and thus dismissed. Sometimes he rejects them because they are so alien that his mind simply cannot encompass them. For many people, this early value system remains stable and unquestioned throughout life, with the person accepting the inevitable happy or unhappy consequences of that system.

The saintly injunctions usually do not become challenged until the child, now grown, feels pain and discomfort because the old code is keeping him from satisfying his own goals, constricting his freedom, confusing his sense of what is right for himself, or causing new people that he cares about to reject him for being so judgmental.

Often the constriction of living with injunctions that have become oppressive and suffocating produces physical symptoms, such as headaches, breathing difficulties, exhaustion, muscle spasms. It is illustrated by the old joke about the doctor who tells his patient who doesn't drink, smoke, go out with girls, that he has a headache because his halo is on too tight.

Usually this constriction is accompanied by rage—rage at his own impotence to exchange the injunctions for a mode that enhances his self-realization.

I'VE GOTTA BE ME

If you have a saintly parent, then your suffering, if not converted to helpless self-pity, your rage, if not expended in ineffectual flailing, can spur a reappraisal of the codes and rules that have been nailed to the door of your mind. Each chafing injunction must be viewed through an attribute you may not even know you have, your *wisdom*. You have wisdom through the millions of times you have observed cause and effect in the way people behave. You may have ignored the data that didn't fit into the most entrenched parental dictates, but the data is there, and you must start to trust your own feelings by testing the rules you live by against reason. Here are some questions to help mobilize your wisdom:

Why am I following this injunction?

Does this way of behaving make sense to me now or am I adhering to it simply because that is what I was taught?

What are the *consequences* of continuing to follow this injunction?

What are the consequences if I break with this injunction?

If I break with the old rule, will somebody get hurt? Will I?

If I break with the old rule, will my life go better or worse?

Am I doing this only to rebel, or to get even with my parents for past injuries, or do I feel I really need to make this change to live more fully?

How much parental disapproval will result from this change? Can I bear their disapproval? Can I get them to be more accepting?

As you probe a particular parental dictate with these questions you may conclude that hewing to it no longer makes sense, is strangling you, and can be stopped without injury to anyone. Wouldn't it be lovely if at that point you could simply chuck it and live differently? But it's exactly at that point that you are rocked by the anxiety that accompanies even contemplating ending the song and dance that has kept that injunction operating. In order to win your sainted parent's respect, you have been stepping with precision to his or her *marche militaire*. The tight choreography allows for little improvisation. Even a slight change in the cadence or direction risks the loss of that respect. This parent, whose judgment of you is still more important than you may care to admit, may withdraw his liking if you change the step. And that can leave you with a feeling of worthlessness so painful that you may begin moving to the old song and dance again to retrieve his approbation.

MY MAMA DONE TOLD ME

To begin to move to a new rhythm, it will be helpful to look again at your song and dance from the perspective of the child in you relating to the child in your parent. It may be difficult to see the child in your sainted parent because his or her grave role as lawgiver seems exalted and agelessly parental, but it is the words of his ungrowing inner child, vibrating through adult vocal cords, that is pronouncing the injunctions. Did you ever see a kid of about five or six screaming to a friend who is doing something forbidden or daring, "Don't! My mommy says you should never touch that! I'm going to tell your mommy you did something bad." There is disapproval, anguish, even horror in the voice of the chastening child. Someone is breaking a parental injunction! Even more, someone is breaking a universal law! This is something wrong, sinful, frightening. It must be stopped.

Now listen to the words of your sainted parent as the giver and reinforcer of rules. The voice is stern, the words include no "my mommy says," but darned if the music of the message isn't the same as that expressed by the little kid scolding his friend! *The part of your parent that is sainted is a recording of his parents,* taped when he was a child, amplified and played through his speaker with enormously high fidelity to the original. (Actually, "original" is not quite accurate because the tape may go back, with variations, for countless generations.) The little child in your parent who was the receptacle for all these injunctions carried them intact and unquestioned, relaying them on to you without ever having held them up to the light of his rational appraisal. This is why when your parent is most sainted he is most being his parents' good little child. The validity of the injunction is not the issue here. The issue is that the injunction has been passed along, with tremendous moral potency, from your parent's parent (grandma or grandpa) to you without ever being filtered through your parent's wisdom. And unless you apply wisdom to it, you will be but another relay station between your parent and your child.

LADY BE GOOD

I think of two young women I have treated who, taken together, illustrate that it is not the validity of the injunction that is at issue, because each of these women were given very opposite injunctions by sainted parents.

Karen was brought up in a little town in central New Jersey. Her mother was a dreary but righteous woman whose horizons stretched from Main Street to Elm Street. The church was the center of religious and social life for the family. Her father was rarely home, possibly chased out by the mother's asceticism, and her mother bore this in a stoic silence that enhanced her saintly bearing. Mother laid down many interrelated injunctions for Karen.

Never get dirty.

You must not talk to your elders or betters until you are spoken to.

Always be polite.

Smile.

Wear pleated skirts and patent leather shoes because that's what they are wearing.

You may wear jeans when most girls from good families wear them.

You should look attractive to boys but you mustn't let them touch you.

You should do well in school but you mustn't do too well. C+ is about right.

Girls should not go to college unless they insist on being a teacher or a nurse.

Girls should be secretaries because it's woman's work and they can meet marriageable men.

Marriage should be as early as possible to a good provider.

You should have children soon after being married.

Karen followed most of these injunctions as a matter of course, except that her school grades were usually closer to B+ and she never did have a child because soon after marrying her good provider when she was nineteen she fell into a depression, he disappeared and the marriage was annulled. When she came into psychotherapy at twenty-three she was dejected and detached, was working as a legal secretary-bookkeeper in a small "one girl" law office and lived in a dark apartment with a girl she had gone to elementary school with.

It took a while in treatment for Karen to realize her depression resulted from blindly living a life pattern that was not at all in tune with her needs, and that her detachment was her attempt to control her hidden rage at this deadening constriction. We began the step of subjecting the injunctions to her wisdom, full knowing that the hardest part was yet to come.

The other young woman I am reminded of is Amy. When she first came to see me she was so taut that she practically twanged as she walked from the waiting room to my consulting room. She was trying to force an appearance of ease but as she sat across from me, she looked like a clenched fist. Headaches, a spastic colon, low back pain and other assorted ills had been afflicting her increasingly and had led her internist to suggest that she consult with me. Amy had received her Ph.D. in experimental psychology at twenty-four and was now an associate professor of psychology who had published several important research papers. She lived alone in a Greenwich Village penthouse, was not married, but had two lovers of long duration. One was a married man about twenty years her senior who did not love her and who abused her badly. The other was a young historian on the faculty of her college who loved her and whom she abused badly. Her life was exciting, active and full of accomplishment but devoid of relaxation, contentment and love.

Amy's father was the edict-making saint in her family. He was an engineer who had been thrown out of important government work when it was discovered that he had been involved in leftist political organizations in college. He went into real estate and made a lot of money. Amy's mother was a giggly, insipid woman who revered her husband slavishly, and exhorted Amy to do the same. Her father spoke his rules in sparse, unemotional tones, but it seemed to Amy that he was a wise, almost holy man, and she never questioned his injunctions.

Children are unreasonable, irresponsible and needy creatures so you must become mature quickly.

Never be flighty or frivolous.

Nothing is more important than intellectual achievement.

The greatest sin is to waste time.

The greatest good is perfection in all you undertake.

Never depend on anyone unless it is absolutely unavoidable.

Romantic love is the worst form of dependency.

Don't marry anyone unless he is serious, brilliant and accomplished.

I had never met a more intent, quick-witted, super-achieving young woman. Amy said she liked the way she was living, if only she didn't have those damn symptoms. As she began to see that she was living her father's rules to the letter while at the same time priding herself on her independence and self-directedness she was very shaken. She felt the contradiction of living his injunction to "Do what I tell you and be autonomous." She began to question the rules she had inherited and found that many did not make sense and were constraining her own inclinations. When she foundered in her initial attempts to discard some of the injunctions, she was dismayed at not achieving what she set out to do—after all, she had a deeply ingrained injunction to achieve and to do things perfectly. She fell into a long period of feeling helpless, weepy and disorganized. She began to see the enormous difficulty involved if she was ever to break the song and dance with her father, because nothing was more agonizing than the thought of losing her father's admiration and pride. If she visited her parents for a weekend and did not want to spend the time working on another research article or playing Scrabble or Backgammon with her father, but preferred simply to lounge at the pool and listen to rock music, she would soon see his look of appalled disdain and she'd feel as crushed as she had felt at three when her father would walk away from her if she wanted to play in the sandbox rather than learn to count. To justify her relaxation she would tell her father she wasn't feeling well and this would encourage the return of her physical symptoms. She became more and more painfully aware of her entrapment in the song and dance.

If we compare the injunctions of Karen's sainted mother with those of Amy's sainted father it is as if each came from different planets. Yet both of these women were being ruled by injunctions their parents' inner children passed unquestioned to them as if they were universal imperatives, and both were held to these injunctions by the fear that the sainted parent—both the replica of that parent that now dwelled in their own heads and the real living, breathing, judging saintly mother or father out there—would withdraw his or her respect.

How do you deal with a little child who feels he has all the answers because his mommy or daddy told him so? Teachers are faced with this problem all the time. They could simply tell the child that what he has learned is hogwash and he must now accept a better way, but their job is to widen the child's horizons and show him new possibilities without making him feel his parents are wrong; feeling his parents are wrong not only threatens his security but is another moralistic judgment, and he's already filled to the gills with them. Very often the teacher's job is not to make the child do the forbidden or "wrong" things but to help him accept these things as a valid and valuable part of the behavioral repertoire of others, instead of disqualifying other people for failing the sainted parent's standards. It is a matter of exposing the child to these new alternatives, of showing him that the people who practice them are not bad, of getting him to reason out as best he can what the consequences of this "wrong" behavior really are, of indicating that his parent's way is one way but that there are other ways. If this effectively opens him to accepting new alternatives for others, it may later permit him to use his wisdom to create the rules he lives by.

The issues are similar in dealing with the moralistic child within your parent. One alternative is simply to tell your parent, "Bug off, this is the way it is from now on and if you don't like it, goodbye." But this usually is unnecessary, and since the moralistic child in your parent may not be able to handle it, it can be a costly alternative. While it rarely means the end of actual contact with your parents, it could mean that you wouldn't be talking to them about anything more than their aches and pains and who died. You would be writing them off, a possibly intolerant and unavoidable action that would needlessly disrupt the continuity of an important relationship. It could becloud whether your new choices reflected a liberation or an insurrection. It could create anger and misgivings that would tighten a negative bond between your rebellious inner child and their moralistic inner child. And even more importantly, it could deprive both of you of the opportunity to accept your differences and, as Rilke says, to love the spaces between you. For one thing that often happens when you see the child in your parents is a sudden flush of understanding and compassion. One woman I know harbored much anger at her mother for always emphasizing "they"—"what are *they* wearing," "what will *they* think," etc. One day, in discussing this with her sister, they realized that their mother had come to America from Europe as a little girl, the oldest child in a bewildered, lost, poor immigrant family. She was the only one who knew any English and as such she was sent out to find out how *they* (the Americans) lived, how *they* dressed, how *they* thought. It had survival value, and it persisted. When these sisters could see their mother as a little girl anxiously scouting new terrain they felt much more tolerant of mother's "they."

So a more sympathetic and effective alternative is to try to teach the child in your parent that there are many possibilities out there. You have to indicate your discovery that different ways of being, which your parent may have invalidated as the practice of sinners or barbarians, have value in the lives of others because others, like you, are different from him or her. You have to make it clear that you have no desire to have them change the rules they live by because that is what seems right to them. Neither do you need their approval of your choices. What you would really like is for them to maintain their respect even when you make choices different from those they feel are right.

You cannot expunge the moralistic child within your parent with all its injunctions, rules and prejudices any more than you can expunge the moralistic child within yourself. That child is engraved in the neurons: "My mommy says . . . !" Attempts to change or deny him will get some kind of hostile reaction from your parent. But you can help open him to new experiences and views if you don't try to change him but keep giving him the message, "You and I are different, and I respect who you are and would like you to respect who I am." If your new choices are working to make you live a fuller, happier life, this will be the ultimate evidence that your choices are valid for you. This evidence may itself be threatening to the saint and may, for perhaps a long while, have to be disregarded or minimized by him or her before he or she can accept it—and you.

The two women mentioned earlier illustrate the difficulties in getting sainted parents to accept your living a life that breaks with their code. Amy, the young, tense experimental psychology professor previously noted, decided to take a vacation at Club Méditerranée on Martinique. Now that may not seem like a cosmos-quaking decision, but for Amy it was as much an injunction-defying step as space travel is a gravity-defying step. To lie on the beach, maybe nude, and do nothing but relax and let the sun caress her, to swim and snorkel for the sheer pleasure of it, to dance and make love under the stars, rather than to visit the cathedrals and museums of Europe or the historic and natural wonders of America was frivolously hedonistic beyond decency. It took courage to tell her father where she was going and he reacted with contempt.

"Don't bother to write."

"Whether I write or not is up to me," she answered. "Whether you read it or not will be up to you."

He grunted and went into his room and though she felt the old tension she did not follow him as once she would have.

Once in Martinique she began to relax. She went to yoga and exercise classes, sunbathed and swam. She could feel her muscles becoming less tight, her movement freer flowing. She met a man, Harry, and for the first time felt she was really in love. They talked end-

lessly, laughed a lot, made love by sunlight and moon-
light, and she allowed herself to fully let go. But when
she realized this might be more than a vacation ro-
mance, that she had feelings for him that would
probably carry the relationship back to New York, she
got very frightened because he was not the kind of
man her father would have chosen for her. She felt
Harry to be a strong, dependable, caring man but he
was not a lawyer or doctor, not a scientist or writer, not
a professional of any kind. Harry owned a gift shop, a
very tasteful and successful enterprise, but Amy's father had long ago indicated that he disqualified store-
keepers as being lightweights. And although Harry was
bright, worldly and well read, he was not an intellectual in terms that her father would define. She had
written some "having a good time" postcards addressed
to both her parents, but then, three days before returning, she wrote a letter to her father.

Dear Dad,
    I may get home before this letter reaches you but
I wanted you to know that I am having the best
vacation I ever had in my life. And I met a very
warm, decent man I may be in love with. I'm not going off the deep end—I guess you gave me enough
of your rationality for that—and I plan to take lots
of time to see how it develops. I know you didn't
approve of my vacation and you probably won't
approve of this man—his name is Harry—at least
not at first—but I think it will mean something to
you that I am happy. You and I are very much alike,
dad, but we are also different in many ways and
I need different things than you do. I hope you
won't hold our differences against me, because I
love and respect you very much and wouldn't want
us to lose the closeness we've always had just because I am discovering how I, me, Amy, can enjoy
life.
    See you soon.

                                    Much love,
                                    Amy

Amy's father avoided talking to her over the telephone the first week or two that she was home, although Amy always asked to talk to him when she spoke to her mother. This was a trying time for Amy. She panicked when she felt the reality of her father's cold disrespect and dismissal. In therapy we conducted many improvised, fantasied dialogues between Amy and her father. In this Gestalt technique she would talk to her father "sitting" in the empty chair opposite her. Then she would switch chairs and respond as her father, then switch again, etc. At times she would cry and beg him to talk to her and love her. At other times she would rage at him and feel wells of hatred. The dialogues would usually end up with her father remaining aloof and Amy saying something like, "Okay, dad, if you won't come along with me I'm sad, but I'm going to make it without you because I'm not a bad, worthless person. I'm good and I'm valuable and I'm sorry if you don't see it."

She stopped asking for her father on the phone although she once said to her mother, "I wish you'd tell dad to stop acting like a baby." A few days later her father called and said, "Mother and I have opera tickets for Saturday night and we can't make it. Do you and Harry want them?"

"Sure. Thanks, dad."

"Maybe you can come over for dinner before the opera."

The other woman we discussed, Karen, had finished two years of college before her brief marriage and was taking courses at night to complete her degree while working as a legal secretary. Her parents offered no financial help with her education though it would have taken considerable pressure off her. In fact, they never asked her about school, were unresponsive when she told them about her courses, and soon the topic dropped completely out of their conversations. She did let them know about her graduation, but her father couldn't take a day off work to attend, and her mother was running a church luncheon that she couldn't forgo. Karen went to her graduation alone and felt a vague sense of shame, but she was unclear as to whether she was ashamed of her parents' narrowness or felt an older shame that always accompanied her breaking with her mother's blueprint of how she should behave. She was ashamed enough so that she hadn't even told them that she was interested in becoming a lawyer, had applied to law school and been accepted to start in the fall.

When Karen finally told her mother about it she said it with all the enthusiasm and excitement she really felt. Her mother was stunned.

"Have you gone mad?"

"There's nothing crazy about being a lawyer."

"We'll never have any grandchildren from you."

"What has that got to do with it? They don't tie my tubes when I pass the bar exam."

"Karen, you mustn't use language like that. I have tried to teach you that there are things good women do and things they don't do. Good women are not men."

"Good lawyers can be men or women."

Karen's mother had stopped looking at her. Just like that, she made it clear that her daughter was no longer worthy of her respect. She said, "I hope you'll get over this soon. Meanwhile, I don't want to discuss it."

"Oh no, mother, not again. You cut me off from discussing my doubts about Peter before I married him, and you have avoided coming to see the new apartment I've been living in since Peter and I split because you thought I should move back home. When I went into psychotherapy, you said you never wanted me to talk to you about it and said I shouldn't tell anyone you knew. You've acted as if I haven't been going to college these last few years and now you're going to disregard my going to law school. Mother, can't you see that we soon won't have anything we can talk to each other about?"

"You used to listen to me when you were younger," her mother said, more wistfully than in anger.

"I used to listen because you were right about a lot of things and I had no idea there were other ways of looking at things. There are."

"They are the devil's ways."

"Oh, mom!" Karen was about to give up but she decided to try again. "They are not the devil's ways, they are simply ways that you're not used to and don't agree with. And that's fine for you. I admire the way you have always been true to your beliefs. But I want other things and I believe other things and I have to be true to what I believe."

"Who's been influencing you?"

"Not devils. Teachers, my boss, the fascination of the law itself. My therapist." Her mother winced. "Mostly me."

There was a long silence. "Listen, mother, I don't expect you to agree with my decision. And I'm going to do it even if you disagree, so you can't do anything about that. But it is in your hands whether we remain friends who can really talk to each other or whether we drift apart so that there's nothing left to say. I'd like to remain friends."

"A lawyer. What will my friends say?"

It took a long time for Karen's mother to accept Karen's profession as well as other facets of her lifestyle but Karen was adamant in her insistence there would be no pretense about her life in her communicating with her mother. On many occasions her mother would withdraw into cool aloofness but Karen, aware that she was dealing with the moralistic girl in her mother, would wait out the silent tantrum. Slowly her mother began to enjoy Karen's development as an interesting young woman. One landmark incident was when she and Karen went shopping for clothes. First, her mother made none of the usual disapproving sounds when Karen bought apparel that violated her mother's usual emphasis on concealing fullness. Second, her mother bought herself a form-fitting bodysuit for the first time in her life. Third, they went to an art museum, something her mother hadn't done since she went on a class trip in elementary school. Lunching in the museum cafeteria, her mother's eyes were sparkling. Their conversations had ranged in many directions—even about sex, which her mother talked about in defiance of her own red cheeks. She told of the ignorance she had been brought up with, she wondered if it had been a mistake not to let herself go more, she dared to speculate about whether that was still possible for her. Karen told of her own sexual development and problems.

When they said goodbye, her mother said, "Karen, this has been a wonderful day."

"For me, too."

"Well, maybe I'm not too old to learn a few things."

So maybe you can teach an old saint new kicks. Or at least to accept yours.

7 | I Don't Know How to Love Him

In an initial session with Leana, I asked her for her earliest memory. "That's easy," she said. "When I was three years old I was on a car trip across the country with my parents. We stopped for lunch and gasoline and I was picking daisies out of the cracks in the pavement and then they drove away without me! I screamed and ran after them but they kept driving. The man at the gas station comforted me and called the State Police. They caught up to my parents who, until that moment, thought I was in the back seat! I can still feel the horror of seeing the car disappear and feeling that they had planned to leave me like that and were never coming back."

In a session with David he told me of a dream he had just had, but which had been recurrent since he was five years old, and which depicted with little change or distortion an actual incident at that time. The dream:

David was at an amusement park with his parents and two older brothers. He and his brothers went on a fast, whirling ride and he began to get terribly dizzy. He screamed out that they should stop the ride and let him off. Nobody heard him and he just kept screaming. Finally the ride slowed and stopped. His brothers leaped from their cars. He barely dragged himself out of his. His brothers ran down the ramp to his parents as he wobbled rubber-legged, throwing up all over himself. His parents didn't see him. They and his brothers started to walk away. He tried to run but fell down in a swirl of dizziness. He tried to call out but only vomit flowed out of him in an endless torrent, flooding the ramp on which he lay panicked but paralyzed.

Leana's earliest memory and David's recurrent nightmare and the real-life incident that triggered it were significant in that they represented their recognition of that part of their parents that didn't love or want them. Everyone has had some experiences or dreams like this. Everyone has had parents who, at some moments, didn't love or want them. But for some, like Leana and David, experiences of being unloved and unwanted have permeated their life space so persistently that it has scarred their entire sense of being lovable, wantable and valuable.

There are some parents who are so obvious in their unloving that their child can't help but know it. The unlovingness has been there, a fact of life, undisguised, open, maybe even brutally apparent. The child growing up in this climate begins to accept that this is the way it is, that perhaps this is the way it is for everyone.

If you have had parents who were openly unloving, who discharged basic obligations to you and little more, then you may remember the puzzlement you felt when you saw other parents giving their children loving attention. Probably you were at first envious, then perhaps you cynically dismissed this display as phoney, like a soupy television family. I recall a conversation with a twelve-year-old boy whose father was rarely there for him because his selfishness left little over for his son. "I didn't mind because I thought all fathers were like that even though I sometimes wished it was different. I used to like to watch this TV program, *The Courtship of Eddie's Father*. Eddie and his father had a real tight relationship and I used to feel, 'what sugary garbage.' But I always watched it. And then I began to look around at my friends very carefully and I saw that some of them really had much closer relationships with their fathers. It made me sad and angry, so I tried to convince myself that they were just putting on a phoney act, too, but I can't stop feeling sad and angry now."

Whether you have accepted your parent's undisguised unlovingness as "that's the way it is for everybody," or "that's the way it is for me," it is a cruel realization, but it has the hard-edged advantage of at least knowing where you stand. The much more common situation is one in which the uncaring feelings are hidden beneath a big-rock-candy-mountain of pronouncements of parental loving. It can be bewildering when what you are being told is dissonant with what your senses and guts are otherwise picking up, and this confusion compounds the tragedy of not being adequately loved.* Parents desperate to hide from themselves and their offspring their uncaring feelings apply, usually unwittingly, many strategies of concealment and distraction, the particular strategy depending on their own style.

I'M ONLY THINKING OF YOU

One of the most common ways unloving feelings are masked is by labeling their expression with the

---

*It is also important to allow yourself to question whether a parent you have labeled as unloving really is so, or whether this was not as true as you were led to believe. A young man was telling his therapist about an incident when he was two years old and his father was bathing him. His mother came in, found that the window was open and screamed at the father for not closing it. "My mother said I almost got pneumonia from that. That's how much my father cared."

"He bathed you," the therapist said.

"Yes, I know, and he left the window open."

"He bathed you," the therapist repeated.

"Right, and he darn near killed me."

"He bathed you."

Slowly the young man began to hear what the therapist was saying. He had before only let himself hear about the open window and not the simple fact that his father, who his mother had long taught him had never loved him or done anything to care for him, had bathed him. It opened him to many early memories of his father (his parents had divorced when he was quite young) that indicated considerably more paternal caring than he had long believed was true.

rubric "It's all for your own good." Angry punishments and deprivations are to teach you a lesson because your parents love you and want you to learn to behave properly. At times the unlovingness in this is revealed by the withdrawing of parental affection or presence as a way of shaping you up. (I think of a man who, as a child, had to eat in the kitchen with the household help until he developed perfect table manners. What he learned from this and countless similar situations was not simply impeccable table manners but that his being acceptable was based on his fulfilling certain narrow conditions rather than his being valued for who he was.) In like manner, a consistent pattern of leaving you alone and not paying much attention to you is because they love you and want you to be independent and self-sufficient; on the other hand, your parents taking you everywhere with them, whether you wanted to go or not, whether they took care for your comfort or not, is because they love you and want you to be with them and have new experiences. (A man who dreamed he was a forlorn coat awaiting the Salvation Army truck recalled that he was brought to parties by his parents and put to sleep on the bed with the coats.) Their not knowing what's going on in your life or being in touch with what's going on inside you is because they love you and trust your judgment to handle things well; on the other hand, needing to know your every thought and to control all aspects of your life is not because they can't tolerate your being an independent being but because they love you and are concerned that you grow up properly.

The big-rock-candy-mountain that conceals the barren valley of unloving can be made of uncounted expressions of affection. At times a parent unable or unwilling to truly love his or her child will dearly and truly love the *role* of mother or father and will perform that role with enthusiasm and zest, but still may not be in touch with the individual needs of the child. Maybe most parents have at times, in a display of parental pride, awakened their tiny children to show them off, but when this type of acting upon their own needs in disregard of the needs of their child becomes a prototype for their behavior with the child, he cannot feel truly cared about even though his parents think that he's being adored. (See the section on double binds and double messages in "Blest Be the Tie That Binds," Chapter 2.) Similar to this are those mothers who are deeply involved with being pregnant and with the birth process as a beautiful or dramatic happening for themselves but are not sensitively in touch with the unique traits and needs of their particular child when it's born.

Again, I am not now focusing on those who have had the almost universal experience of finding our parents to be occasionally unloving, out of touch with us, unable to emphathize with us in some areas, and even just plain disliking some things about us. My concern here is with those who suspect or feel sure that their parents have a deficiency in either their capacity or desire to be basically loving and caring. What type of person is an unloving parent? How did he or she get that way?

One kind of unloving parent is a parent who never wanted a child, or didn't want a child at the time it was born, and whose feelings of not wanting a child were not changed very much by its arrival. Parents have children for many reasons, and only sometimes because they really have a desire to bring a child into the world, nurture it, cherish it and watch it unfold. Sometimes they have a child because they don't know how not to have one. Sometimes it is an accident. Sometimes it reflects a desperate attempt to save a dying marriage. Sometimes it's because the other spouse wants it. Sometimes it's because grandma or grandpa wants it. Sometimes it's because that's what married people are supposed to do. Often, in these situations, the parent wants to want the child, often the actuality of the child flushes out the parent's loving and caring feelings, but sometimes the parent's initial feelings of not wanting that child persist as an inhibitor of truly loving feelings. If that was your situation, the cards were stacked against you while you were still floating around in the womb wondering if you would turn out to be a boy or girl.

And your parents may have been wondering, too. Some of you had unloving parents because you made the wrong turn in following your genetic roadmap— you were supposed to come out as one gender but came out as another. There are parents for whom this little difference can greatly affect their loving feelings. And closely related to this is the question of who or what you symbolize to them, which may be very different from who you are. It is not uncommon for a child to represent his parent's parent. For example, I have seen many fathers transfer unresolved feelings of hatred of and rivalry with their own fathers to their small sons, and these feelings may persist thereafter. I have seen mothers who transfer fear and anger from a domineering or enveloping mother to their children and resent their children's demands, if not their very existence. Perhaps you represent your parent's parent, or maybe you stand for your mother's or father's own despised self, or their hated brother Arthur or contemptible sister Alice. Or perhaps for one parent you stand for everything he or she dislikes about the other, or for both you represent being tied into a marriage they wish they were out of. Whatever you symbolize, particularly when it is someone or something negative for them, the shadow of that symbol falls across you blocking the warmth of their love.

But the most likely reason a parent is unloving is that he is just too involved with himself to have anything left for you. In other words, your parent may be *narcissistic,* and narcissistic people are crippled when it comes to giving love. They may think of themselves as good, loving parents but they don't have any real idea what love is. Narcissists come in many guises, but they have some identifiable traits that run through the whole of the species. Here are the main ones:

(1) The world and the people in it are extensions of themselves and are expected to act the way they would have them act. I am not simply saying here that they would like to have others do as they wish them to do—we would all like that—but that their expectation that this will happen is so great that they are puzzled and

outraged, when it does not. Other people are out-growths of them just as surely as their limbs are. If your nose itched and you wanted to lift your hand to scratch it but it just lay there you would feel astonished, frightened, frustrated and furious. This is akin to the feelings of the narcissist when you don't act in accordance with his expressed or fantasied wishes. So if you've had a narcissistic parent you may have heard things like this:

> "But you must have time for me to visit; I'm right in the neighborhood."

> "You can't mean you wouldn't like to go shopping with me today; of course you want to."

> "How dare you make plans for that day; I haven't yet decided on which day we'll celebrate your birthday."

> "Let your friends wait; this is the time I have to discuss it."

Note that I use semicolons here to indicate that the two statements, though thrown together by the narcissist as if they belong together, are really non sequiturs, joined only by the egocentric logic of the narcissist's view of reality. And not only other people, but other things exist for them and because of them, so a narcissist might say:

> "Did you see that tree shooting up on the front lawn; it grew for me."

Since people are extensions of themselves, the boundaries between the narcissist and others are so blurred that at times the other people may not have a separate identity.

You may have heard things like:

> "I can't look at myself in the mirror if you wear a pink shirt."

> "You'll never learn to ski; I'm so uncoordinated."

"But of course you love tomatoes; I'm crazy about tomatoes."

"I threw out all those old posters of yours; you couldn't have wanted them."

"You couldn't possibly believe in God (astrology, communism, ESP, capitalism, or whatever); it's so obviously wrong."

As part of this blurring of the boundaries, your parent not only cannot see your uniqueness clearly but cannot gauge his or her impact on you. He may give you a gift he believes you would like, not notice the look of dismay or disappointment on your face and say, "I knew you would love it!" And you might feel confused, almost talking yourself into loving it because, after all, you're supposed to love it. Sometimes this confusion becomes so great that it is hard for you to tell your feelings from theirs. A woman told me she was serving yogurt to her friend's little son, Henry. Henry was really enjoying it. Then her friend came in, saw what was happening and said, "My Henry hates yogurt." Henry promptly threw up.

(2) Narcissists are usually overwhelmed by others' needing something from them. The world is supposed to be organized with others meeting their needs, and it is baffling and outrageous when this is reversed. Thus their children, who are totally needy at birth and continue to need them for many years after, are often out of luck. (In some instances, where the parent sees the child as an extension of himself and where the child's needs do, in fact, happen to be similar to the parent's, the child will have a lot of needs met within those boundaries, but of course there will then be lots of reinforcement for his staying within those boundaries, and not discovering his own uniqueness.) The legitimate needs of the child are often felt as intrusive, coercive demands and the response can be enormous anger.

"Don't you dare get sick; I have to go out tonight."

"No, you can't have any of your friends over. I'm not running a social club here."

"I don't want you to go to the party; she'll expect you to invite her back and I'm just not up to it."

"How can you get married in December when you know that's when I always go to Florida."

A corollary of the narcissist's seeing the world as organized to meet their needs is the absence of a real sense of *reciprocity,* of give and take, of you stroke me and I'll stroke you. *What they want is coming to them; what you want is an outrageous demand.* There is enormous frustration in trying to deal with narcissists on a level of mutual exchange of feelings or favors. In fact, they often perceive the relationship as one in which they have done all the giving and gotten nothing in return.

"Just tell me one thing, just one thing, that you ever did for me? You live off my money, I bust my hump to earn it, and you do nothing."

"I don't care if you did wash my car; I'm not getting up five minutes earlier just to drop you off."

(3) Narcissists are usually intensely concerned with their own bodies. When this concern is with their body's attractiveness, much time, effort and money can be lavished on decorating it, exercising it, trimming it, molding it, perfuming it, and dressing it. This is the aspect of narcissism that most literally approximates the legend of Narcissus, who fell in love with his own reflection. Mirrors and the adulation of others must reflect the image of perfection.

"I screamed at the hairdresser and made her reset my hair three times before she got it right."

"I know we owe money to the pediatrician and the

grocer but I just had to have that Pierre Cardin suit. It makes me feel like a million bucks."

"I won't eat that. I really think you're trying to tempt me so I'll be unattractive."

"If you want me to be ready at eight you'd better leave me alone from five o'clock on so I can put on my makeup and get dressed."

A similar concern about appearances and attractiveness can be manifested about their homes and possessions or the way you look or the way your room or home is decorated.

"I threw out your old dungarees; no child of mine needs to be seen so unkempt."

"I know you wanted your room in pink but it's just not in style this year."

"How can you possibly have people over for lunch and use paper napkins?"

"I hardly ever listen to music, but just knowing I have the best stereo components made is what's important."

Concern with the body is often not only with its attractiveness but with its functions and malfunctions. Here we find narcissists who are involved in their every bowel movement, attuned to every ache, focused on every strange sensation, terrified at and fascinated with their every illness. Hypochondria is frequently an offshoot of narcissism, and with it a pressing need to tell others of their bodily symptoms and to involve others in the worry about their health, physical and mental. Much time, effort and money is spent on diagnosing, doctoring, medicating, pampering and observing their bodies. Their children's bodies, as extensions of theirs, are also often objects of their worry, frequently inducing hypochondria in their children. And I have seen the adult offspring of such parents always doing their parent's bidding for fear of the guilt they would feel if their forever-dying parent should really die before they could regain parental approval.

"I've had this headache for three days and I just *know* it's not an ordinary headache. It's always in the same spot, like something's growing there."

"I just happened to look at my bowel movement and it seemed very dark to me, so I thought I better check it out."

"When they put me in the ground, then you'll believe I was sick."

"Leave me alone. If I don't get my eight hours' sleep I'm open to every germ."

(4) Despite their concern with looking attractive and sexually appealing, narcissists may not really be interested in sex except as an expression of their narcissism. They may at times pursue sex avidly to prove their ability to seduce and conquer, but having done this they may get little pleasure from the sensuousness and closeness of the sexuality, because sex is a sharing and requires giving, something narcissists find difficult to do. So other needs often take higher priority than sex, sometimes putting sex on the bottom of the list.

"You know I don't want to make love when I feel so fat."

"Not tonight, I have a big conference tomorrow and I don't want to feel drained."

"You always expect me to have sex whenever you want it" (often translating as "I won't have sex when you want it because that would be giving in to you").

The child may not be aware of these bedroom conversations but the unsexual or antisexual or exaggeratedly sexual tone may be in the air, and the priorities of things are noted by the child. Sometimes these are direct statements to the child that indicate as much.

"No, I can't play with you now; I'm all dressed."

"Be careful of women; they give you this big come-on and the next thing you know they're leading you around by the nose."

"There's one thing your mommy is good for" (patting mommy on the behind).

"You don't give in to a man without something to show for it."

(5) Narcissists lie easily and, in a strange way, they do not know it. They distort the reality to fit their needs and really believe what they are saying is true. They can be fully in accord with the decision as to where the family will vacation and later say, "We always do what you want to do. I never said I wanted to come here." And they will really have rewritten the past so that it does not feel like a lie to them. Or they can rationalize the lie in a way that makes it clear that they see it as a non-lie. ("Did I say I was having company tonight? Oh yes, but they called to say they couldn't make it." Which may be completely untrue, but after all it did provide justification for keeping you from inviting friends over.)

(6) The result of all this—of seeing themselves at the center of the universe with others revolving around them, of not empathizing with the impact of their actions on others, of being distressed at others needing anything from them, of being deficient in a sense of reciprocity, of being involved in their own attractiveness and preoccupied with their health, and of being unwittingly untruthful—is that it is difficult if not impossible for narcissists (depending on the degree of the narcissism) to have close, intimate relationships with other people. And if your parent was a narcissist, it was difficult for him or her to have a close, intimate relation-

ship with you. There may have been a pseudo-intimacy,
the closeness based on your being part of him and of
his trying hard to play his parental role to perfection,
but the caring for and nourishing of your uniqueness
was, to an important degree, absent.

Parental unlovingness always has the general effect
of causing defects in your self-esteem, but there are
some differences based on whether the unloving parent
was mother or father. The mothering job is primarily
nurturant, and demands an exquisite sensitivity to the
child's unique and ever-changing needs. When this is
present, when she is the "good enough mother" Winnicott talks about, the child's bad feelings about himself,
based on the fact that he is quite helpless and inadequate to survive or to deal effectively with the world,
are overcome because he faces the world supplemented
by his mother. His good feelings about himself—his
vitality, zest, curiosity and desire to develop his ca-
pacities—are enhanced. When mother is not "good
enough" and does not effectively supplement the child's
developmental insufficiencies, all the bad or "not
okay" feelings are exacerbated and the good or "okay"
feelings are damaged. If your mother was unloving
you probably are very unloving toward yourself. You
seriously doubt your abilities, your adequacy and your
worth. You may seriously question the point of your
being alive. You may feel shy, unassertive, undesirable
and intrusive. Perhaps you cover this up by going to
the other extreme of being aggressive and demanding,
of being narcissistic yourself, but even then you know
there is a deep flaw in your self-esteem that makes you
very vulnerable to signs of disapproval or rejection.
Your "okay" feelings of zest and enthusiasm for life
may at times be there, but can easily fall away into feelings of flatness or despair. The influence your narcissistic mother may have had on your particular personality
development will depend on the ways you attempted to
get an okay feeling from a mother whose narcissism was
giving you a not-okay feeling.

Males and females are in some ways bent differently
by having a narcissistic mother. If you are the son of a

narcissistic mother, the deprivation of her not being truly responsive to you may have set you on the tragic course of trying to figure out and do the right thing that would draw her warmth to you, as if there were a right thing ("I'm gonna love you like nobody's loved you come rain or come shine"). And, worse yet, you may be running that same grinding course with other women. Literature is filled with such tales—the man who, determined to win the love of the cold, proud beauty, will climb glass mountains, slay dragons, make sacrifices, bring back some valuable prize, even destroy himself just to win her favor. Or perhaps you tried to feel okay by being like your powerful self-centered mother, by assuming many of her characteristics, including those usually connected with feminity, so that by now perhaps you and others see yourself as an effeminate caricature of your mother. Or maybe you are trying to master mother by using and hurting other women. Possibly you've given up on getting love from a woman and your theme song is "I'm gonna buy a paper doll that I can call my own."

If you are the daughter of a narcissistic mother, the unavailability of her nurturing may cause you to seek mothering in relationships with both males and females. It can put you in a little-girl position with both sexes, and is at times a basis for a lesbian preference. Another solution you may have chosen, particularly since girls tend to use mother as a role model, is to identify with mother's narcissism, to become that extension of your mother that she always saw you as anyway. So perhaps you've become a living Barbie doll, or a precious princess, if this was the way to feel okay as part of mother. If mother's narcissism centered around being hypochondriacal and trying to be the center of the universe by being the biggest victim, you may have become an extension of her through trying to make the world revolve around your anxieties.

Son or daughter, a narcissistic mother has left you hungry for love and recognition, and your attempts to get it or to deny that you need it have made up the theme of your life.

It is a lot different when father is the unloving parent. The fathering role (see Chapter 4) is to help the child see and become acquainted with the wider world beyond his mother's skirts and the family kitchen, to help him loosen those parts of the attachment to mother that would stand in the way of his development and individuation. A good-enough father presents his child with an alternative to mother's life space and can be a guide and source of strength to the child as he explores these new territories.*

If your father didn't give much of a damn about you, it may have showed itself in several ways. For one thing, he may rarely have been around (it is usually easier for narcissistic fathers to stay away from home than narcissistic mothers). Maybe you saw him at night before you went to sleep; maybe you caught a glimpse of him on weekends; maybe sometimes you didn't see him for long stretches.† Possibly he was home often enough, but as far as you were concerned, he might have been an astronaut in distant orbit. When you were

---

*I am aware of the sexist nature of these descriptions of the mothering and fathering roles. I am also aware that each parent is most effective as a parent if he or she has the capacity for mothering *and* fathering, for nurturance and "exquisite sensitivity to the child's unique and ever-changing needs" on the one hand, and a "guide and source of strength to the child as he explores these new territories" on the other. Further, I would agree that a child brought up by a mother and father who each embody only the mothering or fathering paradigm is presented with a false and constricting view of people and of his or her own role. But the fact is that in the nuclear family that now exists, even with the enormous changes that have been evolving, the most usual situation is one in which the child's earliest needs for nurturing and his earliest close, dependent relationship is with his mother, and the father will more often than not be with the child less than the mother and, more often than not, represent the world outside the home more than the mother does. I am not saying that this is good or bad, whether or how much it should be changed, or what the results of changing it would be (although changes now taking place will soon give us more data); I know only that *it is usually the case*, and that therefore the mother or father being unloving has, in this time and place, differing effects on the child.

†Father's absence does not in itself prove he didn't care about you —his type of work, shifting circumstances, or not being able to stand being around your mother may have kept him away from the house. If he arranged to take you with him or to do things with him when he *was* around it would indicate his caring even if he stayed away from home a lot. The key would be in the interaction between you, and in your guts you know if he cared.

a child, trying to get him to leave the TV set long enough to play with you, to come out of his workshop or get up from his desk long enough to throw a ball, to cut down on his nap time in order to take a walk with you or help you with your homework, or simply to take the time to sit and talk with you, was so rarely a fruitful effort on your part that it may have become not worth the cost, and you soon became resigned to letting him orbit light-years away.

One effect of being psychologically fatherless, besides the corroding of your self-esteem that lack of love from any important person in your early development can cause, is that it may have been harder to leave mother's magnetic field without the guidance and encouragement of a good-enough father. Perhaps you still haven't accomplished that. Or in trying to diminish your dependency on your mother without his help, you may have made it a violent rupture. Your anger at your father after years of making futile attempts to get him to care may have hardened into a cynicism that impairs your own ability to be loving.

In some ways, sons are affected differently than daughters by a narcissistic father. If your father was not only self-centered but was belittling, a common and castrating combination, then you, as his son, know how this has tended to blunt your assertion and to make you passive in pursuing your own needs and preferences. But perhaps, long ago, you determined to prevent such impotence by grafting that narcissistic part of your father into yourself and being like him. Then you, too, may have a difficult time being close to others, empathizing with them, or easily putting yourself out for them. Maybe you feel this to be a shortcoming, or maybe you are only aware of it as a problem because people in your life complain about it.

If your father was self-involved he was not only unavailable to you but he may have been unavailable to your mother, which can mean that mother was (is) more available to you. Maybe this has left you too attached to her, but more likely you defended against your Oedipal feelings by a prickly or angry relationship with her. If you are at the same time trying to break your dependent tie with her, the combination of these two motives can all but destroy any possibility of something positive occurring between you and your mother. Add to this the possibility that you have identified with your father's narcissism and it is likely that you have a strong need to seduce and manipulate women, and you are probably very good at it.

Narcissistic fathers leave their daughters with deep doubts about whether a man can love them, since the first important man in their life was so in love with himself that he had no love left for them. If you are a daughter of a narcissistic father you may have withdrawn from men and bound yourself to mother, either overtly or emotionally. Or you may be engaged in a self-destructive attempt to be his kind of girl, whatever that is, as you try desperately to extract his love. Perhaps you have transferred this into a masochistic position with other men, finding a narcissistic man incredibly attractive as you try to master the mystery of winning his unwinnable love. And narcissistic men appeal to you because you wish you could be that way yourself—assertive, not giving a damn, self-important —but you lack the confidence to do it yourself so you identify with the man who has their quality, even if it's at your expense. (I have often seen this revealed in those instances where a woman has suffered through a degradingly submissive and abusing relationship with a man, or a series of men, and then, gaining the strength to break that kind of bondage, violently overturns the tables and abuses that man, or the next man in her life, as degradingly as she was misused. It's not just revenge, but the release of a hidden desire to be powerful and to be able to control father and make him beg for her love.) Maybe Sylvia Plath exaggerated when she said that "*Every* woman adores a Fascist," but if you've had a narcissistic daddy there's a pretty good chance that you do adore self-anointed narcissistic men and repeatedly find yourself in relationships where you do most of the accommodating. And maybe you fool yourself into thinking that's what love is about, and sing with misty eyes songs like, "As Long as He Needs Me," "It Must Be Him," and "Can't Help Lovin' That Man of Mine."

Breaking the song and dance with an unloving parent may seem even more painful than continuing it, because it involves some excruciating recognitions, the first of which is fully acknowledging your parent's unlovingness. Some of you may have long recognized it, others of you have not dared. But here is where it must begin, in letting yourself say, "Mostly, my mother (parents, father) didn't love me." And letting that sink in, letting yourself know what you've known all along.

The second piercing recognition is that your parent's unloving has left you with profound feelings of worthlessness. You learn to value yourself to a great extent from how your parents value you from the start of your life, if not before, and you probably came to feel that if your parents did not love you there must be something basically, terribly unlovable about you. It's useful to face that feeling before you can begin correcting it.

The third agonizing recognition is that your parent's unlovingness has left real defects in your own ability to be loving. This is almost inevitable. I do not mean that you can't be loving at times and in ways, but that there are limitations because one parent, at least, did not help teach you how and because there may be an emptiness in you that makes true loving difficult. It is hard to feed others when you are starving. At times you may fool yourself into thinking that you are more loving than you really are because you are showering the kind of loving onto others that you wanted, but this may blind you to seeing it's not the kind of loving the other person wants. As a father you may take your son out on the boat every Sunday, feeling you are doing a loving thing and not noticing that he hates it but is going along with you because he's learned he can only be with you on your terms. As a wife you may feel you are being loved by keeping the house clean and your husband's shirts laundered and not notice that he is longing for an affectionate touch that you may find difficult to give. It is these kinds of impairments in loving that it would be helpful to let yourself see, but you must step back from your own narcissism in order to see it.

Finally, there is the recognition of the particular songs and dances you enter into with your unloving parent that keeps the awful not-okay feelings alive even though they are supposed to make you feel better. The songs and dances are varied, but they are based on a few main themes:

There Must Be a Way—in which you are still trying to get milk from a statue, the statue being your parent and/or other people you are trying to wring love from.

I'm Sitting on Top of the World—in which you are trying to feel okay by joining your parents in self-aggrandizing or in a mutually aggrandizing *narcissisme à deux*. This puts you on shaky ground because it is based on being an extension of your parents' narcissism and not on an accurate self-appraisal. You can be easily wounded or enraged when others don't see you in the same exalted light, or fail to act as extensions of you.

I'll Walk Alone—in which you withdraw from the hope of and striving for love from your parent or anybody and see any intimacy as a threat and a trap. Your feeling of being unlovable becomes a self-fulfilling prophecy as you turn yourself into a mole, a porcupine, or a skunk, according to your style, in order to keep people at a distance.

Who's Sorry Now—in which you are asserting your victim's right increasingly to accuse your parents of not loving you and to extort love tokens or substitutes from them through this accusation. This only works with parents who feel guilty about not loving you, and will go on as long as they're willing to pay this guilt tax. You, of course, must arrange to keep your life a vale of misery in order to be a bona fide victim and to keep your extortion license intact.

Having recognized all these painful feelings and futile songs and dances, and seeing the high price you pay to keep them going, you are faced with an overwhelming question: If I did not get the loving I really needed from my parent and if this has stunted my self-esteem and misshaped my relationship with others, can I repair such a basic and early damage? Or am I not better off maintaining the songs and dances that at least give me some illusion that I am okay or that I will some day find the way to get my parent to love me?

Being unloved by a parent may always leave scars, but the wound can be healed and healthy growth can begin anew. It is worth giving up even those songs and dances that have helped you to survive parental unlovingness because there are better ways to feel okay. In exchanging the old songs and dances for more authentic movement, *it is crucial to begin to accept that your parents' not loving you is a statement about them and not about you. In other words, it bespeaks a defect in their ability to love rather than a defect in your lovability.* It becomes particularly important to see the child within your parent because it is the inner child, too big a part of your parent, that made him or her unable to love you. If your parent had you to please his own parents, or his spouse, or society, then it was the little child in him trying to be the good, conforming child, trying to get approval or avoid disapproval, that made the decision. You were brought into this world by a child, and children can only play at being loving parents.

If you were unloved because of whom you represent rather than who you are, it will be useful to try to discern whom you stand for. And there will be many clues, if you just look. Whom did your unloving parent compare you to, say you looked like or acted like? Whom, in your parent's life, does he have feelings about that seem to be similar to the feelings he has about you? Is it one of his parents? Your other parent? A part of himself that he hates? If he treats your sibling or siblings more lovingly than he treats you, whom does that sibling stand for compared to you? If you symbolize someone unlovable to that parent, to what extent have you assumed the role of that unloved person? To what extent are you acting out the role your parent projected onto you?

If your parent's unlovingness stems from his own narcissistic self-involvement, then it becomes necessary to see him or her as a little child arrested at that stage of development where he felt at the center of the universe, where his needs took precedence over all others. This is not to say that he was well loved by his parents, but that he himself was badly loved, perhaps by parents who "spoiled" him through substituting tokens and plastic affection for real loving. It left him stuck as a needy child, perhaps assuming the grandiose position his parent assigned, never sufficiently developing his capacity to empathize or be concerned about others except as gratifiers of his needs. His or her inability to love you is a tragedy, but it's nothing personal.

So the wounds of unloving, originally inflicted through no fault of your own, are there. Where can you begin the repair job? You can begin, first of all, by not constantly rubbing and reopening the wound through self-destructive songs and dances. Your need for loving is real, but if you take as your task trying to get your unloving parent or other unloving people to love you, you will end up "confirming" your unlovability. Your need for loving is as real as a powerful thirst on a hot day, but if you were unbearably thirsty you would reach for a glass of cool water, not a glass of hot sand which you hoped you could convert into cool water. The needed task, then, is to reach for love where it is available rather than try to get it from someone from whom it is unattainable.

But that is only part of the repair job. The main question is, how can you begin to feel truly loving and nurturant toward yourself when you have no videotapes in your head of parental lovingness toward you? First, it is probably not true that you have no videotapes in your head of early loving experiences. Even your unloving parent may have been genuinely loving at times, your other parent may have offered real loving, and other people—relatives, teachers, friends—may also have stored caring videotapes in your head. You may have enough loving in you to be quite giving to others but have not yet learned to turn this same givingness toward yourself. It will be helpful to note how you are with people you care about most—perhaps a friend, a lover, your spouse, your child—and see if it is possible to embrace yourself with that same warmth, acceptance, tolerance and nurturing.

There is an exercise that I have found gratifying that might help you to develop your own inner nurturing parent and teach it to feed the hungry child inside you. Think of a photograph of yourself as a child. Picture the child you are in that photo as standing there in the corner of the room. Let yourself into him (or her) so you can feel what he feels and know what he needs. Then go over, get that child, put him (or her) on your lap and tell him everything you think that little child wants and needs to hear. For example, a man in his forties, who felt his father never loved him, sat his little boy self on his knee and said, "You're a fine kid. You're fun and warm and sensitive. And I'll teach you how to be strong and how to fight because you'll need lots of strength and self-confidence. I'll teach you not to be afraid to reach for what you want. I can do this for you because I love you and want you to be strong and able and happy. Let me give you my love." As he was telling this to himself as the child on his knee, he was discovering what the child in him wanted from his father and didn't get, and he was learning how he can now give more of this to himself. And a depressed, suicidal, self-deprecating woman of about thirty who felt that both of her parents were cold and unloving held her little girl self in her arms and, tears flowing, told her, "Oh, my darling little girl. You're really so kind that I even like it when you're naughty. Don't be frightened and don't be shy. Be strong and stand up for yourself. Because I'll tell you a secret: You're just the little girl I always wanted, that I always dreamed of having, and I'm so glad you're here and alive." She was letting herself feel what the child in her so desperately wanted and never received, and she was learning how to be nurturing to that child or, more simply, learning to be good for herself.

It is a matter of re-parenting. Of allowing yourself to be a more loving parent to yourself than your parents were, of allowing others to love you in ways your parents could not, of allowing all the loving experiences you've ever had to make their statement about your value.

8 | Don't Sit Under the Apple Tree with Anyone Else but Me

Each infant enters the world not only needing to be fed and cleaned and protected, but needing to be physically stimulated by being held, cuddled and stroked. There is overwhelming evidence that an infant who does not get this physical stimulation will become depressed, withdrawn, ill and may, if the deprivation is extreme, even die. It is also clear that infants who do get enough pleasant physical stimulation are more joyous, content and display a greater sense of vitality and well-being.

Fortunately, most parents love their children tenderly and like to express this affection physically. The infant's need to receive affectionate stimulation and the parent's need to give it complement each other beautifully, and form the basis of an early reciprocity of emotional satisfactions. Although parents may differ in the amount and mode of physically expressing their love, almost all do cuddle, caress, hug, rock, and tickle their infants. As the infant gets older, the loving feelings remain and continue to be expressed. Parents hold their children, sit them on their laps, ride them on their shoulders, tussle with them, bathe them, brush their hair, tuck them in, hug them, nuzzle them, kiss them. The child continues to grow, the love is still there, and the physical expression of it, though modified by the child's development, is still needed. Hopefully it is still expressed by the parents. An embrace, a touching, even the ritualized good-night kiss be-become an important part of the parent-child way of being together. What all this means is that the natural inclination of both child and parent is to feel and express sensuality with each other through pleasure in skin contact. Another way of putting it is that there is a *sexualized* aspect to the parent-child affection that is totally normal, natural and healthy. And I use the term "sexualized" here to indicate that there is often an arousal involved, a desire for more extensive and continued physical enjoyment on the part of both parent and child, and I again state that this desire is normal, natural and healthy. After all, the child is a living, pleasure-seeking, affection-seeking being with the capacity for sexual arousal. What could be more natural than that he would feel this arousal with the people he is closest to, attached to, loves the most and who love him? And the parent is also a living, pleasure-seeking, affection-seeking being with the capacity for sexual arousal. It is natural and common (although many parents repress their awareness of such feelings for fear that having them is wrong or even perverted) for the parents to feel some sexual arousal in the intimate body contact they share with their children.

The child's desire for pleasant, loving stimulation is often centered on the parent of the opposite sex. This forms the basis of what Freud labeled the Oedipus complex. Freud was aware of the perils in this nearly universal phenomenon. First, there is the danger that the child, at ages going back to three or less, can be flooded by feelings and sensations that are so intense that they can overwhelm his adequacy to make sense of them, cope with them, gratify them or control them. Secondly, it could lead to an intensification of the bond to the parent that may abort the child's motivation to move into the larger world. And finally, Freud noted that the child's desire for the opposite-sex parent is possessive and exclusive: the little boy wants his mother *all* to himself and the little girl wants her father *all* to herself. This means the child wants to eliminate his (her) rival, the parent of the same sex, and therefore harbors death wishes toward that parent. This secret, deadly competition makes the little boy fearful of horrible retaliation by his father and the little girl fearful of horrible retaliation by her mother. Ideally, as the child sees the futility of his desires, largely by noting that the parent he wants to possess does not want the same kind of relationship with him, he gives up his Oedipal wishes for the opposite-sex parent, experiences the relief of identifying with rather than competing with the same-sex parent and is free, at a later time, to find a mate all his own. It is here that the parents' ability to respond appropriately to their child's sensuality is crucial, for as natural and understandable as a child's sexual feelings toward his parents are, and as natural and understandable as a parent's sexual feelings toward his (her) child are, it is destructive for the parent to go *too far* in his expression of sensuality with the child.

What is "too far"? It is too far when the parent's own drives become more powerful than his (her) judgment as to what the child needs and what the child can handle. Feeding a child is nurturant and healthy, but when a parent is acting more out of his (her) own drive to get food into the child than out of his sensitivity to the child's needs, or when a parent gluts a child's cravings (for example, by feeding him all the candy he wants) despite the fact that this goes counter to the parents' judgment as to what is best for the child, he has gone "too far." In the area of sexual and affectionate interplay between parent and child, it is "too far" when the parent's arousal or needs for affection have taken over, causing him to lose sight of whether his stimulation of the child is a loving, benevolent act or a selfish imposition of his own needs; it is "too far" when the parent is blind to how his actions foster rivalrous feelings with the other parent and precipitate a dread of retaliation that can terrify the child and interfere with the development of a good and open relationship with the parent of the same sex.

A child cannot cope with an intensive, overt, sexualized experience with a parent without its doing some damage to his development. It is therefore one of the crucial responsibilities of parenthood to find that blurry boundary between gratifying some of the child's sensuality on the one hand and helping the child to contain his arousal on the other hand so that he will not become confused, frightened and overwhelmed. The mature nurturant part of the parent can make this discernment and act to optimally gratify and optimally contain his offspring's longings. But if the child within the parent has taken over, the parent will be driven by his own desires and by the tendency of his inner child to want instant pleasure with no delay, no restrictions, no thinking about consequences. It is when the parent's inner child is in control of the dimension of affection-intimacy-sexuality that great psychological damage can be done to the offspring. And very often, when this situation exists, there is at least passive participation of the *other* parent's inner child who is either subtly aiding or in some way reacting inadequately to the seductive interplay between his (her) spouse and child.

DADDY'S LITTLE GIRL

I once treated a little girl, Judy, who came into therapy at about age ten with anxiety symptoms, a sleep disturbance and impaired concentration. I had interviews with both of the parents, separately and together. Her father, Ed, was the head of an advertising agency, an energetic, vigorous man who told me he had always had strong sexual urges that were not met to his satisfaction by his wife. He had many affairs during their marriage. He described his daily homecoming: "I always looked forward to getting home to Judy. I would come home with a noise, with a hoopla, and Judy would come running down this long corridor to me screaming, 'Daddy, Daddy.' I would grab her and throw her up in the air and we'd hug and tussle on the floor. It's not exactly the same way now because she's too big to toss around and she's more reserved," Ed said, "but there's still a lot of physical affection between us and we go out hiking every Sunday, just the two of us. My wife hates hiking."

Judy's mother, Louise, was a quiet, restrained and introspective woman, and though not particularly withdrawn or unsexual, she seemed befuddled and outside the close, rambunctious relationship between her husband and her daughter. Judy's mother and father seemed to have little to say to each other, though from most outward appearances theirs would seem like a good marriage. All the elements of a troubled Oedipal situation were there and it seemed to me that this was the basis of much of Judy's turmoil.

What are the elements of a troubled Oedipal situation? Shouldn't a father be physically affectionate and spend time with his young daughter? Of course he should—it's a marvelous and special human sharing and gives the growing girl a sense of her worth and her lovability as well as giving her the experience of enjoying and being comfortable with males. What makes Judy's situation an upsetting one is the sexual nature of Ed's play—almost as a spillover of his ever-brimming sexual neediness, his greater emotional involvement with Judy than Louise, his wife (note his statement, "I always looked forward to getting home to *Judy*"), and Louise's helpless, left-out stance. The family is structured for Judy to feel either that she could triumph over her mother, which is frightening because she loves and must depend on her mother, or that her mother will vindictively attack or abandon Judy, a thought at least equally terrifying for a child to live with.

It was not long after treatment began that my hunch that Judy's anxieties arose out of this intense Oedipal situation was dramatically confirmed. Ed had to attend a business conference in Chicago and since Judy had some time off from school, he took her with him. They had a good time, shared a hotel room, went to the natural history museum, walked along the lake, ate in good restaurants and flew back the next day. Soon after their return to their suburban home, Judy went into an uncontrollable screaming panic. She was certain that atomic bombs would be dropped, that the oil burner of their home would explode, and that other nameless terrors were imminent. Through it, she wouldn't let her mother out of her sight, clung to her, and would not let her father near her. The little "honeymoon" with her father had so intensified her sexual, possessive and competitive feelings that her whole world had become a nightmare.

It is not my intention to discuss how Judy was helped but to illustrate the role played by the child within her parents in the formation of her disturbance. As I got to know Judy's father I began to see him as a little boy who felt terribly small and inadequate and who early in his life tried to counteract these feelings with a display of sexualized cockiness. As a child he was a show-off, particularly in front of girls. As Ed became a teenager he had to make conquest after conquest to prove his adequacy. As a man he needed to carry on this pattern, even to his own daughter, as if the tiny, inadequate-feeling little boy in him was screaming, "Look at me, everybody. Look at me, Judy. I'm strong and wonderful and manly. Maybe you can make me believe that if I can get you to adore me."

In Ed's feelings, his wife, Louise, had become for him the cold mother of his childhood, his mother whose narcissism and ungivingness had helped him to feel so worthless in the first place, and all that little-boy hostility at his mother was coming out in his rejecting behavior toward his wife. So Judy became for Ed another mother to conquer, and his wife became the mother he despised. But poor Judy did not know that the father she worshiped was a woefully vulnerable little boy. She saw her father as a big, powerful, handsome man and gloried in his attentions. This made it easy for her to be swept into a song and dance where she played the ever-adoring ingenue to his Prince Charming.

The dance, then, was between two children, a worshipful, sensuous, possessive little girl and a love-starved, show-offish little boy. This mutually seductive song and dance is the most dangerous kind of puppy love.

And Louise, Judy's mother? Clearly there was a little girl in her that never had known feelings of adequacy and worth. Louise had long ago surrendered her self-confidence to a powerfully critical mother (Judy's grandmother), a woman who possessed and controlled her husband (Judy's grandfather). So the child in Judy's mother still felt undesirable, still acted like a loser. The little girl in Louise actually saw Judy, her own daughter, as her overpowering mother and just sat it out, bewildered, as her daughter and her husband traipsed around the ballroom.

Judy's family illustrates how the normal Oedipus triangle is exacerbated by the child within both of the parents. Similar forces are at work when it is the *mother* who is the seductive parent.

In a seductive mother there may be—

—a little girl who was the apple of her father's eye and who sees all males, including her own son, as fair game for the continuation of her conquests.

—a little girl who feels forlorn, unattractive and undesirable but who can hope that her son will see her as a goddess.

—an angry little girl who feels competitive with males, maybe because of rivalrous early feelings with a brother, maybe because of other early experiences, who uses her seductiveness to control her son.

—a frightened little girl with such doubts of her lovability and such fears of abandonment that she is seductive with her son as a means to hold on to him.

—a narcissistic little girl whom everyone must find attractive and sexy, even her son.

—a love-starved little girl who projects herself into her son's place and showers him with all the love and attention she has always wanted for herself.

—an unhappy little girl who was deeply disappointed by her father, continues to be disappointed by her husband, and who turns to her son for salvation and adulation.

There are doubtless many possibilities as to what type of child within a parent leads the parent to be unwittingly seductive, but it is never the mature grown-up part of the parent. *In fact, if you have a seductive parent of the opposite sex, you can take it as evidence that the child within your parent may still be stuck in his or her own Oedipus conflict and that you have come to represent his/her desired parent of the opposite sex.*

But it is not only parental seductiveness with the child of the opposite sex that makes the Oedipus complex endure long after it should have faded into one's personal museum of ancient history, but also parental *competitiveness,* real or imagined, with the child of the same sex. When a parent is seductive with his or her child of the opposite sex, the arousal of the child's fearful feelings toward the same-sex parent is unavoidable, even when the same-sex parent is *not* being competitive. In fact, it can occur even when the opposite-sex parent is not *deliberately* seductive. I recall seeing in therapy a little boy named Joey who was severely disturbed at the start of treatment, even to the point of seeming retarded. Treatment took several years, but when we stopped he was a spontaneous, happy, bright youngster. I saw his parents for a final session. We were all delighted with his progress. I remarked to the father, "The only remaining problem is Joey's fear reaction to you. I don't understand it fully, but it's enough improved so that I don't think he need remain in therapy for it." The father was an enormous man, tall and wide, with that particular gentleness you sometimes find in big men who've never had to prove their strength and toughness. At this point he looked at his wife, a petite and very attractive woman. Then they told me something they had never mentioned in all the time I was treating Joey—that they were nudists and that all their summer vacations were spent in a nudist colony. In other words, Joey was frequently in a position of being nude with his attractive nude mother and big, powerful nude father. The feelings and fantasies this aroused made him feel so strongly his wish to eliminate his father, that he lived with a constant fear of his father's retaliation. (To those who might scoff because, after all, the human body is beautiful and natural so that openness about family nudity should be liberating rather than cause problems, I can only say that such a viewpoint ignores the unconscious. And, I might ask, why did Joey, in four years of treatment in which he described in such detail his summer vacations in the country—all the ball games, the frogs he caught, the family fun—never mention that during all this nobody was wearing clothes? And why, in all the sessions I had with his parents, did they never mention it either, at least not until the end, and as a way of responding to my statement that Joey was still afraid of his father? Certainly there are societal taboos about nudity that might pressure a nudist family to be cautious in revealing this information, but more than social pressures are at work when they don't reveal it to a psychotherapist in so many years. There was an awareness that it was arousing disturbing feelings in their child, which they were not adequately helping him to deal with.)

So if rivalrous feelings can be aroused even when the same-sex parent is *not* being competitive but can spring from the inner life of the child, it is not difficult to see how the Oepidal conflict can be further intensified when the parent of the same sex *is* actually competitive with his or her offspring. Like the Queen in Snow White, a parent who needs to ask, "Mirror, mirror on the wall, who's the fairest one of all," can be deadly and frightening. Often the child is driven away, sometimes into the arms of the opposite-sex parent just as Snow White was driven into the arms of the seven little old men. But Prince Charming does not always come to the rescue.

At times the competitive parent's effort to keep his/her child of the same sex from having a close relationship with the other parent is successful, and this not only prevents a natural working through of the Oedipal conflict, but deprives the child of having the kind of relaxed sharing experiences with that other parent that are so important to growing. The part of the parent that destructively competes with his/her own offspring is a little boy or little girl who feels woefully inadequate compared to others. Perhaps it is the child within your parent that felt so tiny and inept in relation to the huge and able father or mother, perhaps the child that felt unable to compete with the cuteness and demandingness of a younger sibling.

The rivalrous child within your parent may not have surfaced until you began to date peers of the opposite sex. Then your same-sex parent may have become chronically critical and disparaging. He or she may have begun to sabotage your relationships, often under the guise of its being all for your own good, perhaps because your date was no good for you, or you were too young, etc. At times, like Mrs. Robinson's rivalry with her daughter for the affections of "The Graduate," a parent may be seductive with the dates of his/her own offspring.

If competitiveness from your parent of the same sex is familiar to you, you can take it as evidence that the child within your parent may still be stuck in his/her own Oedipus conflict and that you have come to represent his/her rivalrous parent of the same sex.

MY HEART BELONGS TO DADDY

One of the most difficult-to-resolve forms of Oedipus conflict occurs when the same-sex parent pushes the child into the arms of a seductive opposite-sex parent, sometimes actively, sometimes by abdication. At its extreme, it is this combination that leads to those rare cases of incestuous behavior. I recall one woman who had a sexual relationship with her father that spanned many years. Her mother was a long-suffering, depressed, complaining woman who offered little joy to her husband or daughter. When I asked the daughter how she felt after starting her affair with her father when she was an older teenager she said, "It felt okay. After all, I would try to take the burdens off my mother by doing the dishes and the laundry so this seemed like another way I could help out."

Again, we see here the mother's inner child afraid to win in the Oedipal battle with her own mother and therefore assuming the role of the loser, even to the point of surrendering her husband to her daughter. And we see a father whose inner child so needs to possess and conquer, that it overrides his adult judgments and parental protectiveness.

If you can realize that you are still caught up in an Oedipal situation, you may still be getting so much gratification from it—from the closeness, the attention, the intensity—that you might question why you should do anything to change it. You might ask, "Oh, theoretically I know it's not supposed to be good for me, but what harm does it do, really?"

A lingering Oedipal involvement can have bad effects within your relationship with your parents and keep you from growing outside of it. To start with an extreme, the young woman just mentioned who helped her mother out by having a sexual relationship with her father did get married, but picked a husband so passive, so ineffectual and so unaware that she was able to continue her affair with her father without his noticing! But what an empty marriage, what inadequate parent figures she and her husband became to their own children!

That example is so extreme that you may not be able to identify with it. But I recall another situation, also a bit unusual but close enough to the truth of many relationships that you may find something of yourself there. I got a call from an old student of mine telling me that she had a close friend who had just married, and whose marriage had reached such an intense and explosive crisis that she wondered if I could see the couple immediately. I had the couple come over after my usual hours and we worked far into the night because it was, indeed, an emergency. They had been married only a few months. The wife, Beth, was an attractive, vivacious woman of twenty-two whose father was a self-made millionaire—a dynamic, charming, aggressive "captain of industry" type. He had always been a heroic figure to Beth. Beth's husband, Larry, was an unassuming young man, who had just come out of the Peace Corps shortly before Beth met him. He had recently completed his degree in social work and was counseling disturbed families in a community agency. Soon after their marriage, Beth found herself flying into unreasoning rages at him, not even able to identify what she was furious about but just calling him demeaning names and throwing things at him. He was bewildered and would try to calm her, but the night before he had finally blown up and slammed her around; a neighbor had called the police and Beth had had to be taken to the emergency room of the hospital with a broken wrist.

They both felt desperately unhappy and hopeless sitting in my office, as if victims of forces they couldn't control or comprehend. As Beth spoke of her father she glowed, and she compared Larry contemptuously to him. But as she described incidents with her father in more detail it became clear that he could be a ruthless man, a man with little social conscience and a distorted sense of ethics. After a while I said, "Beth, is it possible that you're afraid to acknowledge that Larry is in many ways a better man than your father?" She looked stunned, and then began to sob deeply for many minutes. Larry went to her and held her. As we talked later it became clearer that her need to hold on to her father as the big man in her life, her own shining knight, made her furious at Larry when his good attributes threatened to depose her father in her feelings.

This is a common theme, though it is usually more subtle. It's hard to be in a really loving, committed relationship with a peer of the opposite sex *when you are still deeply involved with your parent of the opposite sex*. A closely related theme is that it's hard to be in a happy, fulfilling relationship with a peer of the opposite sex *when you're still feeling guilty about triumphing over your parent of the same sex*. An example of this is David, a man of twenty-eight who has really never had a girlfriend—that is, other than his mother. They had been very close, intense, and personal with each other. David's father was a very passive and withdrawn man who would sit silent and far away at the dinner table, never noticing that David got the better servings, rarely participating in the animated discussions between his wife and son. When David was seventeen, his mother died after a brief illness. David grieved, and canceled plans to go to college out of town. He stayed to take care of a father who seemed to want little taking care of. And although David would date young women, as soon as a relationship began to feel good and important, as soon as it gave him pleasure and excitement, David would pull back and end it. As we looked into this it was clear that David was not simply remaining loyal to his mother or afraid of commitment, but that the unrecognized guilt accumulated over years of beating his father out for his mother's affections had now made it impossible for him to feel that he could have a woman of his own while his father had none. He was atoning for his triumph over his father by depriving himself of that kind of happiness. So success in the Oedipal struggle can be a very guilt-drenched victory, and if you have experienced any version of that triumph, you may still be paying your penance with some form of self-defeating behavior.

There are many instances when, like David, the offspring in an unresolved Oedipus conflict, in an act of appeasement, attaches himself or herself to the parent of the same sex. At times this can be a factor in a preference for homosexuality. But even when such a reactive attachment to the same-sex parent does not occur, it frequently and sadly develops that the child and the opposite-sex parent, out of guilt and anxiety about the presence of feelings of loving attraction, withdraw from each other, often angrily. I have heard so many women say, "My father and I were so close till I was in about seventh grade. Then suddenly he pulled back and it seemed like we were always fighting."

As we look more closely we see that not only did father pull back, if indeed he did, but that the young girl, with her hormones now thrusting her into puberty, retreated in panic from her intensified sexual feelings. At that point some girls turn their feelings toward a boyfriend and get deeply involved; others pull back so powerfully that they never let themselves become fully involved with any man. I have also seen many a boy with a close relationship with his mother withdraw dramatically from that closeness as he entered adolescence, not as an appropriate resolution of the

Oedipal attachment but as a rebellious retreat that may take him in the direction of a profound adolescent attachment to a girl he idolizes and worships (an unrecognized mother substitute) or in the direction of untender, cavalier or disinterested attitudes toward women. These defensive reactions against Oedipal feelings, as much as acting out Oedipal attachments, can cause a serious impairment in the ability to love.

These examples are a few of the ways that maintaining an Oedipal song and dance can distort your relationships with others. But maintaining that kind of song and dance makes for a deeply disturbed relationship with both your parents as well. You are always uncomfortably perched on the sharp apex of a triangle. Your attachment to the parent of the opposite sex is usually a love-hate bond—you hate the loving closeness because you know it is a trap that has impaired your growth and kept you from getting close to your parent of the same sex. (At times, the tie is mostly expressed through hate, particularly when the need to deny the love and the sexuality is very great. I recall a sixteen-year-old boy I treated who often got into violent fights with his mother. They would often reach the point where she would pick up a lamp or some heavy object to hit him, or he would grab her arm, the two of them would fall onto the bed or to the floor and tussle till they both were panting, their clothes in disarray, immobile with exhaustion. What intense lovemaking is so thinly disguised in these fights and what powerful attachment is hidden in this rage.)

If you are still dancing to an Oedipal tune, your relationship with the parent of the same sex has also got to be all screwed up. If you feel triumphant you may be feeling guilty and reacting to your guilt with an endless choreography of atonement and appeasement. Or you may be feeling contempt for the weakness and inadequacy of the parent you have defeated. It is impossible to have a close relationship and good communication with someone when you feel guilt or disdain about an inappropriate victory. And if you have not had a clear-cut victory, if your parent of the same sex and you are locked in an ongoing struggle to decide who is number one, what a futile, growth-stopping, energy-consuming and absurd conflict that is.

Yes (to go back to the question), there is much in the Oedipal closeness to the opposite-sex parent that is appealing; it is exalting to feel like a winner. But the price, like the cost of a lifetime contract with a dance studio, is the draining of your resources for a dubious and increasingly hollow joy. That first flush of recognition that you are caught in an Oedipal bond is often accompanied by rage at the seductive parent for taking advantage of your vulnerability, starting when you were so young. I recall treating Tom, a young man who had come to New York from a small Texas town to study music at Juilliard. He was an interesting person, an accomplished cellist, both aggressively extroverted and deeply introspective. He came into treatment concerned about his own promiscuity. His charm and attractiveness made him very appealing to women and he would have sexual affairs with one after another. He wanted desperately to have a close and more lasting relationship with a woman and would repeatedly find a woman he really liked but then would pull back, dismiss her and rush on to another to try to forget his loss. As we explored this pattern and his history it became apparent that Tom's mother was extremely seductive with him and I called this to his attention, noting the many ways he had been her "little husband" when his father, a geologist, was away on field research. He denied this interplay, at first vehemently, and then began to look at it with a more open but skeptical mind.

Tom went back to Texas for Christmas vacation and when he returned he sat down, looked at me for a long time and then said, "Damned if you weren't right about maw." He then proceeded to recount his arrival, the hugs and kisses, the special dinner for two (dad was away again). "That all seemed okay, like maw was glad to see me. Then that night I was in bed reading and my mother came in wearing one of those shorty nightgowns and sat down on the edge of my bed and began asking me all about school and New York. I couldn't talk, I felt so damned tense. I was thinking of the hundreds of times she had done something like that and how it always confused my head but I never let myself notice. Then I felt all this anger. She had stopped talking and was waiting for me to say something. Well, let me tell you, I sure did. I said, 'Maw, get your ass off my bed or I'm gonna fuck you.' She jumped up and screamed, 'But Tom, I'm your mother.' I looked her right in the eyes and said, 'That's just the point.' "

After that incident, as painful as it was, Tom and his mother were never able to slip back into the old song and dance and as we worked further in therapy he was soon free enough from his bond to his mother and his guilty fear of his father to form a close relationship with a young woman that lasted for a considerable time. And he reconstituted his relationships with his parents on a more appropriate level.

The expression of anger that frequently accompanies becoming aware that you have been seduced and used is usually not as helpful as it turned out to be for Tom, because most often the seductive child within the parent is shocked and bewildered, literally not understanding what you are talking about. In fact, even trying to get your parents to see the Oedipal interaction in a genuine attempt to have them understand what's been going on will be met by denial unless your parents are unusually open. The denial may be absolute and total and will be buttressed by pointing to the rightness and goodness of parental love. So don't expect to make headway here by explaining it all to mom and dad. About the only good thing that will come of it is that in explaining it, it will become clearer to you. (In fact, that was the main benefit for Tom.) The biggest danger in angrily accusing your parents of such an involvement is that dumping this anger on your parent can become a way of avoiding recognition of your own willing participation in the song and dance. Because in this interaction, perhaps more than any other, it takes two (or three!) to tango.

If you let yourself recognize that you are actively participating in an Oedipal tango, and see the big price you are paying for it, you probably will be motivated to stop the dance. But, as we have seen in other songs and dances, the desire to stop, though essential, is not enough. It is never easy to give up a complicated pattern of interacting that has been gratifying. It is not easy to face your parents' anger at your ending such a time-worn way of relating. Oedipus complex can never become Oedipus simplex. But I think the task of stopping the old routine will become easier when you can let yourself see that there is nothing either romantic or nurturing in this dance. There couldn't be, because *it is a dance between two (or three) needy, insecure little children.* The more you can see the interaction occurring between the little child in your parent and the little child in yourself, the harder it will be to take it seriously.

Look at the moves of your seductive parent. Try to see him or her as a little boy or girl, perhaps coquettish, perhaps conceited, perhaps pathetic, perhaps bossy, perhaps flexing muscles, perhaps clinging. But just a child, masquerading behind an adult's body and demeanor. And look at your own moves. Try to feel the child in you, perhaps coquettish, conceited, pathetic, bossy, muscle-flexing or clinging, but just a little child trying to look like you're in an adult dance. Try to picture these two children on a big ballroom dance floor. They may look silly, but that's where it's at.

When you see the puppy love of you and your parent and it helps you to stop the old way of relating, you must be prepared to deal with the hurt and anger of your jilted parent, or a serious disruption of your relationship may occur. Again, it will be helpful to see the child within your parent, a child who is in pain and rage because he feels suddenly unloved. It is the reaction of a child when the newborn sibling is brought home, or when mommy and daddy go off on a vacation together leaving him behind. How would you react to such a child? Good parenting would lead you to be understanding and to reassure him that you still love him in a parent-child way, but that you stand firm about your other relationships.

I recall working with a girl of eighteen who had always had a close relationship with her father. When she had begun dating, he always seemed to pick a fight with her before a date, or found some unfinished chore she had to do before leaving. One day, after such a scene, she finally left the house with the young man she had been seeing steadily for a while. As she did she heard her father mutter in a stage whisper, "I pay all the bills and he has all the fun."

She had been in treatment for a while and we had discussed this Oedipal involvement so that while she was momentarily stunned by his remark, she was not completely surprised. She had also gone beyond her anger, and could see her father as a rejected little boy. So she made it a point to be warmly loving to her father the next day in a daughterly, considerate manner, while at the same time talking openly about the qualities she liked in her boyfriend. It was telling the little boy in her father, "I love you very much in a parent-child way but I love my boyfriend in a different, special male-female way and one relationship does not compete with the other." It took time, but as she insisted on this message, her father was able to accept gracefully the end of the outlived song and dance.

9 | Don't Fence Me In

"I really think I love my parents, but I hate visiting them. You see, it's not them that I hate. I *hate the way I am when I'm with them*. No matter how much I decide not to fall into certain stupid, aggravating patterns with them, as soon as I walk into that house it's as if something takes over and I'm drawn inexorably back into an old role that I really detest."

Throughout this book, with the purpose of clearly delineating some kinds of songs and dances, I have caricatured martyred mothers, despotic fathers, saints, narcissists, etc. This type of categorizing can be helpful in explicating, in bringing a sense of recognition. But it is simplistic in two ways. First, parents are striving, struggling complicated beings, not animated cartoons. Rarely are they even purely one of the types depicted here (anyone got a martyred, despotic, saintly, weak father?). Secondly, the song and dance is almost never a duet, almost always at least a trio. In other words, while I have focused on the interaction between one aspect of the parent and one aspect of his offspring, this interaction is always in the context of a network of very intricate established patterns within the entire family. The emotional homeostatic balance of the family may depend on your playing out particular songs and dances with both parents, if not with siblings as well.

The quotation at the start of this chapter about being drawn "back into an old role that I really detest" was spoken by Vivian, a woman of thirty-nine, a mother of two college students, who has for several years been running her own small business. She was describing her reaction to spending some time with her parents the previous weekend. She had become well acquainted, through noting her own responses and through observations made by her psychotherapist, with her tendency to regress in her parents' presence to ways of relating she had hoped she had outgrown.

Vivian's mother clearly saw herself as the strong head of the family and made no pretense to be otherwise. "After all, someone has to be in charge around here," she would say loudly in the direction of Vivian's father, who sat, seemingly unhearing, in front of the television set. "Someone has to be in charge around here" was a maternal phrase Vivian had grown up with from the earliest days, along with "It's easier to do it myself than ask him to do anything," "Have you had too much to drink again?" (said to her father), "If I could support you children I wouldn't stay with him," and "You have to show respect for your father."

Vivian had some memories, when she was very young, of her father standing up to her mother firmly and effectively. She recalled being about three or four; a fluffy snowfall was filling the gray air and marshmallowing the streets and houses. Her father wanted to take her sledding and her mother was telling her he could not do that while the snow was still falling, but her father insisted, dressed her in her snowsuit himself, and together they left a sullen mother (she had also refused an invitation to accompany them) and had an idyllic day on the hills in the nearby park. But her later memories, particularly after the birth of her sister when she was almost five and her brother when she was nine, was of a father who was a passive, defeated presence, mostly withdrawn but given at times to violent, object-throwing rages. As an adolescent she realized these rages came about when her father was drunk. Mostly his fury was directed at her mother, though it often spilled over to her and her siblings.

A pattern began to be established. Vivian took the role of her mother's ally, helper, and second adult in the family; her sister, brother and father were the children. There was much gratification in this position, and certain status and privileges went with it, but one price she had to pay was that she had to maintain a condescending and contemptuous distance from her father. In later years there were some shifts in this family structure, but the basic emotional positions remained the same. Her sister, a sulky, obstinately defiant and quite beautiful girl, ran away and got married at seventeen and was now living thousands of miles away with her third husband. Her brother had become a dropout, was into every kind of drug, was frequently in minor scrapes with the law and often, even now at thirty, lived at home with his parents in the same attic room he had occupied as a child. Vivian had married a college classmate who was a flamboyant but immature and dependent man who went into his uncle's business and was still there. Vivian had started a small boutique with a friend after all her own children were in school and it had become a very successful enterprise. She lived within ten minutes' drive of her parents' home.

Because she had increasingly fallen into depression, she began psychotherapy in her mid-thirties and as she looked at the pattern of relationships with her parents (and the continuation of some of these patterns with her husband and children) she worked on ending some of the old songs and dances. As part of this, since she was looking for a new and smaller house now that the children were mostly away, she and her husband bought a house that was a much greater distance from her parents and she opened a branch of her boutique in the town she now moved into. She expected flak from her mother and she got it, her mother criticizing the move from every possible angle, the criticisms laced with, "It's none of my business, but . . ." and, "I don't want to interfere, but . . ." Vivian did not expect a negative reaction from her father, who she thought couldn't care less, or might even be pleased that mother's old ally against him was moving away (although Vivian had been trying to extricate herself from that role). But her father, who was in real estate, told her what a bad deal the house she contemplated buying was and that it was an out-of-the-way area, came up with many houses available nearby and, finally, even offered to pay the down payment on a new house that was close to where they lived. Her brother reacted by getting into trouble with the law again. Her sister did not respond to anyone's letters about these events.

Vivian withstood the full force of her parents' opposition to her moving, and learned a lot in her therapy about her role in the equilibrium. She saw her parents as terrified of having to be alone with each other. Her mother was so afraid of giving up control, so afraid that her unrecognized needs for closeness with a man might cause her to surrender that control, that she had early enlisted Vivian's help in holding her power position and driving her husband into an innocuous passivity. Her father, afraid both of his potency and of his dependency, accepted this arrangement because he could feel safely weak and yet have a pivotal place in the emotional life of the family as its negative pole. Both parents also tried to triangle her sister into this arrangement but her sister, smarting with the nowhere feelings of the middle child, withdrew. But her brother, by becoming a "problem child" and an increasing source of concern, had taken on much of the burden of keeping his parents from directly dealing with their needs for each other by having them always in some sort of worried uproar about him. This was particularly true after Vivian had gotten married.

THERE, I'VE SAID IT AGAIN

At the time Vivian made the visit to her parents that made her feel, "I hate the way I am when I'm with them," she had been living in her new house for a year, the new branch of her boutique was thriving, she and her husband had entered a new era of deep caring, and her brother was living with her parents again, sleeping most of the day and going out at night. Vivian's husband had to spend most of that Sunday preparing for an important business meeting, and Vivian took the opportunity to make one of her now infrequent calls on her parents. She was looking forward to this visit because she was determined to use her insight about the family's patterns to help keep herself from falling into her old position. She felt good as she drove down, singing with the music on the radio. As she got closer to their home she noticed a strange thing happening. First there was a vague discomfort, a thin cloud of anxiety. Then she became aware of many unbidden thoughts and images intruding into her consciousness. She imagined her father sitting in front of the TV set when she came in and heard herself saying, "How can you sit watching TV on such a beautiful day?" She fantasized her mother agreeing with her and shrugging with weary disgust. In another image she and her mother were preparing dinner in the kitchen, saying bad things about her father. Vivian could see what was happening and gave herself a pep talk about not falling into the old song and dance, but her discomfort did not go away.

When Vivian got to her parents' house her father answered the bell. They exchanged quick kisses and he told her how nice she looked and then said, "Your mother will be downstairs soon."

"Good," Vivian said, "that will give you and me a chance to talk."

Her father seemed startled. "Fine, fine. There's only about ten minutes left to this TV show. Come and watch it with me."

Vivian was going to say something like, "Do you have to watch TV all the time?" but she caught herself and said, "I'd like to. What are you watching?"

When her mother came down she saw her husband and daughter sitting together on the couch watching a television program. After saying hello she asked Vivian to come into the kitchen with her to make coffee. "Not just now, mother. I'm watching this show with dad." Her mother didn't say anything but went into the kitchen looking vaguely annoyed. Vivian felt a surge of anxiety at these new steps she was taking. In the past, she would have gone with her mother as automatically as breathing. But despite the anxiety, she felt good. Her father had smiled when Vivian said she'd stay with him but very soon he started to stir uncomfortably and said, "Vivian, you'd better help your mother."

"That's okay, she knows how to make coffee."

Her father grunted, not knowing how to handle this.

"Ouch," her mother yelled from the kitchen. "Vivian, I burned my hand!" Vivian started up and then said, "Dad, mother burned her hand. You'd better go see if she's all right."

"She asked for you," he said, his eyes not leaving the TV screen.

"Damn!" Vivian muttered and went into the kitchen. "Let's see the burn, mother," she said angrily.

"It's nothing. It will be a little blister. What are you so mad about?"

"How come you called *me* when you burned yourself? He's your husband?"

"Him? Who can count on him for anything? He heard me say I burned myself but did you see him come running?"

Vivian pointed out again that her mother called her, not her own husband, and her mother rebutted at greater length. Within five minutes she and her mother were having a conversation about her father's shortcomings. They went back into the living room and her father agreed to turn off the TV while they had coffee, but her father was soon an uncomfortable spectator as Vivian and her mother talked. Her brother came down in his bathrobe. "Hi, sis," he greeted. He poured himself some coffee and took it back upstairs with him. Soon her mother was talking worriedly about her son and here Vivian's father joined in, saying they should throw him out and force him to make it on his own. He accused his wife of coddling him. Vivian's mother attacked him for not caring about his son, and before long Vivian heard herself saying to her father, "If you had presented a stronger image for him to model himself after he wouldn't be like this." She was using sophisticated, psychoanalytically tinged terms but she knew she was back in the old song and dance. It seemed to have a compelling force greater than her resolve. In the remaining hours of the visit she was helplessly in its grip, and she left her parents' home feeling defeated and dejected.

There is much in this brief interchange to show how

families work to keep each person in his or her established place. We can see the discomfort of one-to-one relating between any two members of the family. Even Vivian and her mother cannot talk to each other without "triangling in" a third person, such as her father or brother, if only through talking *about* them.* Real intimacy is avoided in the playing of these scripted, predictable roles. The people in the family act as if they know each other but they do not, they only know the mask that has been assigned. When Vivian briefly left her assigned role her father and mother were each perplexed, as if this familiar person had become a stranger, although Vivian was then being her most authentic self.

When Vivian attempted to differentiate herself from the family by breaking with the songs and dances that kept her in the family's particular emotional system, family forces, particularly in her parents, were obviously very threatened. When she had wanted to relocate, both parents had put much pressure on her not to move any great distance. In fact, there had been subtle guilt provocations and other attempts to make Vivian feel uncomfortable about her move. When she tried to break her alliance with her mother against her father, even her father joined in to push her back into the old alignment. This is how families usually react when one of its members refuses to accept the family's version of togetherness and insists on being an individual.

But what is of even greater interest is that *before* Vivian reached her parents' home, *before* they had a chance to bring her back into line, she herself felt a powerful tug back into the old way of reacting. It was as if the family had a gravitational pull of its own, compelling her to stay within her set orbit. I think of Dr.

---

*Murray Bowen, M.D., a leading family theorist and therapist, says that two people in a relationship will tend to bring in (triangle in) a third person, if even through gossip, when there is tension between the two. For more on "triangles," and as the source of all other references to Dr. Bowen, see his "anonymous" article entitled "Toward the Differentiation of a Self in One's Family," in James L. Framo *et al., Family Interaction: A Dialogue Between Family Therapists and Family Researchers* (New York: Springer, 1972), pp. 111–166.

Murray Bowen's term, "undifferentiated family ego mass."* When I first heard the term it conjured up for me a science-fiction image of a huge, pulsating mass of protoplasm, a blob of an organism made of several people so fused together that all boundaries were lost, an organism with such a magnetic pull that all its parts were continually drawn to the center. It was the pull of this "undifferentiated family ego mass" that Vivian felt as she approached her parents' home in her car.

Of what is this mass composed? Mostly it is composed of the dependent inner child of each member of the family, the part of each member of the family that fears being cut off or abandoned or punished and therefore seeks the safety of fusing with one or more of the others. And all these frightened, needy children are merged together not just by the power of their needs, but by the shared rituals and beliefs, the shared assumption that the others share their assumptions, the learned and practiced songs and dances that keep the family mass from being broken apart by each member's idiosyncracies. An attempt by any one of the members to differentiate himself and claim his uniqueness is felt as a threat to all. Even the unspoken thought of seeking greater autonomy is a threat to the one who thinks it. So the mass pulsates faster and the pull it generates becomes stronger in the feelings of the person attempting to break out. Families may differ in size, composition, beliefs, emotional style, but they all have some pull toward this kind of togetherness.

Part of the belief system that holds the family mass intact are certain myths. There are many common myths that set the climate for different families. There are myths called:

"We are a very happy family."

"We would be a very happy family if only . . . (mother wasn't depressed, dad wasn't so angry, sister wasn't so rebellious, brother wasn't on drugs, baby wasn't sickly . . .)."

"We've always had bad luck."

*Ibid., p. 121.

"We all love each other."

"We always keep our chins up even when things are bad."

"Nothing is ever going to change around here."

"Our family is special."

The myths vary, and their differing natures make for differing families, but what all family myths have in common is that they serve to make those family members who accept the myths *blind* to what the people and the interactions within the family are really like. There were many myths in Vivian's family:

Mother did not want control but it was foisted on her by father's weakness.

Father had never been nor could ever be anything but ineffectual. Mother, not having a strong husband, needed Vivian to be her helpmate and ally.

Sister was a bad girl because she would not help her mother or get involved in the family tensions and dramas.

Brother was a pitiable fellow who had no strong father to help him become a man and therefore was not responsible for what he did.

Everything would be fine if only father would show more interest, take charge and be strong.

As long as Vivian accepted these myths, she had to remain blind to her mother's need to control and not to notice how tenaciously her mother held on to her power. She had to be blind to the complexity of her father, who was afraid of his strength and abdicated too easily but fought total submission by negativistic withdrawals and periodic drunken rages. She had to keep herself from seeing that her brother was weakened not just by a lack of a strong father but by her mother's need to emasculate or infantalize males because she feared them. She had to obscure from herself that her sister was not bad, but that there was no room for her to be her mother's close ally because Vivian was there, no way to divert the family's attentions by being the problem child because her brother had cornered that position, no way to get close to her father because she would win her mother's wrath and get little support from him, no way to become a friend of Vivian's without feeling she had two mothers, so she withdrew from the family game in self-protection and self-respect. And Vivian had to be blind to herself so that she would not see that she was not being a "good girl" but a girl and woman who longed for her mother's approval, feared her mother's anger, and was terrified of her own repressed wishes for a close relationship with her father.

In the course of psychotherapy and of life, the scales began to fall from Vivian's eyes and she saw the realities beneath the family myths. Even more, she began to see the pulls that were holding her in the family as emanating from the inner child of all parties:

She saw a little girl in her mother who had been hurt and rejected by an uncaring, self-serving father and who was determined not to let her yearning for a loving father ever put her in a dangerous submissive position with a man again. Vivian saw that the little girl in her mother had never been able to count on a protective alliance with her own mother and therefore had tried to make Vivian a dependable female ally—*i.e.*, to make Vivian the close mother she always wanted.

She saw a little boy in her father who had been dominated all through childhood and adolescence by a tough, loud, angry mother. He had tried to hold on to some corner of his masculinity and independence by spending much of his time with a neighborhood group of boys. While still very young he married Vivian's mother, who consciously, he saw as a softer, more loving woman than his own mother, and as someone to whom he could transfer his needs for mothering.

She saw how the little girl in her mother, who was afraid that her needs for a man's love would lead her to be subordinated and abused, and the frightened little boy in her father, who wanted to be taken care of at almost any price, had led them into this marriage of a selfish, controlling little girl and a passive, ineffectual little boy. Vivian could also see how deeply disappointed the little girl in her mother was that she had not found the strong, caring father of her dreams, and how bitterly disillusioned the little boy in her father was that he had not married the warm, nurturing mother he had craved from his earliest memories. They were two hurt, betrayed, angry children, clinging to each other in the only way they could.

She saw how she, Vivian, had been born into this setting with her own needs for nurturing and strength from each of them and how she learned, as a child, that her mother would be most loving when she felt in a happy, content mood, so that it was to her advantage to keep mother happy by figuring out what mother needed and giving it to her. She also had learned that mother was not happy when Vivian got too close to her father, and that because the little boy in her father also had a stake in keeping mother from being too angry at him, he would not help Vivian sustain closeness with him. So the little girl in Vivian accepted the role of her mother's parent and with it a parental role with her father and then with her sister and brother when they arrived. She saw how it crippled real closeness between her and any member of the family, and how she had carried this role into her own marriage with near-disastrous effect.

Vivian began to use her awareness of the family's mythology and the fused interactions between her inner child and the inner child in each of her parents to take steps toward greater individuation, despite the many setbacks she encountered. Anyone who has tried to achieve his own separate identity has become aware of the family's compelling pull, both in the actual reactions of the family and in his own internalized reactions. Considering that each of us is born into a structured, intimate group upon which we are then immediately and prolongedly dependent, it is impossible to avoid being enmeshed in its intricate and insistent emotional network. Dr. Murray Bowen has written:

Theoretically, emotional fusion is universal in all except the completely differentiated person, who has not yet been born. Usually, most people are not aware of the phenomenon. There are those who can become aware if they can learn to observe more and react less to their families. There are others so intensely "fused" they probably can never know the world of emotional objectivity with their parents, see and think of them as people without either downgrading or upgrading them. Some people are "comfortably" fused and others so "uncomfortably" fused they use hate or a covert negative attitude (either is evidence of fusion) to avoid contact with parents. There are those of "positive fusion" who remain so attached they never leave home. There are also those who kid themselves into believing they have "worked out" the relationship with parents and who make brief formal visits home without communication; they use as evidence of maturity that they do not see their parents. . . .*

If emotional fusion is universal and unavoidable, the question becomes, Can I ever come to withstand the compelling pull of that emotional magnet I call my family? How can I come within its force field and still remain a separate, differentiated, autonomous being? Murray Bowen has given a clue to the process when he talks of learning "to observe more and react less" to one's family. What exactly has to be observed more and reacted to less? As with all the two-person songs and dances, the first step is to become aware

---

*Ibid., p. 139.

that you are caught up in it. There will be little incentive to do this unless you have some discomfort with the way things are. For some, there will be little doubt that interacting with your family is a painful or oppressive or frustrating or depressing or infuriating experience. With others, if you are to feel motivated to observe the workings of the family system, you will first have to note if vague feelings of discomfort or annoyance or constriction, or some mild symptoms such as headaches or stomach pains are connected with your contacts and interaction with your family. If there is discomfort and a feeling that you do not really like the person you are when you are with them, then you will feel more compelled to step back and ask, "What goes on here?"

When the song and dance involves the entire family rather than just you and one parent—and it almost always does—the song and dance may expand into a troika, a quadrille, a hora circle or a whole corps de ballet. The increased complexity when you are dealing with more than just one person can make for many difficulties in getting sufficiently "outside" the system to observe it but, unless you are a part of the most important and inflexible triangle in the family, the fact that there are so many interactions going on may make it easier for you to slip out, step back and get some perspective on how the family works.

In viewing your family's patterns of interaction, the most important question is "What is my role in the family's emotional system?" You and your family have cooperated to give you a particular part in the family drama. What is that part? Why was it assigned to you?

There are some classic family roles just as there are classic theatrical roles—a few of them are listed below. Perhaps you can see yourself in one of these roles, and perhaps you see the roles of other family members. If you see a role that fits another family member, note what your interaction is with the person in that role.

CLOWN   There are two versions of Clown: (1) making yourself the butt of ridicule or (2) making others the butt of ridicule. (At times you may do neither but simply use humor to keep family situations light or to point up family absurdities.)

The first version of Clown is most damaging to you, in that it involves making yourself look foolish and therefore is a colossal self-put-down. You are playing the part of an irrelevant, inappropriate lightweight who is not to be taken seriously. Your Clown mask is a coverup for your pain, your anger and/or other feelings and desires that you are afraid to have yourself and the family see. You can also use this role to conceal your own strengths, which you may have learned are threatening to others in the family. Although they may at times be exasperated by your antics, the family is happy to have you play this role because they don't have to deal with your real needs or your effectiveness. And besides, you serve as an entertaining diversion, a distraction from other family conflicts. Consistent playing of the self-ridiculing Clown role can lead you to merge it with the roles of Victim or Failure with the attendant gratification these roles hold for you and your family. On the other hand, consistent playing of the Clown directed at making others look foolish holds some of the gratifications of Persecutor.

As frequently as the family might say in exasperation, "Can't you ever be serious?" or "Stop acting like a jerk," if you do let your feelings, needs and real strengths be seriously known, it upsets just about everyone and you'll soon feel tremendous pressure to put your Clown face on again.

DOLL   This is a simple role—all you have to do is be beautiful, cute, adorable, ever appealing and seductive. There are different variations on the doll role—the ingenue, the glamorous woman, the sex symbol, etc. Male versions involve being some sort of Prince Charming, playboy or stud.

The rewards for you in this role are mostly obvious: you can get much attention, positive stroking, even adulation, both inside and outside the family, without making much effort toward producing, accomplishing, self-development or giving. The advantage to the family (or at least one family member) is that you are an extension of their narcissism and thus bring them gratification of their own sometimes unfulfilled needs to be beautiful and popular. Besides, they are relieved of having to consider you a real person with other needs and feelings to which they should pay serious attention. Trouble may come when your role fails to work as well as it used to or when you tire of being two-dimensional (maybe even getting angry or depressed about it) and you demand responses to other facets and depths of yourself. The family may in essence say, "What do you want? You're lucky to be so beautiful, popular, etc." These pressures from them plus your own anxieties about being in touch with your own deeper needs, pain and self-doubt, your fears of developing yourself in new directions, and your reluctance to surrender the enormous satisfactions of the Doll role, may cause you to retreat from any thrust toward change.

FAILURE   You never could quite make it in at least one major life arena that was important to you and your parents—school, social life, career, marriage, etc. It is not the same role as "Victim" since you do not use the role to provoke guilt. As a matter of fact, you often feel somewhat guilty or ashamed of yourself for letting the family down and for disappointing their expectations and hopes. There are two variations of the Failure role:

(1) Sad Sack—in which an air of being one of life's losers hangs over your shoulders like a wrong-sized overcoat. Continued long enough, that hapless feeling can sculpt slack defeatedness or despairing anguish into your facial muscles and your posture. The family's reaction: either constant chiding for your poor track record, or a sympathetic condescension. When they're nice to you you're never quite sure if they like you or feel sorry for you.

(2) Black Sheep—in which you more actively get into trouble or eschew success. Family members

may be angry, hurt or puzzled. They can't quite understand how you could come from their family and act the way you do. They express hope for the return to the fold of their prodigal offspring.

Much of the family interaction revolves around their concern with the Failure. If you are in this role, consider the possibility that very early you and your family cooperated to set you up as a sacrificial offering. Your unspoken assignment was to keep other members from unpleasant confrontations and maybe even to hold the family together by redirecting their conflicts into an intense concern with your poor, inappropriate or provocative behavior. I recall family therapy with a ten-year-old boy and his parents. At this young age he had already managed to make much of his life a shambles—academic work was a disaster area despite his high intelligence, there was continuous conflict with his peers and his parents, and he had a general sense of inadequacy and sadness. There was much hostility between his parents, and every time their anger toward each other would emerge in therapy, the boy would do or say something so provocative that their rage would turn on him. When I pointed out this pattern and they were all able to see it the boy said, "When they fight I'm afraid they'll get a divorce." Thus he sacrificed himself to prevent this terrifying possibility. The parents began to see, too, how they let their anger be directed toward him because of their fear of where their arguments would lead. This pattern of making oneself the Failure, the loser, the scapegoat, the underachiever, the goat, can continue well into adult life.

HERO/HEROINE   This is a glory role. You will be the shining light that will bring pride and redemption to the family. Through your attainments or character you will make up for mother's deep disappointment in father, or father's deep disappointment in mother, or your sibling's deep disappointment in both of them, or the entire family's deep disappointment in life, or your own deep disappointment in the family (or yourself). There may be subdivisions of this role: The Financial Success, The Genius, The Celebrity, etc., or the one who married the Financial Success, Genius, Celebrity, etc.

It is elevating to be the one the family looks up to and in whose reflected glory they bask but, like the Doll, you may find it very disheartening if you want to be reacted to as a total self, with your own needs and anxieties. Ordinary human needs, particularly those arising out of your inner child, can be seen as disappointing weaknesses in a Hero, so the family may try hard not to see that those needs are there, or to come down on you very hard and unempathically when the needs become obvious. And your role of Hero may be openly or secretly resented by some other member(s) of the family who will enjoy shooting you down, or who will rejoice when you flop. It is hard for the inner child in you to get real nurturance from your family beyond the kudos directed at your Hero role.

PERSECUTOR   You are scripted to give at least one member of the family a hard time. Maybe you grew up torturing, either physically or psychologically, one of your siblings (which may have also thrown you into the role of Victim if your parents punished you for it). Maybe you attacked, provoked and made life miserable for one or both of your parents. You have gotten yourself into a role of vindictive self-righteousness; you didn't get loved right or loved enough or loved as much as someone else in the family, or you were unfairly treated, or you were hurt, so you feel justified in making yourself a thorn in the hide of at least one family member.

The family member(s) you are attacking may be getting the masochistic reward of the role of Victim so he (she, they) has little stake in stopping you from playing Persecutor. Other family members may be vicariously enjoying your tormenting the Victim because you are acting out something they would (consciously or unconsciously) like to do or are doing along with you (which makes them your allies if you both have the same target). And you have a role that is a central hub of family interaction without getting really close to anyone, a good position if you want attention but are afraid of intimacy. You may also be getting other gratification if part of your persecuting is to explode what seems to be a hypocrisy or phoniness of the victim, which has damaged you. Underneath it all is your plea, Please love me, which you dare not voice aloud for fear you would have to face pain, humiliation and rage if it is scorned, or face being overwhelmed by your own needs to fuse and surrender selfhood if it is fulfilled.

RESCUER   This has the appearance and appeal of a glory role. People in the family are looking to you to come riding to their aid. You can don the garb of Minuteman, Don Quixote or Florence Nightingale and help one or both of your parents with their battles with each other or the outside world. You can protect the parent who seems to be the greater victim by fighting off or mollifying the one who seems to be the persecutor, you can try to assuage hurts and make up for the disappointments one parent feels with the other, you can label both parents as helpless and habitually defend them in encounters with landlords, banks, utility companies, government agencies, stores and relatives. You can also play Rescuer with siblings, particularly but not necessarily younger ones, defending them against parental injustices or pressures, against another sibling or against societal demands, thus assuming the position of their good and effective parent.

A particularly sophisticated version of the Rescuer role is to play Family Therapist. Here you interpret to the family what is going on and what the interactions mean (e.g., that your father is not really angry at your mother but is expressing unresolved anger at his own mother, etc.) and you try to facilitate communication ("Mom, you fly off the handle so fast that you don't hear what dad is really saying. Just listen to him for a moment and try to understand how he feels.") Yours is a peacemaking service. You offer support, solutions and advice in an attempt to keep the family happy and together. The rewards are obvious—the family turns to you and depends on you, you can maintain the heady belief that you (and maybe only you) have the power to keep the family from disintegrating or one of its members from being victimized. In playing the role of Family Therapist or any form of Rescuer, there is a sense of being above it all. But the fact is that, far from being above it all, the terrible fears of family conflict and disintegration that have long been lodged in your own inner child and that led you to assume your rescuing role have you hooked into the family system just as tightly as those who are being Persecutors or Victims. For as has long been understood in transactional analysis, the Rescuer can easily become Persecutor, Victim or both. If you go to the rescue of one family member, another may attack and victimize you. Even worse, the victim you are trying to help may turn on you for giving him or her the very advice and succor he asked for. Soon your frustration will lead you to rage, and you can do some pretty heavy persecutory attacking yourself. You may want to throw up your hands and say, "I give up trying to help anyone in this damned family," but nobody is going to let you put down your Rescuer role so easily— it plays too big a part in the family's emotional ecology. And *you* can't easily put it down either because the gratifications are great, and your inner child may feel frightened and sad about accepting that maybe there's nothing you can really do to rescue the family or some of its members from their conflicts. This can be a liberating acceptance, but it comes with all the growth anxieties of becoming an autonomous person.

VICTIM   If you are in this role, something bad must always be happening to you to justify a persistent complaint that you are being malevolently or unfairly treated by life, the family, or a particular family member. "Look what you've done to me" is your theme, and you and your family must cooperate to produce the insults and injuries that enable you to maintain this theme.

What you get out of being Victim is lots of attention, justification for your anger at not being loved well enough, revenge on the accused through arousing their guilt, the possible reparations the accused may offer, an avoidance of the alarming responsibility of taking charge of your own life and making it better. That's a pretty substantial reward for playing the Victim role. And what the family gets out of it is the discomfort of wearing you as a hair shirt that increasingly punishes them for unresolved guilt feelings of all kinds, a distraction from other more threatening family issues, and the unending busywork of reassuring you of their love. Of course, they must in overt or subtle ways participate in keeping you victimized or they may lose the advantages of having you in this familiar role. So the family ego mass, including you, has a stake in your remaining miserable.

All the members of the family may not have had the same reasons for choosing you for a particular role. For example, while the role of Failure may largely have been a son's sacrifice to keep his parents from facing their real conflicts with each other, father may want this son in that role to keep him down as a competitor, mother may need him there to keep him from growing away, big sister may want him there because she's always resented this male coming into the family and usurping so much attention, little brother may be glad to see his big brother cut down to size, etc. This Failure may be responding to the script requirements of them all, thus keeping himself the sacrificial offering, no threat to father, mother's poor little boy and an inept rival of his siblings. His role is a gift to everyone. It is a safe, secure and miserable part.

Why it was you and not someone else who was chosen for that particular role is also complicated, having to do with what was going on in the marriage and the family when you arrived, who or what you represented to the others, and the gender, appearance and temperament you brought to the situation. So your role and how you got into it are multidetermined and it's going to take much determination to step out of it.

At times some of the roles within a family system are interchangeable and it is important to become attuned to the melody of the family interaction and not only who is playing what at any given moment. A middle-aged businessman was trying to figure out who was the precipitator of all the fighting and turbulence that persistently rocked the household of himself, his wife, his two sons and his daughter. First it would seem that one was the Persecutor, another the Victim or Failure, another the Clown, and then the roles would seem to switch. Although I was seeing him individually as a patient we thought it would be helpful to have a prolonged session with his family. They were an articulate group, and in a very few minutes their voices were raised and they were verbally shredding each other. I watched for a while, trying to grasp the pattern, and then I saw it. Whenever any member of the family felt hurt, or frightened, or any emotion that was soft or needy, he or she immediately converted these more vulnerable feelings into anger and attacked. It was the family style, a style set long ago by my patient and his wife. I told the family what I observed. There was a silence. Then Jenny, at twelve years old the youngest, said sadly, "Anger is strong, hurt is weak." We began to talk about how their anger was misused, and I encouraged each member to talk of his pain, his disappointments and his needs.

They were terribly awkward at first, but as they spoke the entire atmosphere in the room changed. The hurt inner child in every one of them came out and began to get a sympathetic response, even if only tearful silence at times. An incredible amount of hidden affection began to emerge. It was clear that the path for differentiation of each person in this angry family was at least in part through getting out of the family pattern of immediate conversion of pain and disappointment into anger, and to begin to express directly their other feelings and to ask each other openly for what they wanted. Several members of the family began working on changing their response after this session.

Stepping back to view the family drama and your role in it is crucial, but you won't be outside looking in for very long before your absence will be noted and the coercive efforts to bring you back into the system will begin. When this happens, how can you withstand the pressures from the family and from inside yourself that urge you back into the old interactions? One factor that can be helpful is to *anticipate* that whenever you stop your song and dance, even for a brief while, there will be an inevitable reaction. Anticipating this reaction means a certain amount of preparedness. If you are going to step outside the family system to find yourself as a separate person you have to ask, What can I expect to happen? What responses will I get from the family as a whole, from each member individually, from inside myself? Without this anticipation you may be surprised by the backlash, and in that stunned state you will easily fall back into line. But if you have some notion as to what to expect you can also plan ways to deal with it and mobilize yourself to remain apart from the system longer. The longer you can stay out of the family song and dance, the more opportunity you have to observe how it all works; the more opportunity you have for observation, the greater the probability of your seeing new ways to react; the more you see and try new ways to react, the more you will experience yourself as an individual person. But each step is always met by the pull to return to the fold.

Here is an excerpt from a letter a man in his thirties wrote on his father's birthday in the midst of his struggle to become free of old and angry songs and dances with his parents.

Dear Dad . . . and you too, Mom, because I know you'll read this,

No flowery card this year . . . the words are mine and I wish you the happiest of birthdays and many more healthy ones . . .

Like everyone else much has happened to us over

the years, but all things considered we've been fortunate in many ways. What hasn't been good is the deep chasm between us and it is too apparent to avoid the issue. Whose fault? *All of us*. Were you too strict and too judgmental in my formative years? Yes. Did I let my anger get in the way of our relationships? Yes. You never really got to know me so I didn't want to know you.

We like to think of ourselves as near perfect—the ideal parent, husband, wife, son, daughter, friend——but we're not nearly as ideal as we like to think and it's difficult and painful to make oneself better.

Through analysis . . . I've been trying to work out my problems. At first, it was casual. Circumstances have made me more intense about myself. The process works . . . changes are already happening . . . but they sure take a long time.

For the time being, let's co-exist in a better frame of mind . . . let's understand each other better . . . and love will be easier.

I have never known anyone, even those who have made much progress toward autonomy, who did not regress to the old ways many times before attaining substantial differentiation. Thus it is important that you not berate yourself for not achieving instant individuation. If you fall into a self-deprecating state because you regressed to the family ego mass, this self-derogation will in itself become part of a weakening that makes you more vulnerable to the old songs and dances. You would in fact be saying, "That proves it, I don't have the strength it takes to differentiate myself from the family expectations, so why fight it?" It becomes important to see each foray outside the family system as of value in itself, having given you a new chance to make observations and experience yourself as separate, and thus leading to more frequent and more sustained periods of autonomy. And it may be heartening to know that experience indicates that unless a family is pathologically rigid (see the final chapter) the chances are they will appreciate your efforts to stop doing the family song and dance routines. In fact, as a pioneer in such differentiation, they may well find you intriguing and appealing. But if you are seduced by this into playing for that reaction, your inner child will be hooked again into the family system. The reward of true differentiation is not the family's awe or adulation, but your own self-respect.

10 | Two Different Worlds

In a book about child psychotherapy, I told of a play therapy session with a little girl whose parents had a very strife-filled, angry marriage.

I had seen Helen, a nine-year-old girl with a variety of fears, for several months. In one session she seemed particularly distraught and anxious. When I asked what was troubling her she said she had been kept awake the night before by an argument between her parents. But then she would talk no more about it. A few minutes later she went to the doll house and began enacting a stereotyped domestic scene. Soon, however, it began to take on a more personalized and emotional tone. The mother and father dolls got into a violent quarrel and began to hit each other. They were made to pick up pieces of doll furniture and hurl it in such a way that first one and then the other would be buried under a huge pile of chairs, sofas and beds. As a result of this furniture-throwing it wasn't long before all the furnishings were out of the house and there was nothing left but the mother doll, father doll, and baby doll. So the parent dolls began to hurl the baby doll at each other. All this was accomplished by yells of anger by the parents and squeals of fear by the baby. Then Helen began to shake the doll house.

"Suddenly there's an earthquake," she screamed. "The two parts of the earth split apart right in the middle of the living room, right between Mommy and Daddy. And they get further and further and further apart, until Daddy is as far away as one star and Mommy is as far away as another star." Holding the two dolls at arm's length she paused and said solemnly, "And baby fell down, down into the deep hole in between them!"*

The terror Helen so powerfully expressed in her play is lodged in the inner child of every adult whose parents had an unloving or angry marriage, whether the parents remained together or separated. There is the fear that the foundation on which his or her security rests is shaky, that his world can fall apart, that the people on whom he is dependent will destroy each other or disappear, and that something unknown and unspeakably horrible will happen to him in this process. This haunting possibility begins to shape the child's personality as a defense against these fears.

In Helen's case, her anguish erupted in a variety of symptoms, such as nightmares and an overwhelming fear of going to school (would her house, her family disappear while she was away?). Her parents were temporarily brought into better harmony through their common concern about her well-being, which made me wonder if her symptoms were not only manifestations of her fears, but also an attempt, consciously or unconsciously, to get them to stop fighting and be more nurturant to her. But more about Helen later.

If you come from a marriage where your parents split up, your age at the time of the split is an important determinant of how this event affects you and, as we saw with Helen, young children, dependent and vulnerable, suffer the greatest impact. But even if you are much older when the marriage dissolves, the effect can be very powerful. A young woman was away at her first year of college when she got the news that her parents, married almost thirty-five years, had separated.

I felt terrible, like the rug had been pulled out from under me. But then I noticed I also felt relieved.

---

*Howard Halpern, *A Parent's Guide to Child Psychotherapy* (New York: A. S. Barnes, 1963), p. 29.

At first I couldn't understand that, but as I thought about it I realized it was no accident that my parents split up so soon after I went to college. My older brother and sister had been out long before so I was the last one at home, and it was clear that the children were the reason they had hung together. Somewhere inside me I must have always known that, and the relief I felt was of no longer being burdened by that awesome responsibility of keeping two people together that didn't belong together. I also realized how much of my personality had developed around that task. So I felt lost, confused, very sad, and liberated.

A man of thirty said, "I'd been living thousands of miles away for years but when I heard my parents had split I felt as if I no longer had a home. And it was true. They soon sold the house where we all grew up and I could no longer think of it as a haven that was always there. It was a large suburban house, and when I used to come back to the East Coast for a while I always stayed there, in the same room I had as a kid. Now it was gone. My parents each had separate studio apartments in the city and I'd stay first with one, then the other, sleeping on the couch. It was so strange and sad."

A woman of twenty-one said, "My parents were always clearly my parents and I looked up to them. Suddenly they were two babies, crying, having tantrums and very lost. They wanted my advice and my support and it was clear each wanted me to say he or she was right and the other was wrong. It blew my mind. Each wanted me to be his parent, and I tried, but soon realized I couldn't. I felt in trouble with one or the other of them, but mostly I felt like an orphan. So I did what I should have done a few years before anyway—I moved out. If I was going to be parentless anyway, I might as well be out on my own. I think their breaking up was probably good, but it's so sad."

Note the repeated emphasis on sadness, because a broken family is often a bereaved family and must go through a mourning period. Sometimes, even when the offspring is no longer a child, guilt can enter into his or her feelings. A twenty-seven-year-old guidance counselor said,

> My mother was telling me for the hundredth time how my boyfriend wasn't good enough for me, how I should find someone more dynamic and less passive. I blew up and told her that maybe she was talking about her feelings about daddy and that she shouldn't try to solve her problems through choosing the type of man for me that she wanted but should get it for herself. She started to cry and said I was all wrong. But then a month later she told me that she had thought about it, that I was right, and that she's leaving dad. I was really shook. She knows what she's doing, and she's right, but I feel so guilty, particularly when my father looks like a lost sheep.

There are many other variables that determine the impact of the break on you besides your age at the time. The circumstances surrounding the breakup are very important: Who left whom? Was it mutual? Was the one who left forced out by an impossible situation? How much bitterness and hostility was there? How long had the situation been bad before the actual split? What has the aftermath of the breakup been? The combinations of factors that determine how all the people in a broken marriage situation will interact are infinite, but several statements are as close to axioms as you can get in this impossibly imprecise arena:

> In most (legally or emotionally) broken marriages, at least one parent has a very hurt and/or angry inner child.

> The child within your parent will, to some degree, turn to you for solace, as an ally, as a rescuer, or as an antagonist on whom to vent rage and blame.

Your own inner child will be rubbed raw with hurt, anger and bereavement by the breakup, particularly if it occurs in your childhood or early adolescence, and will make you very vulnerable to falling into narrow and self-destructive songs and dances with one or both of your parents.

In other words, a marital rupture can turn all parties involved into wounded, outraged or broken-hearted children. And it is frightening to the real children, the offspring of the marriage, to see the parents, on whom their security has rested, being too childish to be protective. It is also disillusioning to the young offspring that even when the parents try to be nurturant and protective, they cannot save them from the reality that the marriage is actually, inexorably, irrevocably over. As with Helen's doll house scene, the whole world is shaken, never to be the same.

I'LL NEVER SMILE AGAIN

I return now to Helen because developments within Helen and in her life illustrate so many of the difficulties that are encountered and the songs and dances that are often developed when a marriage breaks up. When I saw Helen for treatment as a nine-year-old, her parents had not yet separated, although talk of it was always in the air. Through psychotherapy with Helen and related counseling with her parents, Helen's nightmares and school phobia abated and soon after, treatment was terminated. It was clear to me that although they were all handling the situation better, the marriage was a deeply troubled one.

My next contact with Helen was when she was thirteen. A few months earlier, her father had left the marriage to live with another woman. Helen's mother had become very despondent and, for a few months, was unable to continue her work as an elementary school teacher. She spent much of her day in bed, with Helen taking care of her and assuming many of the household chores.

After Helen's mother came out of her depression,

Helen went into one. She became disinterested in school and food, and soon lost twenty pounds. It was at this point that her mother brought Helen to see me again. Helen at first said she couldn't care less about getting better, that she wanted to be depressed and even to die. But there were so many feelings bottled up in her that soon she was talking with much emotion.

It became clear that Helen harbored enormous rage at her father for leaving, but had never expressed much of it. Her mother had often ranted bitterly against her husband, almost inviting Helen to join her, but as soon as Helen would say negative things about him her mother would say, "You shouldn't talk that way about your father." Helen's father, in his guilt and concern about leaving, called Helen often, took her to interesting places and bought her many things. This also blocked Helen's expression of her anger.

Another factor that soon emerged was that Helen felt very sorry for her mother, whom she saw as an innocent victim of her father's need to have a younger woman. Besides, Helen had a lot of secret guilt about the breakup because, as we discovered later in therapy, Helen had a deeply hidden idea that her father really left because Helen had grown more defiant and abrasive as she entered her teens. Helen's guilt in relation to her mother led to her becoming very self-punishing, including a loss of appetite that was almost a penitent fast.

After a while it also became obvious that Helen loved her father deeply, but her unexpressed anger at him for leaving, and her guilt that maybe she was the cause of his leaving, made her very uncomfortable and on guard when she was with him. Just as she would not show him her anger, she would not show him her affection. And besides, her loving feelings toward him made her feel she was being disloyal to her mother. Her mother never overtly demanded such loyalty but Helen had noticed little things—like when Helen would return from a day with her father looking happy, her mother would seem disappointed and morose. In fact, once or twice when Helen returned from something

particularly special with her father, she found her
mother in bed in a darkened room saying, "I hope you
had a good time, darling."

In Helen's feelings and conflicts, we see several common *myths* that occur often in a family split by separation and divorce. These myths are often contradictory because they are spawned by parents whose views
of what went wrong in the marriage are even further
apart than their views on many other things. Myths are
also produced by the confused emotions within the
offspring. The common myths we see Helen holding
are:

Mother was a good and loving woman who was unfairly victimized by her husband.

Father left because he was irritated by Helen's defiant
adolescent behavior and he blamed mother for
bringing up Helen badly.

Father left because he was selfish and unloving and
cared about nothing but his own ease and pleasure.

Mother was deeply wounded and can't make it
through life without Helen's taking care of her.

If Helen remains unhappy herself she will not be
deserting her mother; they will still be bound together in their misery as two females abandoned by
a male.

Helen must choose a primary loyalty to one parent,
in this case her mother, and to get too close to her
father would be disloyal to or even rivalrous with
her mother.

Her angry feelings to her father can't be expressed
because father is being so nice and might retreat
from Helen further if she expressed them.

Her father's new wife, the woman her father had
left to live with, was a seductive snake who was the
cause of the family breakup. She deserved nothing
better than a coolly civil response from Helen, and
this only for her father's sake.

Much of the therapy with Helen at this point revolved around uncovering and challenging these myths. As a result, they were sometimes replaced by other myths which in turn had to be challenged. For example, at one point Helen saw her mother's helplessness and suffocating dependency (previously seen as a product of her being abandoned) as the *reason* that her father left and she now blamed her mother for failing as a wife and therefore depriving her of a father in the home. During this stage she saw her father as a hero, a dashing man who courageously left to find a better life, who loved Helen totally and only left her at great pain in order to do justice to his selfhood. Also during this stage, she saw her father's new wife (the woman she had previously hated as a homewrecker) as everything she felt her mother was not—independent, joyous, and very feminine. These new myths created even greater feelings of conflict of loyalties in Helen and we worked hard to replace the myths with the reality of seeing all the members of this drama as multidimensional human beings instead of heroes, heroines, villains and victims.

Besides the trauma, the hurt, the rancor and the mythology that surround a marital breakup, the offspring is confronted with the fact that now there is not simply one family system, one "undifferentiated family ego mass" to differentiate yourself from, but three! Becoming autonomously separate from one family system is difficult enough, and now the task is suddenly much more complex. What are the three systems.

One system includes your mother and your siblings and whatever relatives have grouped around your mother and possibly your mother's new husband or lover and his children.

A second system includes your father and your siblings and whatever relatives have grouped around your father and possibly his new wife or lover and her children.

A third system includes both your mother and father and perhaps all the others mentioned above. It is an overarching system stemming from this intact family of the past, and in which you are still playing a role *between* your parents even though they have long been apart.

For Helen, the first system included primarily her mother and her mother's mother. While it underwent changes in mythology, from the myth of mother as helpless victim to mother as self-defeating loser, the intensity of the bond in this system was always there and was based on feelings that far antedated the termination of the marriage. From Helen's earliest days her mother had made Helen the source of much of her pleasure as well as the meaning for her life. Her time was structured primarily around being Helen's mother. Helen took in her mother's neediness with her mother's milk and responded by becoming as exquisitely attuned to her mother's needs and moods as a fine radar, and by acting to keep mother's loving approval. A symbiosis based on Helen's mother's needs for Helen to mother her and Helen's needs to be mothered was powerfully forged. (In the background was always grandma, who had a volatile love-hate relationship with Helen's mother and a saccharine love relationship with Helen. After the break in the marriage, grandma alternated between sniping at her daughter for losing a husband and commiserating with her about how awful men are. She was consistent in telling Helen how hurt and unhappy mommy was and that Helen had to be nice to her.)

So Helen's *mother system* had Helen hooked into songs and dances based on always acting in ways that would make mother feel taken care of, protected and nurtured. It meant she could never do anything to upset mother without feeling anxiety and guilt herself. After father left, this tie with mother intensified dramatically. Years later, she rebelled against it, became defiant and condemning with her mother, got involved in love affairs with men who abused her badly, ended up literally or figuratively dumped on her mother's doorstep again, and they resumed their roles as two wounded women mothering each other.

Helen's *father system* was shaped to a large degree by her father's need to be admired and idolized by just

about everyone, particularly Helen. He was a successful television personality, which for Helen added to his
charisma as her own Prince Charming. In her early
years, Helen could easily maintain her love affair with
her father despite her bond with her mother because
the friction between her parents seemed minimal. In
fact, whatever Oedipal guilt she felt because of her attraction to her father was assuaged by being her mother's good little-mother. As discord in the marriage grew,
Helen became so confused in her loyalties that she
developed the symptoms that brought her to therapy at
the age of nine. When her father left the marriage
Helen was stunned, not by his leaving mother but by
his leaving her! It was impossible, unbelievable, that
her daddy who loved her so much would move out,
and would move in with another woman. It was acceptable that daddy shared a bedroom and a life with
mommy, because after all she was there first and was
his wife, but to leave to go to another woman was shattering. Her hurt and anger temporarily took her out of
the role as daddy's cheery, unambivalent, starry-eyed
admirer, but her father's efforts plus her own needs
soon won her back into the old song and dance. She
went through many changes in attitude toward her
father's new wife and his new wife's young child by
her previous marriage but then found a place for this
woman as a kind of sophisticated older sister, and for
the child as a dear nephew. So she was deeply involved
in the father system as an admiring neophyte in Came-
lot, seeing her father and his new family as two-
dimensionally as if they had been created by a public
relations agency. When, in her father's narcissism, he
disappointed or hurt her she rationalized for him and
made excuses, denying her pain just as Sally Bowles
(*I Am a Camera, Cabaret*) pushed aside her hurt to
maintain her image that her father (who never shows
up) really loves her more than anything.

BRIDGE OVER TROUBLED WATERS

The *joint system* governed Helen's role *between* her
parents after the breakup of the marriage. She was

faced with the dilemma, How can I maintain the comfortable, mutually protective mother-system songs and dances and the exciting, romantic father-system songs and dances when, now that my parents are antagonists, to be in one system could seem disloyal to the other system?

In the months soon after the breakup, Helen had tried to be a peacemaker between her parents, or perhaps a matchmaker would more aptly describe it. When she was with her depressed and angry mother she would tell her that daddy was really a nice man and bring her tidbits of positive things daddy said about her in the effort to keep alive mother's hope that he was coming back. When with her father she would talk of how pretty mommy was looking and what a good mother she was. But as it became clear that her mother's anger toward her father would not be appeased, and that father had no intention of returning, she became more guarded with each, even deceptive, telling them just what they wanted to hear. She could return from a fun-filled visit with her father and tell her mother she had a lousy time and what a bitch his new wife was. She could refuse to do many enjoyable things with her mother and then tell her father that mommy never did anything exciting. She was telling each of her parents, just as one would with needy children, "Of course I love you best." And she often got into the role of the go-between, asking her father for money for things her mother said she couldn't afford, asking her mother for permission to go to the Caribbean with her father and his family, etc.

But the most pernicious way Helen tried to cope with this dilemma of two opposing family systems was to get sick, either physically, emotionally or both. Her illnesses (colitis, mononucleosis, depression, anorexia, etc.) enabled her to be close to her mother's nurturance and to get attention from her father without either parent overtly or silently criticizing her for her relationship with the other. Perhaps the most important function her illnesses had in the joint system was to keep her worried parents in contact with each other, through phone conversations, consultations with physicians, visits to her therapist, and so on. This pattern of illness bedeviled her well into her twenties.

All three family systems, Helen's mother system, father system and joint system, were phoney and impaired Helen's functioning. Changing these systems could only begin with Helen's recognition of this. If you are hooked into songs and dances with parents of a broken marriage, changing them must also begin with the recognition that you are really hooked. Each parent who is making demands that you relate to him or her in a particular way and (usually much more subtly) that you relate to your other parent in a particular way must be seen as a spoiled, self-centered, angry, hurt little child. Not that *all* of each parent is such a child—your parent is much more mature and complex than that—but the part that is demanding that you structure your relationship with him (her) and the other parent certainly is. And, as in all songs and dances, you have to recognize how the vulnerable child in you, the child that has experienced the trauma and insecurity of a family falling apart, no matter how long ago, is engaged in taking care of the child in each of your parents, often to your real detriment, in your attempt to feel more secure by preventing one or both parents from being upset.

Recognizing the songs and dances also means looking at the myths and false ideas that you may have absorbed or developed long ago and that, though now maybe largely unconscious, may still be governing how you relate to your parents. Here are some common misconceptions:

The marriage breakup was your fault. Sometimes this idea is propagated by one of the parents, sometimes it is picked up from a remark not meant that concretely, sometimes it arises out of the child's own thoughts. For example, Helen believed her adolescent defiance made her father leave. A middle-aged woman held the belief that she was the cause of her father's leaving when she was three and a half because her mother, in a distraught and angry state right after the breakup, said, "No wonder your daddy left you when you still wet the bed." A man in his twenties realized he was still carrying guilt that was shaping his behavior with his parents stemming from a time when he was six years old and his older brother said to him angrily, "Everything was fine in this family until you were born." A young woman had overheard her parents quarrel and her mother tell her father to get out when she was eight years old. It occurred the night after she and her father had showered together, so she felt sure her mother was throwing her father out because mother was aware of the sexual feelings the shower had aroused.

There are countless such examples, and it is important to become aware that you harbor ideas like these and now, as an adult, to challenge them with your adult knowledge *that a parent leaves a marriage because of unhappiness with a spouse, not with a child.* Most often, the parents have hung in there together longer *because* the children did exist, and for many parents, the effect of the breakup on the children is the most painful part. A marriage crumbles because for at least one of the parents it was extremely dissatisfying or even intolerable to remain living with the other. Looking at this with your adult eyes, instead of the distortions seen by the child, should enable you to put down any guilt as a homewrecker that you may be carrying around.

The parent who left didn't love you. This idea is often planted by the parent who feels left behind ("If daddy really loved you he wouldn't have left," "If mommy really loved you she'd come to see you more often," "If daddy really loved you he'd give more money for your support"). Sometimes the child develops the idea by himself: "If mommy (daddy) really loved me she would have taken me along," "If mommy (daddy) really loved me she wouldn't leave me with such an ogre (witch)," "If mommy (daddy) really loved me she would come back for me."

This is an idea that must be challenged with great care and courage for, as we have seen (Chapter 7), there *are* times when parents do not love their children very much and this may be the case with you, but in the great majority of the cases it is untrue. This idea was picked up when you were small and vulnerable, lodged itself in your inner child, and may sit there still, untested by your mature judgment. It is important to ask such questions as, Who gave me the idea that mommy (daddy) doesn't love me? What evidence do I have that this is true? Does the fact that she (he) left the marriage and didn't take me or come back for me mean she doesn't love me? Or did she (or he) not want to hurt daddy (mommy) more by taking me, too? Did she (or he) think daddy (mommy) could really be a better parent for me? Were there formidable legal difficulties in taking me along? Did the remaining parent make life so unbearable during both the marriage and the separation that the leaving parent was driven further and further away? Or was the leaving parent really an uncaring or narcissistic person who did not have much capacity to love?

In challenging the first two myths and discovering that the marital rupture was not your fault and that the parent who left did love you, your inner child can be left with a bitter sense of the unfairness of it. As one ten-year-old girl said after being reassured that the breakup was not her fault and that both her parents loved her very much, "If it wasn't my fault, why should I suffer? It's like being put in jail for a crime I didn't commit." But it is better to face the fact that here is true unfairness, that this is part of life's capriciousness, and that sometimes one is an innocent casualty rather than to maintain the fiction that you caused something you did not. The price of maintaining such a misconception is to make you vulnerable to falling into whatever songs and dances your parents require.

One parent is good, the other a villain. This simplistic idea may be based on the propaganda of a parent, may be the child's distortion as he defends against certain disturbing feelings, may reflect the child's limited understanding of the complexity of human relationships or may, in certain instances, be close to the truth. In almost every broken marriage, each parent believes his/her spouse's actions and failings were the cause of the breakup. Often this belief will be communicated directly to the child: "I tried so hard but daddy (mommy) was just too selfish (cruel, unloving, irresponsible, cold, thoughtless, passive, aggressive, crazy, drunk, promiscuous, or whatever)." Perhaps that's the way you see it, too. Or perhaps you were a boy left with mommy and had to see mommy as the bad one because your Oedipal wishes to possess her felt too frighteningly possible with daddy out of the house. Or maybe you were a girl who had to see mommy as bad because of the fear that you would be swallowed up by her with daddy not there. Maybe you had to see your father as bad because of your hurt and anger at his leaving, or your mother as bad because she threw daddy out and deprived you of him (since most often it is the father who leaves the domicile when a marriage dissolves, no matter what the reason, these are common misconceptions). Maybe you see mommy (daddy) as all good because look how she (he) is suffering, see how deeply she (he) wants the marriage to continue, see the sacrifices she (he) is making. Or maybe you see her (him) as the good one because you have long idealized that parent and don't want her (his) image tarnished by seeing her (his) role in the split; or maybe you persist in seeing one parent as good so you don't let yourself feel the rage at that parent for leaving, or for making trouble, etc.

Once again, it is vital to call these basic ideas into question and, not through your child eyes but as an adult, try to see each parent as flesh and blood beings so that you can understand in human terms what went wrong in the *mix* between two people who, probably in hope and love, brought you into the world.

Your parents didn't dislike each other but just grew apart. Sometimes this is not a myth but a truth. What you have to try to discover is whether it's really true, because if it's a coverup for all kinds of unexpressed rage and hurt ("Let's be very adult about this"), the chances are that that rage and hurt have been communicated to you in subliminal ways that have influenced your reactions to your parents without your knowing it. This can be terribly confusing. Your antennae are picking up anguished and angry vibrations, but you may not permit this information into your consciousness, or you may be unable to cope with their feelings responsively and directly because, after all, everybody is supposed to feel so terribly accepting and mature. Worst of all, whether the parental calm and non-belligerency was a coverup or real, you may have felt that you had to suppress your own feelings of pain, rage, despair and fear at what for you, as a child or adolescent, was a catastrophic happening. You may even have convinced yourself that everything was fine and you had no strong feelings about it either.

To challenge this idea you have to push it aside for a while and permit yourself to check out your deepest feelings, to review a host of memories and the emotions that come with them, and to listen with unclogged ears and look with unclouded eyes at your parents' words and actions.

To get outside the more complex family ego mass of a split family with its several systems (mother system, father system and joint system) it is, as always, important to see the operation of the child in you with the child in your parents, and to challenge the myriad of myths with your most objective judgment and with close attention to your deepest, unbrainwashed feelings. And you must pose the question, "How do I feel about each parent, today, as a separate person?" As important as it is in general to come to relate to each parent as a separate and different human being instead of to mom-and-dad or Mr.-and-Mrs., their actually being separated makes it even more crucial, because it involves avoiding the blackmailing idea that to relate closely to one is to be disloyal to the other. *The malignant songs and dances in this situation can end only when you insist on your absolute right to relate to each parent, and to each parent's new family system, as separate persons and separate systems, and to develop whatever relationship you can and wish to have with each of them.* Insisting on this may cause strong reactions. You may be accused by one or both parents of siding with the other, back-stabbing, ingratitude, etc., but if you persistently make it clear that you are not choosing sides, if you yourself avoid stating any comparisons between one parent and the other, and if you set it forth as simply your right to relate to all people as you wish, the chances are that your differentiation from the songs and dances will come to be accepted and even respected.

11 | Darling, I Am Growing Old

Throughout this book I have talked about the child within your parents as an inappropriate aspect of them which, when in control of their behavior, can cause considerable trouble for you. I have urged you not to go along with the process of taking care of the feelings of your parents' inner child at the high cost to your independence, your freedom to be yourself and your energies. But when we think of relating to parents who are aging and incapacitated by the ravages of years we must shift our perspective, because their leaning on us may not be inappropriate or manipulative and may not be part of a song and dance as we have used the term.

The process of aging often, if not inevitably, will bring the child in the parent to the fore. So many factors, social and biological, interact to make this true. There is the slowing down of movement and reflexes, the loss of strength and sensory acuity, the gaps in memory and clear thinking that, in making the older person less able to cope with situations from crossing streets to dialing phone numbers, bring a return of the early childhood feelings of inadequacy and inferiority. Illnesses are often debilitating and deteriorative. Accidents are more frequent due to losses in agility and perception, and the effects of the accidents are more serious and lasting due to the increased porousness of the bones and lack of elasticity in other systems. All this increases the *actuality* of helplessness and brings back the early terrors and dependence of this helplessness.

The dependence may be exacerbated by your parent's retirement from work that has structured his (or her) time and made him feel worthwhile for years. He may now feel bored and useless. And in addition, there is the loss through death of many dear friends, and possibly of his (or her) spouse. The slipping away of important, life-sustaining relationships often brings a sense of inconsolable loneliness, despair and resignation. Finally, the aging parent is aware of his own approaching death. Since one of the greatest fears of childhood is of separation and abandonment, the inner child of the parent is filled with this dread, which surges powerfully forward at the contemplation of this ultimate separation, this utter abandonment. It is small wonder that the imploring word that comes so frequently from the aged person in pain or in terminal illness is "Mama."

With these unhappy developments which so often accompany getting old, it is not inappropriate for your aging parent to turn dependently to others for help and support and, most often, he will turn to his children as the main source of that help. As Edith Stern has written, "The facts of life are more than the process of reproduction. It is equally a fact of life that in the course of time the roles of parents and children become reversed, and the younger must take care of the elder."*

Despite the fact that you know this fact of life to be true in the abstract, it is often a shock when your parent's dependency first becomes obvious. Part of the shock often has to do with the abruptness of the onset of infirmity. Suddenly he (or she) will have a stroke and be partially paralyzed; suddenly his eyes, which for years he's been saying were going bad, are practically sightless; suddenly he falls on a patch of ice and breaks a hip, leaving him unable to walk without support; suddenly his minor forgetfulness becomes a major neglect of things necessary for his health and safety; suddenly his cynicism about people becomes a

---

*Edith M. Stern, with Mabel Ross, *You and Your Aging Parents* (New York: Harper and Row, 1965), p. 9.

delusion that someone is poisoning his food; suddenly his sadness about getting older becomes a profound depression with weeping or almost catatonic apathy. Sometimes you are struck by your parents' aging even without such dramatic developments, but by their simply turning to you more and more frequently with questions like: "What should we do?" "Should we keep the house?" "Should I have the operation?" "Should I move to a retirement home?" And what will strike you with force about this is the reversal of the parent-child roles, for even though the child within your parents may have long been prominent in their relationship with you, they have still, in most instances, been indisputably the parents and you have related to them as their child. But now *they* are like little children turning to you for succor and comfort, and there is likely to be a sense of loss on your part: no longer can you maintain the feeling (which may have been there only in your unconscious) that you can always turn to your parents.

Your own sense of the loss of a parent you can go to may be compounded by the fact that often the dramatic event that makes one of your parents turn to you dependently is the death of the other parent. Just at a time when you are in mourning for the one who died, the surviving parent may be plunged into an abyss of loneliness, despair and confusion that severely impairs his independent functioning. This is particularly true when the marriage has been long and close (the kind of *duprasse* that Kurt Vonnegut talks of in *Cat's Cradle*), but it can even occur when the interaction between the parents has been full of intense conflict. For you, it is like losing both parents at once even though only one has died. Psychologically, you are orphaned. Practically, to some extent, you have just become the parent of another child.

How you will react to your parent's becoming dependent on you will be a function of several factors. One of the most important of these is the relationship you have had with this parent in the years before his infirmity. Obviously if there have been loving closeness, mutual respect and friendship between you and your parent, you will be much more willing to shoulder some of the burden of the responsibility of his (her) welfare than if there have been years of antipathy, hostility and estrangement. Particularly important will be the kind of song and dance routines that have existed between you, and the progress you have made in modifying them, because most often the role played by the child within your parent will become more salient in a crisis of aging. If your parent has played the martyr role he (she) is likely to be a martyr-supreme when age's miseries give him more reason than ever to provoke guilt. If your parent has been a tyrant he (she) may become more despotic and crabby than ever. If your parent has been a narcissist, his problems in aging can become the center of the universe for him and he will try to make them the center of your universe. And so on. And even if you have made considerable progress in your reactions to his inner child, you will feel a strong pull to get back into the old song and dance as he resumes his part in it with considerable intensity, less control over his inner child, and greater real claims for your attention. The problem you may face at this juncture would be, "How can I be helpful to my parent when he really needs my help without my regressing to old patterns?" And one of the biggest difficulties you may face in dealing with this problem will be your own rage, because the demands of aging parents can inspire fury.

Why are parents likely to become more infuriating as the aging process sets in? We see that all the old patterns may return in strength, and if we thought we had made progress toward a new and more mature *détente* with our parent, we are likely to experience the frustration of seeing that progress go down the drain. Further, your parent's adult controls over his inner child may be so weakened by arteriosclerotic brain damage and other alterations of his consciousness that his behavior may be unreasonable, self-centered and unmodifiable through rational discussion.

Some of the disturbing behavior may not be directed at you. Dr. Leopold Bellak cautions:

> Your mother may have become absent-minded: her mind wanders or she imagines she hears and sees things, or she complains about people being *after her*. Or your two elderly parents may have started quarreling with a bitterness that exceeds anything you have ever heard before. One may accuse the other of infidelity. Mother may accuse father of trying to poison her; father may say she is always hiding his money. Perhaps they will tell you of the meanness of neighbors who keep them awake by moving furniture around in the middle of the night or by spying on them. Let me reassure you—complaints like these, bizarre as they may seem to you on first hearing—are rather frequent.*

But even when the behavior is not directed at you, your frustrations in coping with it can increase your anger. And some of their irrationality may have you at the eye of it, which has a particular exasperating quality if their demands or accusations are outrageous.

Place all of this in the context of where your life is at this time. The chances are, if you have parents who can be referred to as "old," that you are not newly out of adolescence yourself. As people tend, through medical advances, to live longer and longer, a phenomenon is occurring with increasing frequency—people in mid-life and looking forward to its freedoms are confronted with the care of their aged parents. To quote Bellak again:

> This is the moment, maybe even the very first opportunity, to relax a bit, to take a vacation unencumbered by diapers, childish squabbles, measles, colds or school calendars. But wait, what's this? Suddenly a new crop of "children" has been harvested. The middle-aged adults look around and

---

*Leopold Bellak, *The Best Years of Your Life* (New York: Atheneum, 1975), p. 24.

notice that their parents, while not at present helpless, are approaching the age when they will need
looking after.*

Taking care of elderly parents, even in a limited
way, often places new restrictions on your freedom,
heavy burdens on your finances, and an enormous
drain on your time and your energy. All these things
contribute to your rage. And it is not uncommon,
when these kinds of burdens are present, for there to be
wishes on the part of the children that their parents
would die. These thoughts are not simply the resur-
gence of early death wishes that most if not all children experience toward their parents, but are thoughts
that arise naturally out of the frustrations you face with
your parents in the present. These wishes that your
parent(s) would die often are composed of compassion as well, because of your hope that their suffering,
their slow deterioration and their loneliness will come
to an end. Besides, you want to remember them as
vital, independent people. The danger is that your
guilt about these death wishes will make you too vulnerable to falling back into old song and dance patterns, too ready to let the feelings of your inner child
—be they feelings of rage, guilt, fear or whatever—
overrule your judgment about how the situation should
best be handled. Your angry feelings and your death
wishes, though no basis for action, are understandable
in these circumstances and you need to forgive yourself for them if you are to move constructively.

Shaken up by the reversal of roles, burdened by the
drains on your time, energy and money, enraged at
your parent's behavior, how can you keep yourself
from going back to the old songs and dances when the
needs of your parent's inner child now, in reality,
need to be recognized and attended to? The first step is
the acceptance that the situation really has changed,
that you are now dealing with a person who is in some
degree helpless and dependent, not a person who is

*Ibid., p. 5.

only acting that way as a maneuver stemming from his inner child. But even in recognizing this you confront another question that leads to the core of who you are, what you believe and what your values are. You may have striven very hard for autonomy, for a large measure of control of your life, for freedom to choose your own life-style. You may have adopted as primary values the actualization of your potentials, the enhancement of your experiencing, and the courage to make difficult existential decisions. Where does the draining, constricting task of taking care of aged parents come into this value system?

There has been much emphasis on self-actualization, and it has been an important antidote to philosophies and social mores that arbitrarily limited an individual's range of behavior by tying him to unquestioned and unquestionable codes. But self-actualization, to those humanistic psychologists such as Maslow and Rogers who propounded the approach, has never meant egocentric selfishness. In self-actualization, your self expands beyond its early narcissistic smallness to encompass—through empathy, caring, concern and love —greater proportions of your life space. And your parents are very much a part of your life space. It is not a matter of being obligated to take care of them because society or your religion or your guilt says you should, although these may embrace values with which you genuinely concur. It is more a matter of a human commitment to care for others, particularly those who have been important to you and have some authentic claim to this attention. While what you will do and the spirit in which you do it will depend in great measure on your feelings about your parent, it represents an extension of your boundaries and a growing beyond narcissism to accept some measure of this commitment. Your own inner child may want none of this obligation; he wants to go out and play. But the more mature part of you may make the existential choice to overrule this child and enter into a supportive and helping interaction with the person who once took care of you.

If you have made the decision to be supportive to your aging parent, and recognize that some degree of dependence on his part is now appropriate, it will be helpful in avoiding regressing to the old song and dance if you realize that one of the best things you can do for your parent is to encourage him to be as *independent* as his physical condition allows. Treating your parent as an infant can take away much of his dignity, his spirit and his will to go on creating his life as best he can. Remember, the song and dance you and your parent were engaged in before his infirmity was between his inner child and *your inner child*. His inner child may be more exposed and active than ever, but what is called for on your part now is a mature, realistic, caring and *parental* response, not the guilty or placating response of the child in you that could push your parent into greater helplessness.

OH, MY PAPA

While encouraging your aged parent to assume as much independence as he is capable of managing is important in preventing his (her) regression, there will be times when, from your parental role, you will have to push him toward certain decisions that you can see are clearly necessary. There may even be times when his own judgment is so faulty that you will have to make those decisions for him.* Vinny's father was seventy-eight, and his wife of over fifty years had died two years before. Vinny had never really liked his father. When Vinny was little, his father, who owned a restaurant, was rarely home and when he was he was often tired and irritable. Later Vinny worked in the

---

*It is difficult to make objective judgments about decisions affecting your parent's life and your own. It becomes important to call on the viewpoints and expertise of others. You should confer freely and openly with your own siblings, spouse and children. You should discuss it with friends whose wisdom and perceptiveness you admire. And you should consult specialists in the field of aging in community agencies and family agencies. They will not be able to help you with your emotional conflicts, but will have invaluable information as to the alternatives and facilities that are available. This would be a bulwark against the possibility of acting on the feelings of your inner child, and will keep you focused not on the question of what *should* I do, but what *can* I realistically do, and what will my parent *let* me do?

restaurant for a few years and his father was a tyrannical boss. For a long time now Vinny had had little
to say to his father. There were a handful of warm
memories that meant a lot to Vinny but he could
not pretend, after his mother died and his father
wanted to see more of him, that he felt any strong loving feelings toward his father. In the two years since
his mother's death, certain things had become obvious.
The neighborhood in which his father lived was de-
teriorating quickly into a dangerous slum. His father
had twice been mugged and his wrist had been broken. During a five-day winter cold snap, there had been
no heat in his father's building and the disrepair was
becoming worse. And Vinny could see that his father
was becoming increasingly unable to care for himself.
He was losing weight rapidly because he often forgot
to eat, his clothing was smelly and he rarely bathed.
Vinny began to urge his father to move but his father
clung to his old home desperately, with its memories
of his wife, his friends and the bocci games he had
played in a neighborhood park that no longer existed.
Vinny thought about having his father live with him.
It was a very undesirable solution. Besides the fact that
Vinny and his father often clashed, Vinny's wife was a
nervous, high-strung woman who could just about
manage the household and two children without being
overwhelmed. They were short on space, and their
children were noisy and rambunctious. The total living conditions and a realistic appraisal of the per-
sonalities of all involved indicated that this solution
would be a nightmare. Though it was somewhat
difficult financially, Vinny employed a part-time homemaker for his father; for a while this went well, but
then the homemaker was mugged and quit the job and
he could find no one to replace her. Meanwhile, his
father was becoming more irrational, would go for
walks and become lost, would call in the middle of
the night to say the neighbors were conspiring against
him, etc. His physical health again deteriorated. At this
point Vinny decided he had to become a firm parent
to his father. He came over and told his father that
he would have to move to a home for senior citizens

and that he had no choice in the matter any longer, but that he could have a choice as to which home. He took his father to several places he had heard good things about and his father liked one more than the others. When it came time to move, his father balked and Vinny said it was either that home or a hospital. His father looked at Vinny, saw he meant business and said okay. Then his father said wistfully, but with a definite tone of pleasure, "You used to be my son. Now you are my father."

Taking this decisive role in your parent's life can present you with many internal conflicts:

Am I acting out of guilt or caring?

Am I acting out of reason or out of panic? Or out of old hates and grudges?

Am I blinding myself to my parents' infirmities and real needs because I don't want to be burdened by their needs?

Do I want to keep away from them because seeing them as old and failing is a dread reminder of my own approaching fate?

Am I choosing the solution for them that's best or cheapest?

Am I putting my parent in a "home" for his good or mine?

Am I taking on too much?

Am I taking care of my parent at too great an expense to my spouse, my children, my job, my health,

Would I want my children to care for me the way I am caring for my parent.

Taking over these decisions for a parent always has an air of tragedy about it, as we follow a timeless human cycle of the older taking care of their young and then their young taking care of the old. If you saw *I*

Never Sang for My Father you might remember how Melvyn Douglas, himself aging, talks of last seeing his father alone and dying in a hospital. He leaves his father with a bag of oranges. The movie ends with Melvyn Douglas himself left by his son alone and dying in a nursing home. We can only hope to combine the best of loving that resides in our inner child with the greatest wisdom and nurturance that reside in our maturity so that we can make the most helpful, compassionate decisions for our parents if we must some day assume that role.

It is particularly important, when interacting with aging parents, to be tuned into the themes beneath their words, as their words often obscure their real feelings, especially when parents have become irrational. If you get caught up in the words and don't hear the melody it can be maddening. Ralph was a forty-four-year-old man I was seeing in psychotherapy. His mother had always been a self-centered, controlling woman. Her husband had been dead for many years and she had managed fairly well, although she sometimes made excessive demands on Ralph and his family. Then, as the arteries in her head hardened and less oxygen reached her brain, her demandingness became more pronounced and irrational. One evening, as Ralph sat with his wife and children at dinner, his mother called, sounding very frantic. She at first told him she had nothing to eat but he reminded her he had been there the day before and that the refrigerator and freezer were well stocked. She said that was true but she wanted roast chicken and that she had the chicken but something was wrong with the oven and she was afraid it would blow up. He suggested frying the chicken but she said she couldn't cut it up because of her arthritis. He suggested she fry the fish he knew was there. She said the fish had a funny smell and she was afraid of food poisoning. And so on with about ten other suggestions, with some of her refusals being childish and even bizarre. Her tone became more angry and accusative.

"What the hell do you want me to do?" he found himself screaming. "Bring you a meal?"

"Would that be so terrible?" she answered.

He went into an outraged defense, telling her that he had been there the previous day, that he had a family, that he was relaxing from a hard day at work, that she was incredibly selfish, etc. She said, "You don't care if I starve." He had yelled, "You're driving me nuts. Get off my back." Then he hung up.

Now Ralph sat in my office feeling both guilty and justified about what he had done, but mostly despairing at being trapped again into this kind of exchange. I could see how frustrating it could be and we talked about it. Then I suggested we act out the phone conversation with Ralph playing his mother and me playing Ralph. I explained that since I wasn't really him, and he wasn't really *my* mother, I might just be able to keep my inner child out of it enough to find alternative ways of responding.

MOTHER (as played by Ralph): Look, I have nothing to eat.

RALPH (as played by me): But mother, I was there yesterday and I saw to it your refrigerator and freezer were well stocked.

MOTHER: I know. I want roast chicken, and I have the chicken, but the oven isn't working right. I'm afraid it will blow up.

RALPH: It must be hard sometimes to be all alone and cope with it all.

MOTHER (after a pause): Yes. It's terrible.

RALPH: Are you feeling lonely?

MOTHER: Yes. Sometimes I get so lonely I don't think I can stand it.

RALPH: I'm sure it's rough. I think you're doing very well with it, all considered.

MOTHER: Do you really think so?

RALPH: Yes, I'm proud of the way you're handling things and I'm glad you feel free to call me and get it off your chest when you're feeling it's too much for you.

MOTHER: Yes. Well, it's not always so bad. You must
 be eating so go back to dinner.
RALPH: Okay, but what are you going to eat?
MOTHER: I'll roast the chicken. The oven's not too
 bad.

Ralph was astonished to see that there were alternative ways of responding to his mother if he stayed in
a mature, nurturing frame of mind instead of slipping into variations on the old song and dance. He was
particularly startled to see how he, playing his mother,
began to respond differently, almost in spite of himself, when I responded empathically to the underlying message.

The next week Ralph came in beaming. "I'm beginning to get the hang of it," he said. "My mother
began telling me in that hysterical way of hers about
how she was sure there were men in the house across
the street spying on her, particularly when she got un-
dressed. She said they could see her if the shade was
open even a crack because one of them had binoculars.
She was terribly afraid they would come to her apartment and attack her. I was about to argue with her,
scoff at her and generally get into a frustrating mess.
Then I saw how easy it was to put myself into a
nurturing parent role instead and I said, 'Mom, you've
sure been looking attractive enough so I wouldn't
blame those guys for wanting to get a good look at you.
But guys who peek like that are never really dangerous. They just like to look. So take it as flattering, because it is.' My mother said something about how she's
trying to not let her figure go to pot and she let it go."

The more you can get into a kindly or firmly
parental stance, with your elderly, infirm, dependent
parent, the more you will be able to avoid the pitfalls
of the old song and dance and to respond constructively and with a compassion that is never out of date.

The Song Is Ended (but the Melody Lingers On)

12

One of the earliest, most pervasive fears of childhood is "What if my mother or father dies?" It is the unthinkable thought, yet children brood about this, panic about it when their parents are away on a trip, pray for it not to happen when one of their parents is sick or injured. For many of you, this long-feared but commonly shared tragedy has already happened. If you have experienced it, you probably felt it as a powerful trauma with some sense of unreality about it: "Will I really never see him (her) again?" Just how upsetting the death was and the effects it has left on you will depend largely on what your relationship with that parent was like and your age when he (she) died. The one thing you can be sure of, however, is that the death of a parent does not necessarily end any song and dance routines you may have been engaged in with him. *In fact, one of the most difficult songs and dances to stop is one with a dead parent.*

It is difficult to end a song and dance routine with a dead parent because your interaction with him as a real person who undergoes change and who gives you continuing feedback as you change no longer exists. Your image of him—of what he thought, of how he felt about you and others, of what he expected of you and what his injunctions for living were—became frozen when he died. His death robbed him of the opportunity for further growth and the chance to be influenced by the social developments that have occurred between then and now. And, despite changes that have taken place in you, your images of him have probably remained static. These images replay as immutably as old movies and prerecorded voices in your head. So your interaction with him is stuck because it is not with a real person but an image formed by antique animated pictures replaying inside you.

MEMORIES ARE MADE OF THIS

This image of your parent is built partly of your memories, and many of those memories were collected and stored when you were very young. Before being stored away they were filtered and interpreted by your ways of thinking and perceiving as a young child, and the young child's experience of what he sees is narrowly circumscribed by his limited understanding and by a tendency to view the people around him the way he *needs* to see them. If you *needed* to see your parent as the "best" and "most wonderful" subjects of a Mother's Day or Father's Day card, you will ignore data to the contrary. If your childhood narcissism made you *need* to have your own way all the time, you could see your parents as mean and unfair whenever they said no. What you remember is selected by your needs out of an almost infinite number of memories and you assemble these recollections to form a parental image. As you grew up, your needs changed, your ability to see people more realistically developed, and your interactions with your parents gave you a continued flow of input that began to modify your perception. But when your parent died, this input stopped and your image of your parent became fixed.

Besides your selected remembrances, other people have helped you to create the illusion of who your parent was. The younger you were when your parent died, the more this will be true. If your mother told you that your father was a wonderful, kind, noble man, it would tend to make you forget or extravagantly rationalize incidents in which he was mean or petty or cruel. If she told you what a devoted father he was, you may forget that you mostly experienced him as indifferent and detached. Or if she told you what a thoughtless, selfish, irresponsible man he was, perhaps you've repressed or distorted those memories in which you experienced him as warm or loving.

Despite the fact that others have influenced your view of the parent who died, your view of him or her is a distinctly personal one. For example, since your needs differed from those of your siblings, since you experienced him as a living person up to a different age than your siblings, and because the time he was alive spanned different years in the history and mythology of your family, your memories of a deceased parent can vary widely from the recollections of your sisters or brothers. When adult siblings talk to each other honestly about how they remember a dead parent they are often astonished to find that it's as if they were talking about different people. "Your father is not my father," a woman told her younger sister after they shared impressions of him. The older sister was seventeen when her father succumbed to a deteriorative muscular disease which had increasingly incapacitated him for three years. Most of her memories of him were of a vital, successful, fun-loving man. Her sister was ten when her father died and only seven when he became ill. Many of her sharpest memories of him were of a debilitated, depressed and bitter presence in the house. Even when the age difference is closer and the circumstances less dramatic, the fact that you had a unique place in the family constellation that differed from that of your siblings gave you the experience of a different parent. You were the "brain," or "beautiful," or "clumsy," or "the middle child," or "the baby," or "father's favorite," or "mother's headache," or the "clown" or whatever, and you viewed your parent from that perspective, making your image of him highly subjective.

And the most subjective aspect of the image of your deceased parent is how he or she felt about you.

I've heard many adults say they wished their parent had lived longer so they could have gotten a clearer picture of what that parent's feelings about them were because now it's rather hazy. And I've seen many adults, their parents long dead, who are still trying to win their parents' approval or avoid their disapproval.

An attractive, slim woman of thirty said, "My father always kidded me about being fat, which I was as a child. I'm almost always on a diet even though everyone says I have a good figure. But it's impossible for me to look at the scale and see I've gained even one pound without being swept with that same sense of humiliation as when he kidded me. And he died when I was twelve."

A forty-year-old man said, "My mother always ridiculed me for being absent-minded. Even now, when I forget to do something I can hear her saying, 'You'd lose your head if it wasn't attached to you.' She's been dead for thirty years and I still cringe." The man who said this is the head of a multimillion-dollar corporation, and is known for his competence and effectiveness.

A well-known pediatrician said, "It was always so hard to get my father to take me seriously. He acted as if I were irresponsible and inept. I think I've had to become president of every professional organization I belong to in order to make him proud of me. And he's been dead since I was fifteen."

The image you carry of how your parent felt about you greatly influences the kind of song and dance you have going with him or her. And the injunctions you received from your parent as to how they expected you to act, which behavior they would approve of and which behavior they would admonish you for, also set the tune for many song and dance routines. Parental injunctions are always powerful, but when the parent has died, these injunctions, like the inscription on his tombstone, can seem chiseled in granite. Injunctions then form the basis for songs and dances that are forever going on between you and that parent. Think of common expressions: "Papa would have wanted it that way"; "My mother would turn over in her grave if she knew"; "My father would be so proud of me today." All these expressions assume that you know what the injunctions of your dead parent are, and they further assume that you, or the child within you, still finds it very important to get the approval of the parent who is dead. (Sometimes the assumption that you know what the injunctions of your dead parent would be is based on a wish fulfillment. A young woman, at the birth of her own child, said, "Mama would be so proud of me today," but later she realized this probably was not true—that there never had been any way to make her critical, negative mother proud of her, and that if she were alive now, she'd still find something disapproving to say.)

To assume you know exactly what your dead parent's injunctions are is a fallacy because even when they were explicit, they would still be subject to change with time. Think how much you have changed in the last ten years, and how much other people you know, including the parent who is left alive, have changed. These changes are not only the result of a natural tendency to grow as life's vicissitudes daily teach fresh lessons, but also because societal upheavals have accelerated at a rate that has subjected us to minute-by-minute future shock. There has been a revolution in ideas and practices in relation to the family, marriage, the role of women, sexual frankness, sexually accepted behavior, the meaning of a good life, racial equality, life-styles, and attitudes toward money, romantic love, work and established institutions such as education, religion and patriotism. This revolution, often without our awareness, has influenced the thinking of us all. Ten years ago I frequently heard parents advise their daughters not to have sexual relations till they were married; now very commonly I hear parents say, "Why do you have to marry him? If you want to be together, live together for a while and see how it goes." A short time ago this was unthinkable for almost any parent; today it is said with increasing frequency by parents whose own parents would have disowned them for pursuing such a course.

So often we hear people say, "I was born too soon" or "I wish I had it to do over again." I have heard fathers say they wish they had gone to college when the dorms were co-ed, but ten years before they might have refused to let their own child go to one of the first co-ed dorms.

If you and others have changed so dramatically, what makes you think your dead parent might not also have changed? One woman's mother had always told her that the worst possible thing was to live alone. She had made it seem as if living alone was inherently bad: "A normal person doesn't live alone." This woman's marriage broke up and her mother told her to take a roommate or come live with her but not to live by herself. The daughter fixed her home warmly, entertained, enjoyed a social life, and communicated to her mother that she felt comfortable and secure with it. Finally, in a discussion, her mother talked of her life-long dread of loneliness and said, "Okay, if you like it, go ahead. I'm putting my own childish fears on you." If her mother had died years before, this woman would have assumed that her mother was unalterably opposed to her living alone and, if her need to have her mother's approval had been great enough, she might have made other living arrangements.*

In Shaw's *Man and Superman*† (the "Don Juan in Hell" sequence), Ana, who has just died at seventy-seven, speaks to Don Juan about her father, who died in a duel defending her "honor" many years earlier when he was sixty-four and she was a young woman. She had spent the rest of her life mourning him and model-

---

*If you yourself are a parent, giving your children a sense that your views grow and change can be helpful so that even after you die their views of your injunctions do not remain fixed.

†George Bernard Shaw, *Man and Superman* (Baltimore: Penguin, 1973).

ing her behavior after the pillar of virtue she held him to be. When her father asks Don Juan (the man who had killed him in the duel but is now his good friend), "Any news?" and Don Juan answers, "Yes: your daughter is dead."

"My daughter?" (Recollecting) "Oh. The one you were taken with. Let me see: what was her name?"

"Ana."

"To be sure: Ana. A goodlooking girl, if I recollect aright. Have you warned Whatshisname? her husband."

Ana, who has been listening, is very upset, and when her father informs her (now that they are both eternally dead and for her to continue mourning him and worshiping him makes no sense) that his views of morality and his own marriage to her mother were quite different from what she believed, she is shocked. He makes it clear that in many of his actions, including his fatal duel, he was simply following the expectations of his society, rather than any deep sense of love or commitment. So Ana had been following the injunctions of a dead man who was himself following injunctions she never knew he did not believe in. And not knowing, she couldn't even contemplate that he could accept different behavior from her.

So the first step in ending a song and dance with a dead parent is to challenge the assumption that the injunctions that you experienced coming from him (her) were in reality fixed and unmodifiable.

"Mama would turn over in her grave if she knew I was getting a divorce." Would she? Is it possible that knowing the total situation mother might have sympathized with, if not actually approved, your decision?"

"Papa would never forgive me if I married outside my religion." Possibly, but did your father have no flexibility to change with society's shifts in attitudes? And if he met the person you wanted to marry might he not have felt differently?"

"Mother would never approve if I decided not to have any children." You'll never know, if she's dead. But wouldn't it be something if she were around and told you that she agrees, and that she might have had a more rewarding life herself if she hadn't had any? "My father never wanted me to be aggressive or too successful. He said all the really successful men he knew got there by being underhanded and stepping on others." This doesn't mean that your father might not have enjoyed your success or seen it in a different light. His own fears of competition and triumph may have led him to adopt that viewpoint, but he may be pleased to see his child not similarly sabotage himself."

"My mother was a meticulous housekeeper. She measured a woman by the way she took care of her home and her family." Would she have really thought less of you for deemphasizing that role for a career now? When your mother grew up she and most women who wanted to express their abilities and competence did it through being effective as a housekeeper. Otherwise, she may have felt her life to be wasted and meaningless. But now, with so many opportunities available for women, would she really think less of you for de-emphasizing home-making to pursue another career?"

"It was important to my father that the family name be carried on. When my first child was a girl he looked crushed but he said, 'Don't worry, the next one will be a boy.' He died soon after, and three years later we had another girl. We really can't afford another child but I know a boy would make him happy so we'll try again." Maybe if you had the chance to talk it out with father, he would agree that having another child now would be a hardship."

"My father wouldn't let me go to college after high school—he said that was for boys, not girls. Now I'm in my fifties and have had many opportunities to register, my husband encourages it, and to my surprise I passed the entrance exam with a high score. That took away my last excuse, but I've still never done it. I wonder if it's still my father holding me back even though he's been dead for thirty years." But if her father had lived and had seen the sweeping changes in attitudes toward women's education, isn't it likely he would have approved of his daughter's going to college now?"

But as helpful as it might be for you to see the possibility that your parents' injunctions might have changed if they had lived, the crucial step in stopping a song and dance with a dead parent is, as with a living parent, the recognition that the interaction is between the child in your parent and the child in you. It is the child in your parent because the injunction grew out of his or her need to control and delimit your behavior, and it is the child in you that is still oriented toward getting the approval of mommy and daddy even though you are a self-sustaining, capable and autonomous person. The child in you may be particularly entwined in a relationship with a dead parent because the parent's death made it impossible to gratify the yearning for parental loving and affirmation, or to discover that it never would be gratified. It has been left as an open-ended question, an incomplete task, and this leaves an intense pull to achieve some sort of resolution—a resolution that cannot now, in reality, be attained.

In ending other songs and dances, we found it helpful to get to see what kind of little girl or boy in your parent may be calling the shots by looking at her or his reactions closely. But how can you observe the inner child of your parent closely when she (he) is no longer alive? And since she (he) is dead, why should you even try?

THE WAY WE WERE

The primary reason for trying to become more deeply acquainted with a mother or father who has died is to grasp her or him as a real human being who is subject to change and growth, rather than the two-dimensional static caricature you have been interacting with. Your parent was neither a character in a melodrama nor a legend. He was not created by your needs or other people's myth-making; he existed as an entity of enormous complexity. To see his (her) end of the song and dance you have to see your parent in the colors and shades that make him real. There are several ways that you can do this, if you feel that your picture of your parent has enough gaps to make it a worthwhile enterprise.

You can talk to people who knew your parent in as many different facets of his life as possible, people other than those who gave you your present image of him. Ask for their memories and impressions. Ask what they liked and what they did not like about him. Be aware that you are getting their myths and their distortions, as well as the possibility they may be telling you what you want to know, but see if any consistent image or persistent themes run through what you are hearing. A woman recalled that her view of her father, whom she had seen as a hard, austere and unsentimental man began to shift at his funeral when all the workers at the factory he owned appeared and wept openly. They all had stories to tell of her father's deep kindness to them at important moments in their lives. One worker recalled that during the Depression he was at rock bottom and he had stopped her father on the street for a handout. He had responded, "I won't give you a cent, but if you want to do an honest day's work, come with me." He had become an important and valued employee. She began to think more of various incidents in their family where her father had always seemed to her a stern patriarch and she concluded, "You know, he was really a pussycat."

See if you can find unifying themes as you review your own memories of your parent. Start with your earliest memory of him or her, and set down the more outstanding ones up until the most recent. Are there themes of nurturance, meanness, pride, anger, passivity, honesty, courage, irresponsibility, detachment? Are the themes of your memories consistent with your general image of him (or her)? Are they consistent with the stories you have gleaned from other people?

You can look at photos of your deceased parent (this is a helpful exercise with living parents as well).* Note his (her) posture—is he rigid or relaxed, assertive or passive, firmly grounded or weak and unstable? And how about his facial expression—is it friendly? forbidding? warm? seductive? phoney? open? happy? anxious? depressed? masklike? If you or other people are in the photos, note what kind of interaction is pictured. Is he touching anyone? Whom? Does the touching seem comfortable or forced? Is there warmth and welcome in it? Is it a tentative touch or a hearty embrace? Do his posture, his face and his interaction go together harmoniously?

If you have photos of your parent as a child study them closely. What kind of child was he (or she)? What does his world seem like? When you were his age, would you have wanted him as a friend? How come? How would it feel to have a child just like the child in the photo?

You may be fortunate enough to have samples of what your parent has written. This may be letters he (she) wrote to you when you were in college, camp, or the army, or when he (she) was away on a trip. Or, if he was the writing kind, perhaps some stories or essays. What do you sense of him (her) from what he writes about and the way he writes it? What was important to him?

It can also be helpful to review everything you know of his (her) life history—his childhood, his parents, his education, his career choice, his marital choice, etc.—from the vantage point of the mature person you are now, and see how it all fits together. What kind of story does it make? What would you title this story? What kind of person emerges? How do you feel about that person?

These methods may give a truer picture of your parent than the one you carry in your head, but don't be surprised if you fight accepting this truer picture,

---

*See Robert U. Akeret, *Photoanalysis* (New York: Wyden, 1973).

because the old image in your mind was the only part of him (her) you had to hold on to, a precious thing to surrender.

AFTER YOU'VE GONE

Getting to know your deceased parent more realistically is just a part of what needs to be done if you are to end the song and dance, but the most important change must be in your response. *And just as your image of your parent was frozen at his death, the responses you are having to that image are also frozen at the age you were when he died, and maybe even earlier.* How can you unfreeze your way of interacting with that parent who now exists only in your head? How can you interact with him again in a new and fresh way? Through the technique of the "empty chair" dialogue used so prominently in gestalt therapy, it is possible for you to talk once more with your dead parent.

Bert, a thirty-two-year-old architect, was wrestling with the question of whether to leave the large company he worked for and for which he was doing routine and uncreative drawings, and go into partnership with a friend building innovative vacation houses. It was a risky step, and in the course of discussing it Bert had said, "I have a feeling that if my father hadn't died when I was a kid, if I had had a man to grow up with, this kind of decision wouldn't throw me. I know that sounds like I'm passing the buck, but I'm still mad at him for dying." I suggested he talk to his father about it, and I moved a chair to face his. Bert was familiar with this way of working so he asked no questions. He looked at the empty chair and said, "Dad, that was a mean, bastardly thing to do, going off and leaving me that way. Christ. I was only nine. Do you know how young nine is?"

I motioned Bert to sit in the empty chair. "I'm sorry, son. I didn't mean it to happen that way. I really didn't want to die."

"If you didn't want to you wouldn't have," Bert said as he sat in his own chair again. Bert's voice and his pouting lip made it clear that his inner child was speaking, that he was back to the time his father died. "I hate you for dying."

"Bert, I guess you felt your dad could do anything, including staying alive with a heart whose valves were made of Kleenex. You must have seen me as a super-man."

"You were. I remember the time you hit two home runs at the Cub Scout father-son picnic. Nobody else even hit one."

"I remember how proud you were, and how good it felt to make you proud. I don't think you ever realized how much I loved you. You know, when the doctor first told me how bad my heart was and hinted that I probably wouldn't last too long, the first thing I thought of was you. I really didn't want to die and leave you. I wanted so badly to live to see you grow up and to help you grow up. Do you believe me?"

"I guess so. But it's hard to put down the anger."

"Do you have children?" Bert's "father" asked.

"Yes. One of each, ages eight and five."

"How would you feel about dying and leaving them?"

"I guess that would be the worst part of dying right now. I want to live a long time, but I particular-ly want to hang around till they're on their feet. Al-though I think my wife would do a better job without me than yours did without you."

"Did mother hold you back a lot? She was nervous."

"She was always screaming at me, telling me I couldn't do this because it was bad or I couldn't do that because I'd get hurt. I would lie in bed crying, and cursing you for dying. I knew you'd let me do those things. But at times I wasn't sure of that either. I remember when you were sick that last year and I had to be so quiet so as not to disturb you and I wondered if maybe you really didn't like the noisy part of me that liked to run and jump and do things."

"I loved that part of you. I was a lot like that my-self before I got sick, but you may not remember that part too well. Except for those two home runs. Really, I was an active guy and I wanted you to be strong and go out and live each day fully."

"But look what happened to you."

"Bad luck, mostly. I wouldn't change a bit of the way I lived, except for my smoking. Do you smoke?"

"Yes."

"Cut it out. Life really is to be treasured. And you do have those kids. But aside from that, the main thing I want to tell you is don't live like a mouse. Your mother wanted you to be that way and she wanted me to be that way because she can be a frightened little girl sometimes. But that's no way to live."

"Dad, I'm an architect and I have a secure, dull job with a big company. I'm thinking of quitting and starting my own partnership, but it's scary."

"Is the idea sound? Is your partner someone you can trust?"

"I'd trust my partner with my life. And I've checked out the idea from every angle. There's nothing basically wrong with it, but there's a risk."

"There's always a risk. But you don't seem to be happy with the alternative and this sounds like what you'd really like to do. I think you should do it or you'll always wonder what would have happened. I certainly wouldn't want you to be cautious because you think that's what I would want. You've got a life to live."

Bert was back in his chair sitting silently. I asked him if he had finished talking to his father. He shook his head, looked at the empty chair and said, "Dad, tell me the truth. I know at times I made noise when you were sick. Did I make you die?"

"No, honestly. My heart was so bad I didn't have a chance. Don't think you were so big you could knock off your old man!"

"Where did a haberdasher like you learn about this Oedipus stuff?"

"I've gotten smarter since I'm dead!"

"Yes, you have." Bert paused. "I guess we should say goodbye."

"Why? We can say 'so long' and we can visit again if there's more to talk about. I'm not going away again."

"Good, dad. It's been great talking to you. I'll see you around. And, dad, you died before I ever had a chance to tell you I love you."

"That makes me feel good. I love you too, Bert. You were a great kid."

"Thanks, dad. We'll talk again and I'll let you know how it turned out."

Bert could not, of course, know what his father would really say, but that's irrelevant because the only father Bert has a relationship with is the one in his head. And in this kind of dialogue, it is possible for that frozen father to thaw, change and give Bert new messages, and it is possible for the child in Bert to respond differently.

Not all "empty chair dialogues" with dead parents end up on such a warm note. Phyllis was an attractive twenty-eighty-year-old woman who carefully selected the men in her life to prove mother's teaching that all men are no good and will use you. But she was changing, she was increasingly finding men who really were interested in her, and now had fallen in love with Bill, a man who really seemed to care about her deeply. She ached to tell her mother that there were exceptions, to get her mother to give her permission to let her trust herself with Bill, but mother had been dead since Phyllis was fourteen. At my suggestion, she began a "conversation" with her mother, and she told her mother at length about Bill. Then she switched to the empty chair and replied as mother.

"It certainly sounds like this Bill fellow has your number. He's just telling you what you want to hear so he can get what he wants."

"How do you know that? You've never even met him."

"I don't have to. They're all alike. I tried to teach you that, to give you the benefit of what I learned the hard way, but it sounds like Bill made you forget everything you know."

"Not just Bill. I've been working hard in therapy for years to get rid of some of those sick ideas you gave me about men."

"Sick ideas. Tell me, what happened after I died? What did your father do?"

"He's one man."

"What did he do?"

"Okay, he wasn't around very much. Dad is a self-ish, irresponsible guy and he spent a lot of his time and his money gambling. But you picked him, not me. And he wasn't always that way. There were times when he came through."

"You can believe what you want, but I know better. Where was he when you were born? At the racetrack. Where was he when I got so sick? In Las Vegas. Men just don't have a sense of commitment. My father ran away when I was ten and left my mother with four children."

"I've heard the story all my life. But, mother, not all men are that way. If you met Bill you'd see for yourself."

"I don't need to meet Bill. I know. You just learn to take care of yourself and be independent."

"I can take care of myself and I am independent. But I also am in love with this man."

"I can see you're trapped. If you have to be with him, make sure you don't give anything without getting something."

"Mother, you haven't changed at all."

"Who wants to change? I know what I know."

"Well, I'm not going to try to convince you, then. But I don't want to think the way you do anymore. I believe Bill is loving and caring, and I trust him."

"You'll learn."

"I don't think we have anything more to say to each other. Some of what you taught me has helped me to be tough and self-reliant. I want to thank you for that. But you don't have anything much to offer me anymore."

"Not if you won't listen."

"No, I won't listen anymore. In fact, I'm just not sure I want to talk to you again. It's a dead end." Phyllis paused for a long time. "Peace, mother."

This dialogue did not bring about a rapprochement between Phyllis and her dead mother in the way it brought Bert and his father together. What it did do was to make concrete for Phyllis the extent to which that part of her that distrusted men and could not permit herself to get close to them was largely her mother inside her, the recorded voice of a person long dead. It made it clear that this injunction from her mother came from a little girl in her mother, still smarting from her own father's abandonment, still angry at her own husband's irresponsibility. But above all it clarified that Phyllis had changed so much that mother's injunctions, once so much a basis for Phyllis's thinking and behavior, had now become alien to her. She no longer had any wish to maintain a tie to her mother on that old basis. Phyllis had wept when she said goodbye to her mother at the cemetery half a lifetime ago, but at this parting of the ways she felt joy.

There are many ways you can use this empty chair dialogue to finish unfinished business with a dead parent. In almost every instance where a parent has died, their child, of any age, usually feels that there were so many things they wanted to tell their parent that they never got around to saying. They may never have told their parent how they loved him (or her), or hated him, or respected him, or were hurt by him, or were appreciative of his parenting. In fact, most often they never said goodbye to their parents. Even in those instances where the parent's death was not sudden and unexpected, even where the dying was slow and the child was there, the reluctance to admit that death is coming, or the inhibition against expressing profound and powerful emotions, have often led the offspring to utter such empty farewell words to their parents as, "You look fine today. Tomorrow you'll probably be up and around," or, "I saw a skirt in Bloomingdale's that you would love and it's just your color."

The denial of death often forecloses the goodbye. If this is true for you, give yourself that second chance. If you are not in the kind of therapy where this empty chair dialogue is used, you can, giving yourself the privacy and time, seat your "parent" in a chair opposite you and tell her (him) what has been unsaid. Let it all come out, and give her a chance to answer. Go back and forth, have this dialogue, get to know and express all you feel about her, and all you feel she (he) feels about you. Just as a parent's death does not necessarily put an end to the song and dance, it does not prevent the possibility of putting an end to the old song and dance. Your relationship with her (him) transcends death; it exists within you, and it is never too late to change that.

13 | Let It Be

It's been a major premise of this book that it is usually better to maintain a relationship with our parents than to rupture it. After all, our relationship with those two people is based on experiences so numberless and so early that they are often beyond memory, and these interactions are a primary source of who we are. These experiences are stored in our neurons, and they form part of the everlasting child within us. Our inner child, never completely erased, is, in one of its aspects, always seeking for some form of that peculiar combination of love, nurturance and guidance that is the hallmark of good parenting. Long after we stop really needing this sustenance from our parents, long after we have become able to deal with the world with independent effectiveness, even long after we have become parents ourselves, the child in us may still hark back to that primal wellspring, if only for symbolic gratification. Some may call this neurotic. Others may call it childish.

I won't argue labels, but it seems to me that this ineradicable part of us is only truly troublesome when it overrules our judgment and controls our feelings and behavior. For it is usually not that we still want to relate to our parents as little children, even though our inner child still harbors old dependency wishes. We would like to relate to them adult to adult and, where this is accomplished, it can add a warmth and fullness to our adult lives, and a unique sense of continuity with the child in us that helps us to integrate the disparate, often fragmented shards of our own histories. There is a preciousness in that familiarity over time that should not be easily discarded.

But there are times when the price of perpetuating such a relationship may be too high. We have entered into songs and dances with our parents in which the child part of us accedes to the requirements of the child part of our parents so that we can purchase the hope of their continued approval and caring. Years of this can steadily erode our independence of thought and response and our ability to know who we are and what we want. If we are aware of the songs and dances and the terrible cost involved, and we have struggled to change our end of it but our parent(s) won't budge, we must confront the possibility of ending the relationship. The act of terminating the tie may be taken by us, if we have reached the limit of our ability to tolerate their insistence on the old pattern, or it may be initiated by the parent(s) if he (she, they) no longer can accept the person we now are.

Either way, there is something tragic about it. It may be necessary, inevitable and liberating, but it is the stuff of which both melodrama and true tragedy are made. In novels and plays, some of the most heartrending, painful scenes occur when there is a break between a parent and child, and some of the most heartwarming, eye-misting scenes occur when there is a reunion, through the return of the prodigal child or the relenting of the parent.

How much change a parent can accept in his child is a very individual matter. In the popular musical *Fiddler on the Roof*, Tevye is faced with each of his three daughters choosing paths that differed from his hope and expectations. First Tzeitel wants to marry a poor tailor instead of the rich man or scholar he and his wife had wanted for her. Tevye debates with himself, counterbalancing each statement with, "On the other hand . . ." Then Tevye shrugs, and says, "Well, children, when shall we make the wedding?"

His second daughter, Hodel, wants to marry a radical who is dedicated to the overthrow of the Czar. They don't even ask for his permission, but for his blessing. He is upset, obsessed about "the other hand

. . ." and finally concludes, "Very well, children, you have my blessing—and my permission."

But when he is told that Chava, his youngest and his favorite, has married a non-Jew it is different. When Chava asks him to accept them he talks to heaven, "Accept them? How can I accept them? Can I deny everything I believe in? On the other hand, can I deny my own child? On the other hand, how can I turn my back on my faith, my people? If I try to bend that far I will break. On the other hand . . . there is no other hand. No, Chava. NO-no-no."*

It is a terrible moment, a shocking moment when Tevye drives her away. Our compassion surges toward both of them—toward Chava, who loves her father and craves his acceptance, and to Tevye, who must tear from himself someone very dear.

Tevye's words, "If I try to bend that far I will break," marks that boundary where Tevye cannot go beyond the core of values and learnings carried within him from his earliest days on earth. The degree to which any parent can accept us in a new role, and in a way that differs from their expectations, is largely dependent on where they are on a continuum of flexibility-rigidity. Tevye was flexible about the marital choices of his first two daughters, but when it came to Chava's marrying a gentile he proclaimed his rigidity: "I will break." At this point, he terminates his tie with her, and in the stage version he takes off his shoes and sits on a low box, the traditional Jewish mourning for one who has just died.

When you change your end of the song and dance in accordance with your need to be true to your own inner rhythms, you are testing your parents' flexibility. You will soon discover the boundaries of their ability to change and to accept you as who you are and not how they'd like you to be. Most parents, perhaps after an initial period of bewilderment, anger and a redoubling of their efforts to force you to resume your old,

---

*Joseph Stein, *Fiddler on the Roof.* Based on Sholem Aleichem's stories. (New York: Pocket Books, 1966.)

expected responses will after a while give up, accept the new arrangement, and may even come to be pleased by it. I have seen many instances when a patient in psychotherapy has changed the lifelong song and dance and the parent will say something like, "I've learned a lot from your changes. I can see that I've been too possessive (dependent, domineering, needy, controlling, intrusive or whatever) and, while it's been difficult changing, I feel much better and freer, too." Sometimes they'll even say, "Tell your therapist he's helped me also." Usually this isn't expressed so openly, but there is often an appreciation of the new, more age-appropriate parent-offspring relationship that is now possible.

But for some parents the initial confusion and anger never end; they are so hardened into an old position with you that your change is an intolerable threat. Their disapproval will be powerful and rejecting, their demands will be strident, coercive, even emotionally (or financially) blackmailing. As you withstand their aggressive or seductive campaign to bring you back into step, their rage may increase enormously, possibly even to unreasonable and threatening proportions. Assuming that you have gone beyond being locked into an inflexibly defiant stance against any accommodation to their wishes and suggestions, you will see in bold relief the rigidity and narrowness of the type of relationship they can tolerate with you. Perhaps because of your simply refusing to go along with the old patterns your parent(s), like Tevye, will cast you out. Or perhaps your awareness of the futility in trying to get a more acceptable response from them will prompt you to move to sever the relationship. Sometimes it is hard for you to know who brought the relationship to the brink. In *Fiddler* was it Tevye and the old injunctions he embodied, or was it Chava and her seeking her own fulfillment? Does it matter? For the most part it is irrelevant who carried things to the breaking point. Who is right and who is wrong are also irrelevant, and getting involved in that debate with your parents would be to resume another form of the song and dance. What matters is how adamantly your parents maintain their old requirements of you, and whether you can accept interacting on the basis of these old requirements.

GIVE IT UP OR LET ME GO

There are no criteria that say that after two months or six months or two years or whatever of waiting in vain for a different response from your parent, you've given it long enough. Circumstances differ and relationships differ too much to apply arbitrary deadlines. It is always your feelings and and your judgment of the total situation that determines the decision. And here the main question to ask yourself is "Do I see any signs, even if small, of some consistent progress on the part of my parent toward a more constructive and respectful responsiveness to me?"

The question brings the focus back to the dimension of rigidity versus flexibility. If your parents are *rigidly* stuck in any particular parental position—martyred, despotic, moralizing, manipulative, infantalizing, uncaring, narcissistic—so that you sense no real movement in their response to you, even though you have persisted in responding to them in a new and more mature way, you will eventually be faced with the probability that they simply will not change. There is the danger of jumping to that conclusion too quickly through unrealistically expecting an immediate positive response to your bid for a new kind of interaction. Just as it has taken you time and pain to change, you can expect the same inertia from them. Patience is called for to let reflection and circumstances have an effect. Even Tevye, when the Czar has decreed that all Jews in his town must leave Russia, finally relents when Chava visits to say goodbye. He cannot permit himself to speak to her directly but, under his breath, as he packs his wagon, his prompts his oldest daughter, Tzeitel, to say to Chava, "God be with you!" This is one of those eye-misting reunions of estranged parents and offspring I spoke of earlier.

But there is also the danger of letting the relationship drag on and on without any real signs of a changed response on their part. Wishfulness may even cause you to see changes where there are none. Permitting the relationship to continue indefinitely with you responding in your new way and your parents persisting in their old reactions can be a product of a renewed unrealistic hope that they will change, and this in itself can become another song and dance based on the same old magical expectation. Of course, if you change and they sustain their old pattern and this does not bother you, nor push you back into the old interaction, you may have a viable *modus vivendi* even if you and they are not on the same beam. But if there is no evidence of change over time in their responsiveness, and their response is distasteful or hurtful, you may, in doing justice to yourself, have to face the sad option of cutting this basic tie.

THE PARTY'S OVER

Dr. Robert Goulding, in teaching workshops in transactional analysis, advises three guideline sentences for the handling of phone conversations with parents where you still wish to maintain contact, where you want to avoid the old type of interaction, but where you feel there is little chance for a more authentic relationship. The three sentences he suggests are:

(1) What good happened today?
(2) Otherwise how are you?
(3) Goodbye.

I would like to use those three sentences as a paradigm for the course of your efforts to determine if it is necessary to terminate the relationship but I find it useful to change the second—otherwise how are you? —to "So what's new otherwise?"

What good happened today? This signifies your attempt to move the relationship from the *negative* orientation of the old song and dance, which always revolves around suffering, guilt, submission, fear, placating, constricting, etc., to a *positive* orientation that is life-affirming, joyous, and expanding. And the word "today" says, let's not dwell on past modes and grievances but let's relate in the here and now.

So what's new otherwise? If your parent still focuses on the negative, still goes back to the past, still invites you to join him in the old song and dance, you can refuse to be diverted but can make more efforts to refocus the relationship. After all, we cannot expect him to instantly change such a profound pattern because we are now ready to have him do it.

Goodbye. You accentuated the positive, you kept from regressing to outworn patterns, you persisted in offering a new way of relatedness, but your parent, through disinclination or rigidity, did not change his or her end of the song and dance. Perhaps he even hardened in his position. It is time to say goodbye.

What exactly do I mean when I talk of saying goodbye to a relationship with people to whom you are profoundly bound by blood and history? In extreme instances, it can mean a cessation of all contact, an unfortunate but sometimes necessary measure when the relationship is so toxic to your well-being that any contact brings only some form of great unpleasantness. But more often it means reducing the contact to protocol meetings, such as weddings, funerals, etc., or to infrequent rituals, such as Christmas or birthday greetings, special occasion visits, or "important news" letters or phone calls. At times, it means refusing to participate in ritualized events such as Christmas visits or Thanksgiving dinners. In any event, it marks the end of any frequent, regular expected contact, and an abandonment of further attempts to wrestle emotionally with your parents about the nature of the relationship. It is a unilateral declaration of the severing of old patterns and of the end of any attempt on your part at a close bond.

Terminating a tie as basic as the one with your parents is such a serious step that I again urge patience and tolerance to give your parent(s) a chance to readjust a lifetime pattern of relating. Bear in mind too that your parent not only has to make profound changes within himself (or herself) but that as part of a family system, the role he (or she) plays with you is tied in with the role he plays with his spouse, his other children, etc. Suppose your mother is living a martyred and guilt-provoking script. If you refuse to go along with her, and she stops playing that role, it could disturb the equilibrium she had developed with your father. She may have been controlling him for years through martyrdom, and if she drops that form, there could be a fallout in her relationship with him. Perhaps he will see that he doesn't have to let himself be controlled by guilt. Or perhaps he so much needs her to be in that controlling position that he will do hurtful things in order to push her back into the masochistic role. She may face a similar readjustment in her relationship with your siblings. The point is, there is much in the total situation that militates against changes in your parents, so forbearance is needed and often pays off.

But there is one particular type of parental rigidity that severely limits any possibility of change, and that is when your parent's discomfort or disapproval with your ending the song and dance hardens into an *adversary* position. In this context, your most innocuous attempts to define yourself as a separate and autonomous person can bring enraged and outrageous accusations that you are trying to victimize and hurt him (her). Your most well-meaning or neutral words and actions can be twisted, to your stunned disbelief, into something evil and malicious. This angry, recriminating stance, when it is not a reaction to actual malevolence on your part, can thwart any attempts at rational communication and can quickly propel you into a state of wall-climbing frustration. Entering a dialogue on this basis becomes a new song and dance that is even more futile and unrewarding than the previous one, because all his or her reactions will be based on the simple precept, "I'm good and you're bad."

Any of the types of parents we have discussed can,

with sufficient rigidity, assume an adversary position.
Suppose you have a martyred parent and suppose further that you stop feeling guilty, stop allowing his guilt
provocations to control you, and stop trying to outmartyr him by living an unhappy life yourself. Instead
you try to relate in a more life-affirming and independent way. If he adopts an adversary position, he can
see your freedom and happiness as proof positive
that you don't care about him or even that you despise
him. And any attempt on your part to make your martyred parent feel less victimized, if he (she) is rigidly
entrenched in martyrdom, can be felt by him or her as
a Trojan Horse being sneaked through the gates of his
masochistic line of defense, pretending to offer a mean-
ingful new relationship, but concealing within it hostility, indifference and desertion. The resulting blame
and denunciation of your best intentions can be so un-
remitting and so irrational that, tragically, you will have
to save yourself by making his fear of your abandoning the relationship with him become a fact.

There can be a similar denouement with a *despotic* parent when you break the old submissive or rebellious song and dance and offer, instead, a relationship based on mutuality. If he (or she) becomes locked
into an adversary stance, he will see your attempts to
have a more equal relationship with him as a disrespectful and malicious undermining of his control. Trying to establish a better relationship under these conditions will precipitate further suspicion, insults and
derision. This reaction may become so bristling and distasteful that even if he does not angrily terminate the
relationship, your own self-respect would lead you to
do so.

Or suppose your parent is a *saint,* and that you
have decided to get out of your particular song and
dance with him (her), so you give up trying to
defiantly shock or rationally convert your parent, and
instead just go about using your own feelings and judgment as the basis of your behavior. A parent with some

flexibility can come to accept and even appreciate the person you now are, but a parent who is so rigidly locked into his view that he must defend it by making you an adversary may see you as bad, evil, depraved, perhaps even influenced by the devil. He will either try to save you, by insisting on bringing you back to the Truth, or will see you as someone whose life-style, morals and viewpoints are so dangerous or revolting that he must either punish you or send you into exile. At this point, further efforts at remaining in a relationship with him will be about as rewarding as a black Catholic trying to be chummy with the Grand Imperial Wizard.

The *narcissistic* parent in an adversary posture is an enraged peacock. When you stop trying to win his (her) nurturant caring by being a compliant extension of him, when you no longer exalt him, when you stop following his pre-scribed script, he will react with the indignant certainty, "If you are not a part of me, you're against me." And, if you require reciprocity in your relationship with him, if you insist on a flow of give and take, he will feel that you are trying to take everything from him and always have your own way. He (she) may be willing to write you off rather than submit to such an obviously unfair demand on your part, and unfortunately you may have to let him do just that.

The form a parent's rigidity may take when it hardens into an adversary position will differ with the type of inner child he has, but what they all have in common is enormous rage and outrage if you fail to act as they expect. And theirs is not a transient outburst at unexpected frustration or disappointment—their fury may calcify into a chronic suspiciousness or hatred in which you can sense their willingness to destroy the relationship with you and even to wreck your happiness and theirs rather than accept a new way of relating.

Depending on you, the experience of your parent

perceiving you as an enemy will either so traumatize you that you will chose to regress back to the old song and dance, or will so clarify how impossible it is to have a viable, constructive relationship with him that it will make it easier for you to terminate the tie. You know what going back means; you've been there. Under the circumstances, if you've come so far that you've been able to change the song and dance and this has done nothing but propel them into an adversary stance, it is clearly better to make the painful decision to let it go.

An example of a parent's taking an extreme adversary position in response to her child's changing the old interaction occurred dramatically in the life of a young woman who was once my patient in psychotherapy. I had been seeing her for over a year when she became ill and bedridden with pericarditis, about two years after her son was born. For many months, Dorothy's mother, a widow with a controlling, critical personality, semi-lived with them to help out. While having her mother there was a frequent irritant to Dorothy and her husband, the total situation made her assistance necessary. It wasn't long before Dorothy was back into the unhappy song and dance that had dominated her whole early life—mother would criticize her for everything, Dorothy would become enraged and insult her mother, her mother would be bitter, wounded and accusing, Dorothy would feel guilty, afraid of her mother's withdrawal, and contrite, her mother would interpret Dorothy's contrition as license to become more flagrantly controlling and critical, etc.

Most of the gains Dorothy had in recent years begun to make in separating herself from her old reactions to mother crumbled away as her illness put her in a passive, regressed position. But she also had much time, lying there in bed, to observe her relationship with her mother, to see how the frightened angry child in herself locked into a destructive interaction with the angry narcissistic child in her mother. She saw how afraid she had always been that her mother would stop loving her if she refused to go along. As Dorothy's health returned, and she could go about taking care of her own household and son, she started to phase her mother out of these chores. Her mother was enraged, accusing Dorothy of using her and discarding her. Dorothy said, "Mom, it's true that I desperately needed your help when I was flat on my back, and I am grateful that you came through for me. But I'm better now, and I can take care of my home and family. You're certainly welcome here as our guest."

"Guest! Me, a guest! At my own daughter's house?"

"I mean I don't need you to take care of things now. I'm feeling fine and I can take charge of things again."

"You would give a maid two weeks' notice."

"Would you like me to get back into bed?" Dorothy felt her sarcastic response moving her back into the old song and dance, and she stopped herself. "I'm sure you're glad I'm better, and it would have been very difficult without you. How about coming over Friday night and I'll make dinner for a change?"

Her mother stood up, got her coat and walked out, saying, "That's the thanks I get. I can make my own dinner."

The weeks of lying in bed, observing her mother and herself and working on changing her responses paid off. She fought her urge to call her mother and either fight or beg. Two days later she received an anonymous news clipping in the mail, about some police chief who had given a speech about how disrespect toward parents was the first step toward crime. The next day Dorothy called her mother to inquire how she was, but said nothing about the clipping or her dinner invitation. Her mother was icy, and then said, "Don't think I don't know you want me to come over for dinner to show me up. Anyway, I'm busy."

Two weeks later her mother called saying, "I took care of my grandson all that time you were sick and you never invited me over to see him." Dorothy responded that her mother was certainly welcome to see him. "Sure, as a guest."

"And as his grandmother whom he loves."

"I want to see him Sunday."

"Fine. We'll be home."

"I don't want to come up. I'll ring you from downstairs and you can bring him down. I'm taking him to the Zoo."

Dorothy felt a surge of anger and loss and was about to pick up the invitation to the dance again, but she held back the child in her and said, "Okay, he'd love that."

Her mother took the boy to the Zoo, and dropped him off laden with toys and souvenirs. Two days later Dorothy received a rambling letter from her mother, saying that she obviously was no longer welcome in Dorothy's house, that Dorothy's husband also hated her and that she could see they were brainwashing their son against her. Dorothy wrote back a brief note saying that she was surprised her mother felt unwelcome, that she had several times invited her, and that she still was welcome. Her mother wrote back saying that the clever deception in Dorothy's letter did not fool her a bit, and that she would only like to have occasional visits with her grandson to prevent them from completely turning him against her.

Dorothy and her husband talked it over and decided that although grandma was sounding pretty disturbed, their son, at least at this point, seemed to enjoy being with her so that they would let her take him on visits as long as he showed no ill effects, but that they would make no further efforts to initiate close contact with her. It was a painful decision for Dorothy, but there was much release in it. The relationship became one in which grandma picked up their son for an outing about every two or three weeks, grandma came to her grandson's birthday parties and was not too intolerable, they visited grandma on Christmas so their son could get his presents, and there were occasional phone calls about specific matters. After a while Dorothy's mother began to do a lot of traveling, which made the situation easier, but Dorothy had already said good-bye.

BREAKING UP IS HARD TO DO

If you think that stopping the old song and dance was difficult, you may find that that was nothing com-

pared to saying good-bye. You may find that you are
bound to your parents with cables of feelings that could
hold HMS *Queen Elizabeth II* to her berth during a
hurricane. The many-stranded hawsers that tie you
are in part composed of the deep imprinting of your
parents' presence on your neurons from earliest days.
You experienced being *their* infant, *their* toddler, *their*
child, *their* adolescent. All their facial expressions,
their smiles and their glares, the mouths turned in a
grin or twisted in rage, their eyes lit with pride, wet
with tears, or wide with fear, all passed through your
own eyes and burned into your brain. Their do's and
don't, their ways, their judgments, their blueprint as to
how you should be in general and with them in particular are all there inside you. And your reactions to
your parents, your dependence, your craving for their
love and caring, your fear of their anger or abandonment, your joy at their praise, and all the ways you
learned to win their love, avoid their disapproval or
get a rise out of them are intertwined with their messages to form the cable. And there are also strands of
hope, hope that if you can only wait long enough, or
get them to listen, or put it in the right words, or reason
with them, or show them your need clearly, or touch
the right heartstring, they will finally give you now
whatever they failed to give you in childhood. All your
reason may tell you that you won't get it, that they
either don't have it to give or don't wish to give it, in
fact your reason may tell you that you don't even need
it, but still that inner child in you holds on to the
hope.

Perhaps the strongest strand in the cable binding
you to them is the desperate terror of the child inside
you that if you end this relationship, this primal
bond, you will be all alone and adrift in a cold and
uncaring universe. Again, your reason may tell you
this is untrue. You may know that you are surrounded
by a loving and concerned spouse, children, friends,
etc., but the tiny child that dwells in you can take over
your feelings and all his or her nightmarish fears of
being abandoned, totally helpless and at the mercy of

unspeakable terrors, unending loneliness, or bottom-less despair can cause you to resist mightily the cutting of this umbilical cable.

WITH A LITTLE HELP FROM MY FRIENDS

The anxieties you face in considering terminating the tie make it frequently advisable that you try to restrict the relationship a little bit at a time. It can be helpful to take longer "vacations" from the relationship, or end certain aspects of it (for example, stop regular phone calls) as a way of helping you to experience your fears in smaller, more manageable doses. This will give you a chance to build up your resolve, to calm the frightened child in you, to reason with him, and to call on your other "life support systems"—your friends, lovers, skills, hobbies, pleasures—to help you through that scary limbo between the familiar and the new. It is a time when all the energies and efforts that were once directed at trying to change your interaction with your parents must be turned inward, toward the greater understanding, liberation and development of your own separate self.

Sometimes you may need help in this cable-cutting endeavor. Perhaps you've already discovered that you need professional assistance in stopping your end of the song and dance, for these steps are often difficult to accomplish alone and you may find yourself stuck at a point where you know what needs to be done but can't overcome the anxieties and resistances that block your way. If you are stuck, it may be wise to get the assistance of some type of psychotherapist to get you un-stuck.

Perhaps you know enough about psychotherapy to know that there are many schools of thought (Freudian, Jungian, Gestalt, Transactional, etc)., many techniques (free association, dream interpretation, empty chair dialogues, script analysis, deep breathing, screaming, etc.), many formats (individual psychotherapy, group therapy, family therapy, encounters, etc.). And since exponents of one approach may be in sharp conflict with proponents of another viewpoint, this disarray may present a befuddling and disheartening picture to someone seeking help. But if part of your reason for wanting psychotherapy is because you are locked into a song and dance, there is one encouraging fact you should know: *every approach to therapy basically aims to free people from bonds to the past and learnings from the past that no longer are pertinent.* About this, there is no warfare within the field of psychotherapy; the controversy only refers to the most effective ways to reach that goal, and each school of thought has developed ways that are useful.

For example, if your life has revolved around a submissive relationship to a controlling mother (and to other subsequent controlling "mothers"), a *psychoanalyst* might concentrate on exploring the repressed fears and guilt feelings that underlie such submission, particularly as these feelings are transferred to the analyst; a *gestaltist* might have you involved in fantasied dialogues with your mother or with your fears, etc., to help you integrate the fragmented parts of yourself so that you will become firmly enough in touch with your strengths in the present to make it less likely that you will continue submitting; a *transactional analyst* would help you see how your child ego state is activated in your relationship with your parents, how this leads to living out an unhappy life script and what you must do to change the script; a *behavior therapist* might teach you to relax in the face of your fear of mother's anger, collapse, abandonment or whatever she uses to control you so that you will not be vulnerable to her manipulations; an *implosive therapist* might plunge you into fantasizing your worst fears in relation to your mother and have you experience the anxiety so intensely in the fantasy that the real thing will lose its charge and be easy to cope with; a *primal therapist* would put you in touch with your earliest emotional ties to your mother and the psychological pain that is lodged in you and that you have designed your life to avoid; a *family therapist* would help you to differentiate yourself from the complex and compelling magnetic forces that bind you into old familial ways of relating; etc. This is a gross oversimplification, and there is much overlap, but you can see that all of these approaches aim at freeing you from responses you learned when you were very young and very malleable. And since these responses are so long embedded, and finding a way out can be so difficult, hiring a therapist as a guide often makes sense.

What is the role of such a guide? He can help you to become aware that you are not simply a passive and unfortunate victim of life but that you act to cripple yourself and therefore can act to strengthen yourself. He can put you in touch with the early hurts and angers and disappointments that have led you to adopt such maladaptive modes. He can open your eyes to new alternatives. And he can be there for you in an understanding and supportive way as you endure the pain of giving up the illusions, which stem from deep inside the child part of you, that say that some day mommy, daddy (wife, husband, friend, boss, children) will love you and respond to you in just the warm and healing way your inner child yearns for. He can help you give up the comforting but ultimately shattering magical belief that if you can find precisely the right way to act, and if you discover the magic button, you can make these people respond exactly the way you need them to. That is a treasured illusion, because all seems hopeless without it, so we all fight to hold on to this kind of belief and to continue the repeated patterns, the endless songs and dances that grow out of this belief.

Dr. Fred Hahn, in writing about magic and change, asks what psychotherapy can offer to someone who has been irrevocably cheated by his history if he takes away the illusion that someday he can right and rewrite this history. With eloquent power he states that

> the goal of therapy is to help the patient go beyond intellectualization and rationalization and other resistive maneuvers to the point where he can move into uncharted territories to seek and find the anguish and terror of total realization and discover that he can survive. To know that life can be truly absurb and capricious; that one is not omnipotent;

that without magic as the ultimate defense, there is pain at times which hurts more than words can describe. And after the grief and the mourning, not only for the lost objects of one's fantasies, but for the fantasies and illusions themselves, to be able to live relatively without illusion. To know Time as a friend as well as enemy. To recognize that happiness is not a condition, but an ephemeral and precious experience, that if one lives without illusion one must impart meaning to one's life; that hope must replace expectations and demands; that activity must replace passivity; that realistic hope must be directed towards the expansion and growth of one's potentialities, which implies experiencing more richly both sorrow and joy.

That the gates to that Eden of infancy are closed, barred by angels with fiery swords.

That mother is dead, forever, and ever, and ever.*

Yes, that is the fantasy we must surrender—the fantasy that mother (or father) can fulfill what they long ago fulfilled, or failed to fulfill. If Fred Hahn's picture of what these illusions are to be exchanged for seems bleak in comparison with the illusion, it must be remembered that although we cannot make magic that redeems the old, unrealiable, hope, if we stop the ineffectual sorcery of the song and dance, we open the possibility of being better parents to ourselves than our parents possibly could be for us now. But even though we may know this with our intellect, even though this statement makes eminent sense, giving up this magic feels risky and frightening. For, as I have written elsewhere about the psychotherapy undertaking, "The real challenge is the terror of change. After the receptive opening up to the inner messages and the sharing them with another; after the insights into the irrationality of our behavior and its origins in situations that no longer pertain; beyond the confrontations that open up new vistas and alternatives and deeper

---

*Fred Hahn, "On Magic and Change," *Voices* (10/1975): 4–13.

than the encounters that give us fresh glimpses into who we are and what we can be, we come finally to the great impasse—the fear of using this awareness to actualize these new, beckoning choices. And then it becomes a matter of a peculiar kind of *courage*."*

The kind of courage that is needed is not the same as physical courage or valor, although it may be related to it. The courage needed is to be able to face the fact that one's greatest fears do not reside in our parent's (or in anybody's) ability to harmfully and catastrophically affect us, but that these fears reside in ourselves. In his poem "In Waste Places," James Stephens tells of a man relentlessly pursued through the desert by a lion. He finally realizes who the lion is:

> *I am the lion and his lair!*
> *I am the fear that frightens me!*
> *I am the desert of despair!*
> *And the night of agony*
>
> *Night or day, whate'er befall,*
> *I must walk that desert land,*
> *Until I dare my fear, and call*
> *The lion out to lick my hand!*

A good psychotherapist can help you to dare your fear, and much courage may be needed to say goodbye. Because in saying goodbye to our parents we are not only bidding farewell to these particular people but to our link to the past and to our roots. But most poignantly and most frighteningly, we are saying goodbye to the "if onlys." We are saying goodbye to the illusions built on "if only mom," "if only dad," "if only the world . . ." We are facing life as it really is, with no unrealistic hopes and yet whole new exciting possibilities.

Usually, the saying goodbye takes place inside you before you actually break your ties with your parents. At times, in psychotherapy, when patients have reached that point where saying goodbye seems necessary and

*Howard Halpern, "Catalysts of Courage," *Voices* (9/1973): 5–9.

desirable, we do it first in a session. Brian had long ago ended his old song and dances with his mother and had made many efforts to respond to her in a new and mutually respectful way, but she remained persistently attacking, manipulative and generally unpleasant. He had reached the point where the price of continuing the relationship was more than he cared to pay and he realized he would have to end it. He was shaken and sad about this realization. I placed a chair opposite his, asked him to picture his mother in it, and to begin his goodbyes. He sat quietly for a long time.

"Mom," Brian said softly, "I just can't hack it anymore. I love you, and I've tried to keep things going with us, but it's not working. I'm not going to see you. I'm hardly even going to call you on the phone. It's just too damn painful. I mean, well, I guess I mean goodbye."

I then asked Brian to move to the other chair and respond as he felt his mother would. When Brian got into the other chair a hard and bitter look came into his face. "Exactly what are you talking about? What's painful about being with me? If you weren't always running somewhere, if you acted like a considerate son, we'd never get into these hateful fights. Everything I ever ask of you is a big hardship. Every suggestion I make is unwelcome. So if you treat me like dirt, what am I supposed to do, just swallow it?"

Brian switched chairs. "Mom, I don't believe I treat you like dirt, and I've become convinced that nothing I ever do will stop you from believing that. I'm tired of trying to prove I'm a good son. I'm tired of your acting as if my living my own life is a personal affront to you. And I'm tired of arguing with you about it."

"You're as selfish as ever," his "mother" responded. "No, as a child you were good, you listened to me. But later you began to change. And since you got married it's been one insult after another."

"I've never meant to insult you. But can't you see by this very conversation that you are always hitting that same note, always trying to make me feel selfish? I don't want it anymore. And there's no way to avoid this kind of thing except to stop seeing you. If I see you, I fall into the same pattern, like I'm doing right now. So let's at least see if we can make a gracious goodbye of it."

"A gracious goodbye? My son is disowning me and he wants a gracious goodbye?"

"You're right. That really is too much to ask. I'm still trying to get you to approve, even about leaving you. But I guess there's no easy way to do this except to say it's over. I do love you. I have some very warm memories, like when you'd meet me at school with my raincoat and galoshes when it was teeming, or the concerts you took me to at the Philharmonic, or your saving the pot you used to make chocolate pudding for me to lick, and so much else. That will always be a piece of me. But now it's no damn good and hasn't been for a long time. In fact, there are times when I hate you and I don't want that feeling. I want to end things before I forget why I ever loved you."

"How can you be so unfeeling and so ungrateful? Are you aware what I've sacrificed for you?"

Brian sighed deeply. "Mom, I suspect I'll miss you but I'm not sure. I may not give you a second thought after a while. I may be relieved to get you off my back and be free to live my own way. But for now, I'm terribly sad. Goodbye."

"But you can't! What will I do?"

"You'll manage. You always have."

"If only you'll listen to me."

"Mom, you'll have to deal with your own 'if onlys.'"

"What are you talking about?"

"Mom, goodbye."

Brian sat for a while crying. Then he looked up and his eyes had a shine to them that was not from tears alone. His face was radiant and free. He looked once more at the chair where "mother" sat. He grinned and blew a kiss in her direction. "Bye bye, mommy. Hello, world."

That kind of internal decision to say goodbye to a stifling tie to a parent, that sad but liberating farewell to the "if onlys," is a way of opening the door to a wider world. It signals your discovery that your life is bigger than any one love and than any one relationship, even the primal one. That ending and that new beginning face you with what Kierkegaard called "the alarming possibility of being able." And why is being able alarming? Because it means breaking with all the messages you grew up with that say, "Don't," "You can't," "You're too little." You may have been rooted in muck all this time, but it was familiar muck. Who you were, what was expected of you, and what limitations you had to accept were all clearly marked. Breaking with all this means facing the unknown and, by yourself, without the aid of your old and timeless fixed stars, using only your own feelings and judgment, daring to navigate through terrifying, uncharted and unpredictable space. Being able means severing the vestigial ties that leash you to the past, and standing upright, knowing your ultimate aloneness, knowing your weaknesses and your strengths, daring to turn your wishes and your potentials toward untried risks. If that isn't alarming, what is?

Most of the time you can open up this alarming possibility not through ending the relationship with your parents, but by stopping the old songs and dances. Each has its own risks, and requires courage, determination and compassion. But whether the freedom of your choices and the actualization of your energies are achieved through ending the songs and dances or, if need be, through severing the parental tie, it is a matter of doing ultimate justice to yourself. And that's worth it all.

Mother · gentleness, nurturing
Father · fearlessness, confidence

ABOUT THE AUTHOR

Howard M. Halpern received his Ph.D. in clinical psychology from Columbia University in 1954 and has been on the staff of several hospitals and clinics, as well as on the faculties of Columbia University, Finch College, and the Metropolitan Institute for Psychoanalytic Studies. From 1962 to 1977, he was the codirector of the New York Student Consultation Center for Psychotherapy, and is now their consultant in Parent-Child Relationships. He is a former president of the American Academy of Psychotherapists, currently is a consulting editor of *Voices: The Art and Science of Psychotherapy*, and has published many writings in the field, both as articles and in book form. His most recent book, on ending unsatisfying relationships, is *How To Break Your Addiction To A Person* (Bantam Books). For over twenty-five years, Dr. Halpern has practiced psychotherapy in New York City.

Father
· narcissisticly self involved
· weak man : Ineffective, Irresponsible
*   morally defective*

Bantam
On Psychology

☐	26507	**MEN WHO HATE WOMEN & THE WOMEN WHO LOVE THEM** Dr. Susan Forward	$4.50
☐	34366	**SIGNALS** Allen Pease (A Large Format Book)	$7.95
☐	26401	**MORE HOPE AND HELP FOR YOUR NERVES**	$3.95
☐	23767	**HOPE AND HELP FOR YOUR NERVES** Claire Weekes	$3.95
☐	26754	**PEACE FROM NERVOUS SUFFERING** Claire Weekes	$4.50
☐	26005	**HOW TO BREAK YOUR ADDICTION TO A PERSON** Howard M. Halpern, Ph.D.	$4.50
☐	27084	**PATHFINDERS** Gail Sheehy	$5.50
☐	24754	**PASSAGES: PREDICTABLE CRISIS OF ADULT LIFE** Gail Sheehy	$4.95
☐	27043	**THE POWER OF YOUR SUBCONSCIOUS MIND** Dr. J. Murphy	$4.50
☐	34368	**GOODBYE TO GUILT** Gerald Jampolsky, M.D. (A Large Format Book)	$7.95
☐	34367	**TEACH ONLY LOVE** Gerald Jampolsky, M.D. (A Large Format Book)	$7.95
☐	24518	**LOVE IS LETTING GO OF FEAR** Gerald Jampolsky, M.D.	$3.50
☐	25822	**WHAT DO YOU SAY AFTER YOU SAY HELLO?** Eric Berne, M.D.	$4.95
☐	26009	**PSYCHO-CYBERNETICS AND SELF-FULFILLMENT** Maxwell Maltz, M.D.	$4.50
☐	27087	**CUTTING LOOSE: An Adult Guide for Coming To Terms With Your Parents** Howard Halpern	$4.50
☐	26390	**WHEN I SAY NO, I FEEL GUILTY** Manuel Smith	$4.95

Prices and availability subject to change without notice.

Buy them at your local bookstore or use this handy coupon for ordering:

Bantam Books, Inc., Dept. ME, 414 East Golf Road, Des Plaines, Ill. 60016

Please send me the books I have checked above. I am enclosing $_____
(please add $1.50 to cover postage and handling). Send check or money order
—no cash or C.O.D.s please.

Mr/Mrs/Miss _____

Address _____

City _____ State/Zip _____

ME—9/87

Please allow four to six weeks for delivery. This offer expires 3/88.

Special Offer
Buy a Bantam Book
for only 50¢.

Now you can have Bantam's catalog filled with hundreds of titles plus take advantage of our unique and exciting bonus book offer. A special offer which gives you the opportunity to purchase a Bantam book for only 50¢. Here's how!

By ordering any five books at the regular price per order, you can also choose any other single book listed (up to a $4.95 value) for just 50¢. Some restrictions do apply, but for further details why not send for Bantam's catalog of titles today!

Just send us your name and address and we will send you a catalog!
